WEB SEARCH
GARAGE

Tara Calishain

PRENTICE HALL PTR
Upper Saddle River, NJ 07458

Library of Congress Cataloging-in-Publication Data

A CIP catalog record for this book can be obtained from the Library of Congress

Acquisitions Editor: John Neidhart
Editorial Assistant: Raquel Kaplan
Marketing Manager: Robin O'Brien
Marketing Specialist: Kathleen Addis
Publicity: Heather Fox
Managing Editor: Gina Kanouse
Project Editor: Michael Thurston
Editorial/Production Supervision: Argosy Publishing
Cover Design: Anthony Gemmellaro
Interior Design: Wanda Espana
Manufacturing Buyer: Dan Uhrig

Publishing as Prentice Hall Professional Technical Reference
Upper Saddle River, New Jersey 07458

Prentice Hall PTR offers excellent discounts on this book when ordered in quantity for bulk purchases or special sales. For more information, please contact: U.S. Corporate and Government Sales, 1-800-382-3419, corpsales@pearsontechgroup.com. For sales outside of the U.S., please contact: International Sales, 1-317-581-3793, international@pearsontechgroup.com.

Printed in the United States of America

First Printing

ISBN 0-13-147148-1

Pearson Education Ltd.
Pearson Education Australia Pty., Limited
Pearson Education South Asia Pte. Ltd.
Pearson Education Asia Ltd.
Pearson Education Canada, Ltd.
Pearson Educacion de Mexico, S.A. de C.V.
Pearson Education—Japan
Pearson Malaysia S.D.N. B.H.D.

Dedicated to my husband, with much love.

CONTENTS

ABOUT THE AUTHOR

Tara Calishain is the editor of ResearchBuzz, a weekly newsletter on Internet searching. She's also a regular columnist for SEARCHER and has written for a variety of other publications. Her author/co-author credits include *Google Hacks* and *Official Netscape Guide to Internet Research*.

PREFACE

In the last ten years or so I've been fascinated with the Web. And since the Web started getting large enough to require organization, I've been fascinated with how that organization has evolved. From very basic text pages and Big Red Buttons That Don't Do Anything, we've moved to extensive databases, search engines, and online information collections of all sorts. Since I wrote the *Official Netscape Guide to Internet Research* in 1996, the landscape has changed dramatically.

In 1996 it was possible to maintain a "big picture" idea of resources available online: even if you couldn't track down every last one you had a sense of what was available, where the gaps were, and so on. Now that's impossible. The Internet is growing too quickly. But hey, these are the kinds of problems you want to have, right? A rapidly growing collection of information, with a rapidly growing set of tools for dealing with it.

In 1996 I decided I was crazy about search engines. I loved experimenting with them, learning the syntaxes, trying to figure out how to make them work best. I'm still crazy about them. I'm almost as crazy about trying to teach other people to use the search engines, to help them take advantage of the wealth of information that's appearing online.

Thanks for buying this book. If you, too, get bitten by the search engine bug, join me over at ResearchBuzz.com. There I'll try to keep you up to date with developments in the search engine world.

Thanks for reading.

ACKNOWLEDGMENTS

When you think of a book being written, you think of one person sitting for long hours at a keyboard. But that's just the tip of the iceberg.

John at Prentice Hall has been so thoughtful and so patient with my ideas. Thanks, John. All the folks at PH I've worked with—including Robin, Heather, Raquel, and Linda—have been great. Thanks guys!

Living with a writer, especially a geek writer, is sometimes weird. You ask them to pass the mustard and they start ranting about text searching in titles. My family and friends get my continual thanks. Maddest props to Rachel, Martha, Gerd, Carolyn, and Herbert.

Of course I have online friends, too. There's a whole community of writers as crazy about search engines as I am. How lucky for me that they're also great people, willing to share their knowledge! Thanks to Gary Price (hey man!), Chris Sherman, Genie Tyburski, Danny Sullivan, everybody on the Web4Lib list, and all those other folks out there who share our enthusiasm for finding things online.

I wrote my first Internet search book in 1996. Since 1998 I have been writing an online newsletter about searching and online information collections. It's called ResearchBuzz. Through ResearchBuzz I have made some friends and met some wonderful people. For their suggestions, comments, good wishes, support, and enthusiasm, my grateful thanks to the readers of ResearchBuzz.

INTRODUCTION

What's This Book For?

Pretty much everybody on the Web has to use a search engine every now and again. Some people already know all they need to use one. If that's you and you want to read this book anyway, fine! Welcome. But this book is written more for those people who fall into one of these three categories:

1. People who need to use Internet search engines a lot, either in the course of their work or for their personal interests.
2. People who need to help other people use search engines—librarians, teachers, support people, homeschoolers, and so on.
3. People who have an irrepressible curiosity about the scope of the Internet and want to learn to improve their skills at finding and monitoring new sites of interest online.

What You'll Need

This book is not an introductory Internet text. You'll need to know at least the basics of navigating the Web. Beyond that, this book doesn't require any special knowledge.

What It's All About

No, not the hokey pokey. Conceptually, this book's content is organized around three categories, with the hope of teaching you as much as possible without making you wade through topics in which you're not interested.

The Elements—This is the wheels-on-the-road, basic stuff: what search engines are all about, tools to use with them, and what gadgets and tweaks you can use to make your researching life easier.

The Principles—This is where *Web Search Garage* is different from many other Internet research books. In addition to covering specific topics and showing you how to work search engines, I also try to give you some principles for how Internet searching works. Search engines and online information resources will change all the time, but I think the Principle of Onions, the Principle of Salt Grains, the Principle of the Reinvented Wheel, and all the rest will hold you in good stead even as you learn about new resources and new search engines.

The Examples—These are the topics that cover specific kinds of searching, from genealogy to finding audio online to finding local information. Read the topics you find interesting, and skip the rest (though personally I think they're all fascinating).

The Internet, at this writing, has over four billion pages. Everyone is going to approach it with different needs and interests. Everyone's experiences are going to evolve in different directions: one person might lean more toward medical resources, another legal, and another might learn a lot about publication archives. The possibilities are almost endless.

Whatever your interests and wherever you go, I believe this book will be a solid foundation for you as you learn to explore, seek, and find on the Internet.

PART I
INTRODUCTION TO WEB SEARCHING

1 SEARCH ENGINES

For an Internet researcher the first great tool is the general, Internet-wide search engine. The largest ones encompass huge amounts of data (Google at last count indexed over four billion pages, but even that isn't the entire Web or even, it is speculated, the majority of the Web). They're also your ticket to finding more general search engines and useful information collections.

So as an Internet researcher the first element you must know is the general search engine. There are two that I consider major and a bunch of minor ones. They can be divided into two broad categories: full-text search engines and searchable subject indexes.

Full-Text Engines

Full-text engines are those search engines that try to index the entire content of a Web page. (They don't always do it because many search engines limit how much of a page they'll index. Google, for example, will only index the first 101K of a page no matter how large the page is.) That includes the title, URL, and page content. Google and Teoma are examples of full-text engines.

Searchable Subject Indexes

Searchable subject indexes make no attempt to index the content of a site. Instead, the name and URL of a site—and usually some kind of brief description—are included in a set of categories. The categories are usually browsable, but they're searchable as well. Yahoo and the Open Directory Project are examples of searchable subject indexes.

Mixing It Up

Now, here's the tricky part. Google, a full-text search engine, has a searchable subject component called Google Directory. Yahoo, a searchable subject index, has the option to search a full-text engine. (Yahoo's directory results are from their searchable subject index, while their full-text search matches are called Web results and come from their own full-text search engine.) But primarily, Google is known as a full-text engine and Yahoo is known as a searchable subject index.

Why Have Two Kinds?

Why have two kinds of search engines anyway? What is each one good for?

Full-text search engines are good when you're searching for very distinct types of information—for example, quotes, song lyrics, addresses, less-famous people, lesser-known places, or complicated queries. Searchable subject indexes do not contain enough information about Web pages to answer these kinds of queries.

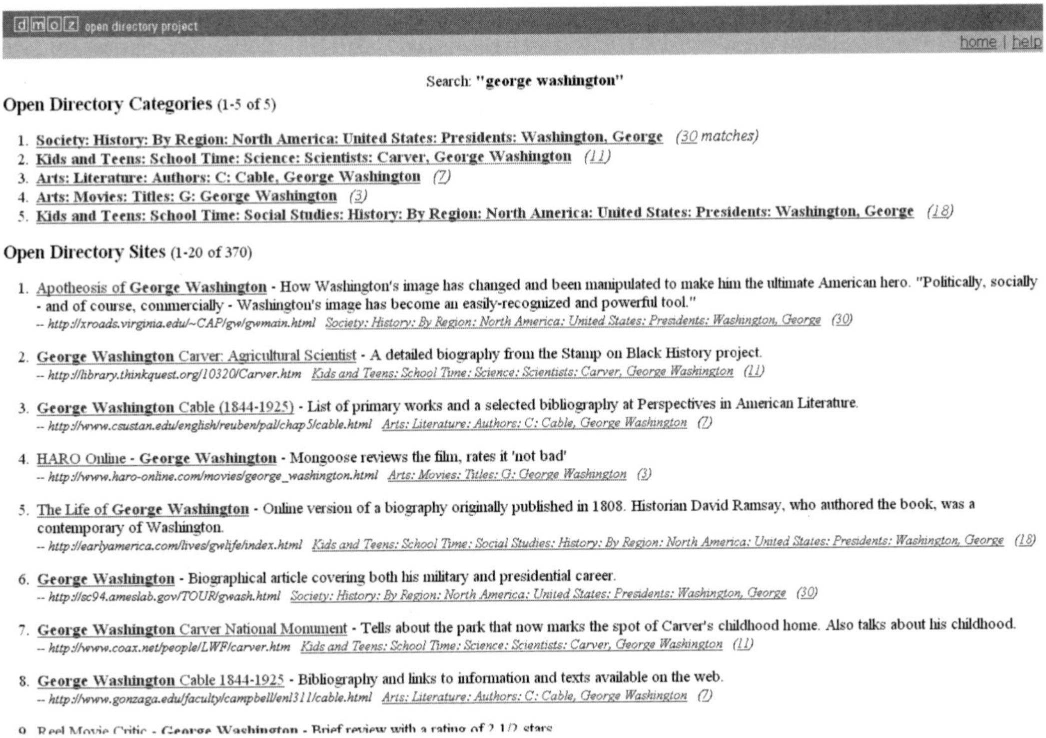

dmoz open directory project

home | help

Search: **"george washington"**

Open Directory Categories (1-5 of 5)

1. Society: History: By Region: North America: United States: Presidents: Washington, George *(30 matches)*
2. Kids and Teens: School Time: Science: Scientists: Carver, George Washington *(11)*
3. Arts: Literature: Authors: C: Cable, George Washington *(7)*
4. Arts: Movies: Titles: G: George Washington *(3)*
5. Kids and Teens: School Time: Social Studies: History: By Region: North America: United States: Presidents: Washington, George *(18)*

Open Directory Sites (1-20 of 370)

1. Apotheosis of **George Washington** - How Washington's image has changed and been manipulated to make him the ultimate American hero. "Politically, socially - and of course, commercially - Washington's image has become an easily-recognized and powerful tool."
   -- *http://xroads.virginia.edu/~CAP/gw/gwmain.html* *Society: History: By Region: North America: United States: Presidents: Washington, George (30)*
2. **George Washington** Carver: Agricultural Scientist - A detailed biography from the Stamp on Black History project.
   -- *http://library.thinkquest.org/10320/Carver.htm* *Kids and Teens: School Time: Science: Scientists: Carver, George Washington (11)*
3. **George Washington** Cable (1844-1925) - List of primary works and a selected bibliography at Perspectives in American Literature.
   -- *http://www.csustan.edu/english/reuben/pal/chap5/cable.html* *Arts: Literature: Authors: C: Cable, George Washington (7)*
4. HARO Online - **George Washington** - Mongoose reviews the film, rates it 'not bad'
   -- *http://www.haro-online.com/movies/george_washington.html* *Arts: Movies: Titles: G: George Washington (3)*
5. The Life of **George Washington** - Online version of a biography originally published in 1808. Historian David Ramsay, who authored the book, was a contemporary of Washington.
   -- *http://earlyamerica.com/lives/gwlife/index.html* *Kids and Teens: School Time: Social Studies: History: By Region: North America: United States: Presidents: Washington, George (18)*
6. **George Washington** - Biographical article covering both his military and presidential career.
   -- *http://sc94.ameslab.gov/TOUR/gwash.html* *Society: History: By Region: North America: United States: Presidents: Washington, George (30)*
7. **George Washington** Carver National Monument - Tells about the park that now marks the spot of Carver's childhood home. Also talks about his childhood.
   -- *http://www.coax.net/people/LWF/carver.htm* *Kids and Teens: School Time: Science: Scientists: Carver, George Washington (11)*
8. **George Washington** Cable 1844-1925 - Bibliography and links to information and texts available on the web.
   -- *http://www.gonzaga.edu/faculty/campbell/enl311/cable.html* *Arts: Literature: Authors: C: Cable, George Washington (7)*
9. Reel Movie Critic - **George Washington** - Brief review with a rating of 2 1/2 stars

01–01

It's much easier to get meaningful results for a famous figure like George Washington using a subject index. (Image from http://search.dmoz.org/cgi-bin/search?search=%22george+washington%22.)

On the other hand, the limitations of searchable subject indexes make them very useful for more general searching—when you're trying to find information on New York, for example. Or George Washington. Or other general topics. Sometimes going through a searchable subject index finds you enough material that you can then get more specific information from a full-text engine. The two types of search engines work harmoniously together—provided you know which one to use first.

What They All Have in Common: Search Defaults

Despite the fact that they're searching very different things, both types of search engines have one thing in common: their search default. This is important, so pay attention.

When you enter a multiple-word query into a search engine and don't enter any search modifiers (like AND or NOT), the search engine has to decide how to treat your query. Broadly speaking, the search engine can do one of two things. It can decide to search so that *all* of your search words *must* be included in any results—in this case it's defaulting to AND. Or it can decide to search so that *any* of your search words must appear in a document for it to appear in search results. In that case it's defaulting to OR.

The first most important thing to know about a search engine is whether it's a full-text engine or a searchable subject index. The second most important thing to know is whether the search engine defaults to AND or OR. If it defaults to AND, you should be more thoughtful about your query words, because all query words you choose must appear in a Web page before you'll get results. If it defaults to OR, you should be sure to put + signs in front of terms that must be included in your search. You can also try to search more for phrases.

How can you tell if something defaults to AND or OR? Do a search with a very odd set of words—say `elderberry chiropractic snowblower brick`. If you get no results (or just a few results), you're searching an engine that defaults to AND. If you get lots of results, you've found an engine that defaults to OR.

Going Beyond Default with Boolean Modifiers

How do you tell a search engine when you want to include something or exclude something from your search? You use Boolean modifiers. These modifiers tell the search engine exactly how you want your search words to be treated. The two main Boolean modifiers are + (must include a word in a search), and - (word must not be in search result pages). There are other ones that we'll look at as we look at each search engine. But for now, a pop quiz: What does this search mean?

```
+"three blind mice" -"see how they run"
```

This is a simple one: the search results for this search must include the words "three blind mice" but must not include the phrase "see how they run." (Most search engines specify phrases with quote marks.)

Beyond Basic Boolean: Getting Special

Boolean modifiers are simple, aren't they? + means must and - means must not. But things get a little more complicated than that. Some search engines have OR modifiers. (Google uses a pipe symbol (|) to specify OR. Look for the \ symbol on your keyboard; Shift-\ is a pipe. You may also hear it called a vertical bar.) Some search engines have NEAR modifiers.

And most search engines go beyond Boolean to special syntaxes. Special syntaxes allow you to do special searching within a Web page or related to a Web page—you can limit your searches to a Web page's title, or body, and so on. Different search engines have different types of special syntaxes, so we won't go into them in too much detail here.

The Next Step: A Search Engine Flyover

A long, long time ago when the Earth was flat, search engines were relatively straightforward creatures. You entered your search query and you got a list of search results.

In the late 90s most search engines (Google was a notable exception) descended into Portal Madness: instead of a place to merely search the Web, search engines became places to get news, weather, sports scores, and other snippets of information.

Portal Madness has died down but there's still a lot of search complexity. Searchable subject indexes like Yahoo contain what I call different "properties": areas to get extensive and focused information (like Yahoo News and Yahoo Get Local). Full-text search engines like Google have, as mentioned earlier, "special syntaxes": query words to enter that can sharply narrow your search focus.

In the next two chapters we're going to cover two major search engines—Yahoo and Google—and a host of less-famous-but-still-very-useful engines. This book doesn't have the space or the format to cover every nook and cranny, but you'll get a good flyover of what the major search engines offer. Later in the book, I'll show you how to delve into the properties of Yahoo and the special syntaxes of Google and get them to do some good search engine tricks. But let's start with the overview.

Google

Overview

At this writing, Google (http://www.google.com) is the most popular full-text search engine out there. It processes millions upon millions of search requests today and indexes over four billion Web pages. It also indexes other file types, like PDF (Adobe Acrobat), DOC (Microsoft Word), and PPT (PowerPoint). Google will return up to a thousand results for a query and limits a search query to ten words.

Boolean Modifiers

Google defaults to AND. Its Boolean modifiers include + (must include), - (must not include), | (or), and ~ (synonym). Phrases are indicated with quotes.

The synonym operator placed in front of a word searches for both that word and any word similar to it. The most obvious example of this is a plural. So a search for ~car would find car, cars, etc. The OR operator, inserted between two words or phrases, specifies that at least one of the two should be found in the search results. Searching for `roses | "white gardenias"` would find search pages that contain either the word "roses" or the phrase "white gardenias."

It's not exactly a Boolean modifier, but Google also supports a full-word wildcard: the asterisk (*). Using this in a query will find any word where you put the *. For example, if you search for `"step * step"`, the Google results will show step by step, step and step, step over step, and so on. Note that the asterisk will find only entire words, not partial words—you can't add a * to the end or beginning of a word.

Special Syntaxes

Google has several special syntaxes for searching.

site: Restricts a search to a specific domain:

```
"Stanton MacDonald-Wright" site:art.com
```

or a top-level domain:

```
"Stanton MacDonald-Wright" site:edu
```

intitle: Restricts the specified search words to just Web page titles:

```
intitle:"Stanton MacDonald-Wright"
```

inurl: Restricts the specified search words to just Web site URLs. This is a tricky one to use since Google matches only entire words and it's hard to guess what kind of full words or abbreviations a site might use in its URL. This syntax works well in conjunction with other syntax, however:

```
"Stanton MacDonald-Wright" inurl:library
              site:edu
```

intext: Finds query words in the text of a Web page only, and not in the page's HTML. Many times this syntax won't make much of a difference in your search unless you're searching

NOTE

inurl: and intitle: have the additional search options allintitle: and allinurl:, respectively. allintitle: specifies that all words to its right should be found in the title, and allinurl: specifies that all words to its right should be found in site URLs. I tend to not use allintitle: and allinurl: because they can be confusing and can completely wreck a query if not used properly.

for a word common to HTML code, like HTML. Do searches of `HTML` and `intext:HTML` and you'll see a big difference in the search results.

inanchor: Finds words in the descriptions of sites that point to a page. If I'm searching for `inanchor:CNBC`, I'll find pages that are linked from other sites using the word "CNBC." For example, say there's a site http://www.example.com, which contains the following HTML:

```
<a href="http://www.cnbc.com">The stock market
        is cool with CNBC.</a>
```

A search for `inanchor:CNBC` would find the page http://www.cnbc.com, and not the page http://www.example.com.

link: Finds pages that link to the page you specify.

```
link:http://www.mit.edu
```

will list pages that link to MIT. This syntax may not be used in conjunction with other syntaxes—`link:http://www.mit.edu site:edu` will not work.

cache: Provides a picture of what the page looks like from the last time Google indexed it. Indexes text only; images aren't included. Caches aren't available for all pages; some pages (like newspaper archives and pay-information sites) don't want their pages cached.

related: Finds pages related to the URL you enter. This doesn't always work. The more representation a site has in the Google index, the better this works. Try `related:http://www.amazon.com` to see the kinds of results you get.

info: Provides some information about a URL, including a current listing for that URL (if any), a link to a cache of the page, a link to pages that are similar, and pages that link to the URL. Finally, there's a link to pages that contain the URL as text.

daterange: Allows you to search for pages that were indexed by Google on a certain date range. Note that you're looking for pages that were indexed (that is, found by Google and added to their database) on a certain date or date range, not created by a Web site during a certain date or date range.

The bad thing about Google's daterange: syntax is the fact that it uses Julian dates instead of the common Gregorian calendar. Julian dates are used by astronomers. They're integers and they roll over at noon instead of midnight (much better for stargazers, right?).

Commands for Special Searching

Not all the special syntaxes Google offers have anything to do with searching Web pages. Some of them are designed to find particular kinds of information.

stocks: Use this query with a stock symbol and you'll get a framed page with financial/stock information from a variety of sources. Try `stocks:amzn`.

NOTE

Not all pages indexed by Google have caches. And not all pages are indexed by Google to begin with! Why not? First of all, Webmasters have the option to ask Google's spider not to index their site, and some folks use that option—they have small sites or private sites and they don't want traffic from Google. Second, many sites are database-driven—they generate pages from the content of a database. Google often can't go through every nook and cranny of these kinds of sites.

NOTE

When you're searching for special content, as is the case with phone numbers and stock information, you can't mix that search with search for content on Web pages. You can't search for phone numbers in the .edu domain, for example. In other words, you can't "mix these syntaxes" by using them with other syntaxes or keywords. The other syntaxes that search just for page-related content (inurl:, intitle:, site:, etc.) can be mixed together. The only other Google syntax that isn't mixable is the link: syntax. Mixing syntaxes is a very powerful way of cutting down your search results, as you'll learn while you progress through this book.

phonebook: You can use the phonebook: syntax in a couple of ways. If you use it in conjunction with a phone number, like this:

```
phonebook:555-555-1212
```

Google will attempt to do a "reverse lookup" on the number. If you use it in conjunction with a keyword, city, and state (or just city and state), like this:

```
phonebook:cheese Madison WI
```

Google will attempt to look up any businesses or people containing the word "cheese" in Madison, Wisconsin. You can restrict your search to businesses by using bphonebook: and restrict your search to residents by using rphonebook:.

Try searching for a keyword and an area code, like `phonebook:cheese 415`!

Google's Non-Web Search Properties

Google's most popular property is its Web search at http://www.google.com. But it does offer other collections of searchable materials.

Google News—http://news.google.com
News from over 4,500 sources around the world, indexed constantly. News alerts send news based on your keyword to your e-mail once an hour or once a day.

Google Groups—http://groups.google.com
Usenet archive that goes back over twenty years, featuring literally tens of millions of messages. Great when you need technical support or a game hint (more about that later).

Google Images—http://images.google.com
Images indexed by Google's spider from around the Web. At this writing Google Images contains over 800 million images. There are two levels of filtering here for you to avoid prurient content.

Google Special Searches—
http://www.google.com/options/specialsearches.html
Google has five levels of special searches that help you find very specific topics. You can search for information on Microsoft, Linux, Apple, BSD, or the Government. Google even has special searches for dozens and dozens of universities.

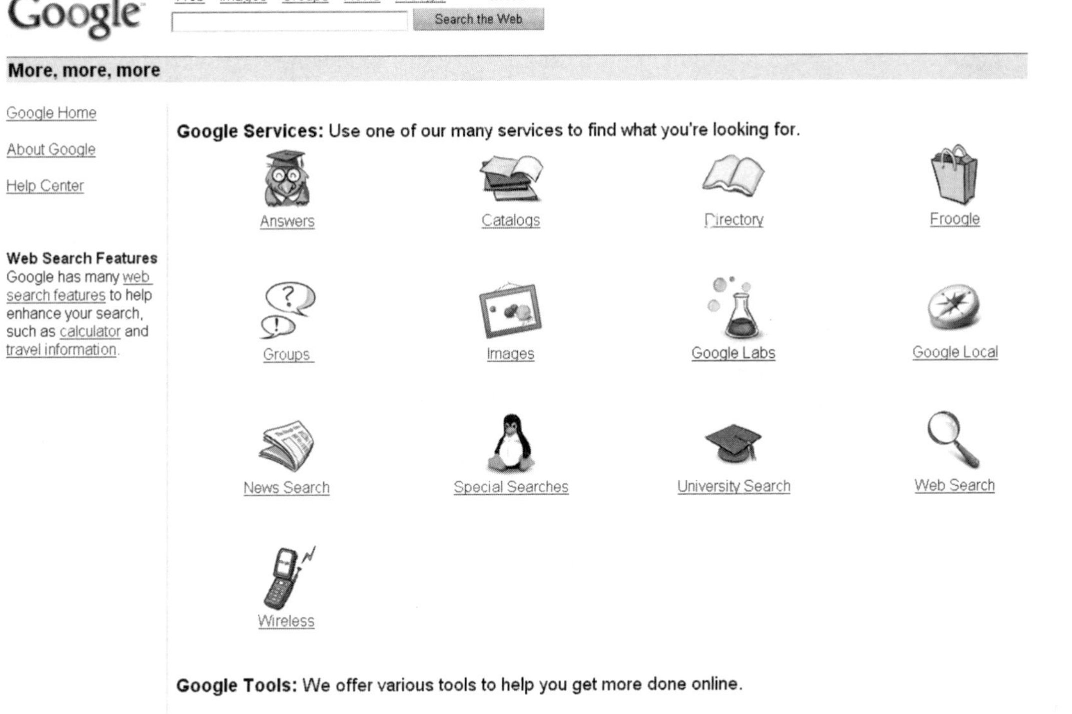

01–02

Google offers many, many different search options. (Image from http://www.google.com/options/index.html.)

Google Catalogs—http://catalogs.google.com and Froogle—http://froogle.google.com

Google Catalogs and Froogle are both for the shopper in you. Google Catalogs is a search of paper catalogs that Google has scanned in and indexed. Froogle is a search of online shopping sites.

Yahoo--http://directory.yahoo.com

Overview

Yahoo is both a searchable subject index and one of the granddaddies of Internet search. I remember using Yahoo when it had only a few categories and only a few thousand Web sites. (That was when I had to walk ten miles through the snow to log on to the Internet.)

That was a long time ago. Now Yahoo has, I suspect, millions of Web site listings, but unfortunately the Web is growing far faster than they can keep up with. Another thing that modifies Yahoo's listings is the fact that they charge money for listing business or profit-oriented sites. (They charge even more money for listing adult sites.) Unless you're shopping, this isn't bad or good. It just means that the listings are going to be different—more oriented towards large businesses, which feel that they can afford Yahoo's annual listing fee. If you're looking for the equivalent of the local street fair's craft booth, it may be hard to find here.

While Yahoo does have a searchable subject index and it's very useful, it's not even the majority of their offerings. They have several other properties—far too many for me to cover in this section. I will cover the highlights, the really useful stuff.

> **NOTE**
>
> The URL on the previous page is for directory.yahoo.com, and not www.yahoo.com. If you go to directory.yahoo.com and search, you'll get results from Yahoo's directory. If you search from www.yahoo.com, you'll get results from the Web search that backs up Yahoo's directory search, and then you'll have to click on the Directory tab at the top of the screen to get directory results. Make it your habit to start at directory.yahoo.com.

Boolean Modifiers

Yahoo defaults to the Boolean AND, but there's a twist. If Yahoo cannot find a match in its own searchable subject index, it'll search its backup search engine and present those results. If there are no results in the backup search, you'll get a "no result" message.

If you search for a more common word—like "cars" or "flowers"—or a place name, you'll get a list of matching categories at the top of the search results. If you truly are looking for information for such a general thing, use the categories first.

To include items in a Yahoo search, use +. To exclude items, use -. To gather words into a phrase, use quote marks (""). To search for either of two items, use OR.

Special Syntaxes

Maybe you think that because Yahoo is a searchable subject index it doesn't have much in the line of special syntaxes. It isn't as extensive as Google, but it does have a couple. In fact it has two sets, one for its subject index and one for its full-text search engine.

Subject Index Syntaxes

The t: syntax limits your search to the titles of items. This is useful when you're looking for a keyword that might appear in many different kinds of listings. Try searching for `books` versus `t:books` and notice the complete difference in the results listings. If you try to use this search in conjunction with regular searches, it can get awkward; you may have to experiment.

The u: syntax limits the search to the URL. Don't use this to find keywords, but instead to find particular companies. For example, were you wondering which Google pages were indexed by Yahoo? Search for `u:google` and find out. Not all the results will be Google, but it'll be easy to tell the Google sites from the news stories, etc.

Full-Text Search Engine Syntaxes

site: Finds results within a specified site and all its subdomains. You can also use this to check for results within a specified domain.

hostname: Finds results for a particular site only. For example, searching for `economy site:cnn.com` will find over 150,000 results. However, searching for `economy hostname:cnn.com` finds only about two dozen results because it's searching in cnn.com only, not money.cnn.com, us.cnn.com, etc.

link: Finds all pages that link to a specified URL. You must use the beginning of a URL—http://—in order for this to work properly.

linkdomain: This finds all pages that link to a particular domain. Unlike link:, you must not use http:// for this to work properly. A properly formatted search would be `linkdomain:cnn.com`.

url: Searches for a particular URL in the Yahoo search database.

inurl: Searches page URLs for a specified word.

intitle: Searches page titles for a specified word.

Yahoo's Shortcuts

Yahoo also has a class of special searches called Yahoo Shortcuts. These shortcuts offer a variety of searches for specific types of information that usually appear at the top of regular search results. You can get more information and a complete list of Yahoo Shortcuts at http://help.yahoo.com/help/us/ysearch/tips/tips-01.html. In the meantime, here are a few shortcuts you can check out.

Encyclopedia Lookup: Get *Columbia Encyclopedia* information about a topic by searching for that topic plus the word "facts." For example, `"George Washington" facts`.

Exchange Rates: Get the exchange rates between two types of currency by using the word "convert" and the two types of currency you want to convert. For example: `convert yen euro`. Even when this doesn't work directly, the search results can provide good points to converters.

Stocks: Enter the word "quote" and a symbol of a stock that's on the New York, American, or NASDAQ stock exchanges; for example, `quote luv`. You'll get a chart as well as a stock quote.

Time Zone: Enter the word "time" and a location to get the local time as well as that location's time zone; for example, `time Tokyo`.

Yahoo's Advanced Search Page. Don't forget to use Yahoo's Advanced Search Page. There are some things you can do with that page that you can't do with special syntaxes. For example, you can narrow your search by file type, by last update, by country, or by language. You can also implement a filter in the advanced search page.

Non-Web-Search Properties

The heart of Yahoo remains its searchable subject index, but by no means is that all of Yahoo. Yahoo is made up of huge numbers of properties—some search-oriented, some not—which cover a wide variety of ground on the Web. Here are some of the highlights.

Yahoo Daily News—http://dailynews.yahoo.com

Worldwide news in a huge number of categories, both searchable and browsable. To see what your fellow surfers are interested in, check out the most popular lists. Multimedia as well as text stories are included here. Read more about Yahoo Daily News in Chapter 14, "News Searching."

Yahoo Get Local—http://local.yahoo.com
Information on U.S. cities. You may browse by state or search by zip code. Information provided includes maps, weather, places to dine and shop, and other information.

Yahooligans—http://www.yahooligans.com
Yahoo for kids. Culture, sites, and news, but no adult-oriented sites.

Yahoo Reference—http://education.yahoo.com/reference/
Integrates many different kinds of reference materials—including a dictionary, thesaurus, encyclopedia, and fact book—into one searchable site. Also includes information on schools, degrees, and study guides.

Yahoo Maps—http://maps.yahoo.com/
Get maps for places as well as driving directions, and get maps to put on your own Web site.

You can get a full list of available Yahoo properties at http://docs.yahoo.com/docs/family/more.html. Don't forget to check out the World Yahoos at the bottom of the page and the editorial resources on the left side of the page.

The search engines are only the first step in your search journey, but when you are researching a new topic, trying to get a quick factoid, or just trying out some new search strategies, you will often start with search engines. So it's important that you have a good sense of how they work.

2 Other Search Engines

Most of the time when you hear about a search engine in the news, you're hearing about Google. Sometimes a story will mention Yahoo or another search engine, but most of the time it's about Google.

Because it's been that way for a few years now, it's easy to assume that it'll always be that way: that Google will be on top, and that all other search engines will be unnecessary. Google's a great search engine to be sure, but there are always other contenders. Until there's one search engine that indexes every page on the Web, offers every conceivable search syntax, and makes everybody on the Web happy, there will always be contention for the position of #1 search engine.

Other Engines

This book is not large enough for a discussion of every general search engine on the Web—there are literally hundreds of them. But I do want to take one more section and discuss some search engines that don't need their own chapters but are worthy of discussion.

Open Directory Project--http://www.dmoz.org

The Open Directory Project, also known as the ODP, is a searchable subject index of over four million sites. Like Yahoo, it's a searchable subject index. Unlike Yahoo, it contains no other properties—no news search, no mailing lists, no nothin'. Furthermore, it's a volunteer effort, maintained by an army of over 60,000 editors managing over half a million categories.

It's an amazing effort, and for the most part it's a very good directory. But because volunteers maintain the site, quality sometimes appears uneven; some categories are more active than others. Search is with plain keywords, with a Boolean default of AND. (You can also specify NOT with - and phrases with quotes.) If you go to the advanced search you'll think that your advanced search options are fairly limited. The advanced search allows you to limit your results by top-level category or limit your search to site listing or to categories (so you might search for "Dallas" and find the 42 categories that include the word "Dallas" but not the 4,000+ site listings that contain the word "Dallas"). You can also limit those search results to kid- and teen-appropriate sites.

If you go past the advanced search page and look on the search page, you'll see that you do have some search syntax options:

t: Search site titles only
u: Search site URLs only
d: Search site descriptions only

Of these three, the u: syntax is the least useful unless you want to get a sense of how many pages in a particular domain are indexed by the Open Directory Project. The ODP also offers the ability to list all pages from a certain domain, if you just search for the domain name itself. For example, searching the Open Directory Project for `AskJeeves.com` finds one category and one listing for a page at AskJeeves.com. (Beware of sites listed under multiple domain names; the Ask Jeeves search engine itself is actually listed under ask.com.)

The ODP also allows some stemming; you can add a wildcard (*) to the end of a word and get all the variants for that word. The search term `mili*` will find military, militia, etc.

The ODP doesn't get all the press that Google or Yahoo do, but it's important because of how often its data is used. The ODP makes its data freely available to other sites who want to use it, so you'll see ODP categories included all over the place. Knowing how to search that data will help you get around far more sites than just the ODP itself.

Gigablast--http://www.gigablast.com

Have you ever heard of Gigablast? Probably not. Gigablast is not a corporation but a guy named Matt Wells who's happened to put together quite a good search engine. Unlike most search engines, Gigablast defaults to the Boolean OR (and warns you about it in the search results, putting those results that do have all your search words at the top of the results and separating them from other results with a blue bar). Gigablast also supports not (AND NOT) as well as or (OR).

```
Skiing AND NOT "cross-country" AND NOT snowboarding
```

is a legitimate search in Gigablast.

Gigablast, though it's a full-text search engines, indexes far fewer pages than Google. So don't expect to get nearly as many results. You can use the following special syntaxes:

> suburl: keyword is in the URL
>
> site: query is from the specified site (you must specify an entire domain—like unc.edu—and not just a top-level domain like edu)
>
> url: searches for an entire URL
>
> title: searches for a keyword in Web page titles
>
> ip: searches for results from a specified IP address
>
> link: searches for pages that link to a specified URL
>
> type: searches for Web pages of a specified type. Types include PDF (type:pdf), Microsoft Word (type:doc), Microsoft Excel (type:xls), Microsoft PowerPoint (type:ppt), Postscript (type:ps), and plain text documents (type:txt).

Gigablast's search results look at first like Google's. There's a place for a cached result (though in this case it's called an archived copy) as well as information about the title and URL of the page. But there's also information about when the

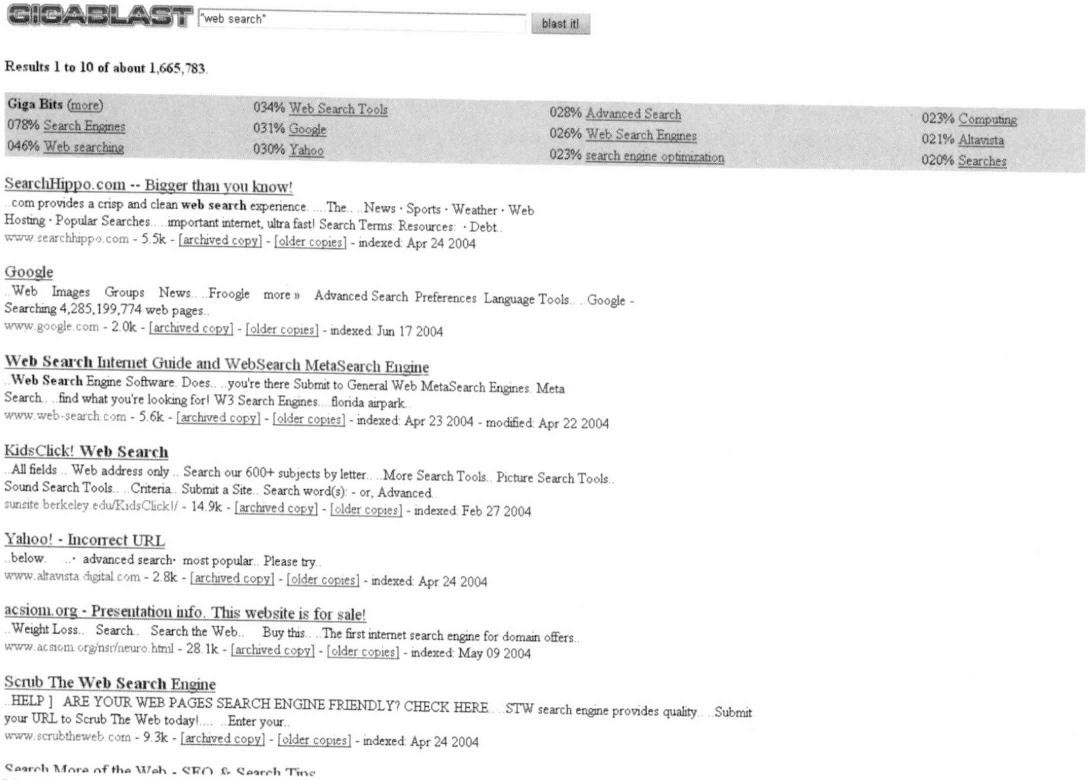

GIGABLAST "web search" blast it!

Results 1 to 10 of about 1,665,783.

Giga Bits (more)	034% Web Search Tools	028% Advanced Search	023% Computing
078% Search Engines	031% Google	026% Web Search Engines	021% Altavista
046% Web searching	030% Yahoo	023% search engine optimization	020% Searches

SearchHippo.com -- Bigger than you know!
..com provides a crisp and clean **web search** experience. ....The.. ..News · Sports · Weather · Web Hosting · Popular Searches.. ..important internet, ultra fast! Search Terms: Resources: · Debt..
www.searchhippo.com - 5.5k - [archived copy] - [older copies] - indexed: Apr 24 2004

Google
..Web Images Groups News.. ..Froogle more » Advanced Search Preferences Language Tools.. ..Google - Searching 4,285,199,774 web pages..
www.google.com - 2.0k - [archived copy] - [older copies] - indexed: Jun 17 2004

Web Search Internet Guide and WebSearch MetaSearch Engine
..**Web Search** Engine Software. Does.. ..you're there Submit to General Web MetaSearch Engines. Meta Search.. ..find what you're looking for! W3 Search Engines....florida airpark..
www.web-search.com - 5.6k - [archived copy] - [older copies] - indexed: Apr 23 2004 - modified: Apr 22 2004

KidsClick! **Web Search**
..All fields .. Web address only .. Search our 600+ subjects by letter.. ..More Search Tools.. Picture Search Tools.. Sound Search Tools.. ..Criteria.. Submit a Site.. Search word(s): - or, Advanced..
sunsite.berkeley.edu/KidsClick!/ - 14.9k - [archived copy] - [older copies] - indexed: Feb 27 2004

Yahoo! - Incorrect URL
..below. ..· advanced search· most popular.. Please try..
www.altavista.digital.com - 2.8k - [archived copy] - [older copies] - indexed: Apr 24 2004

acsiom.org - Presentation info. This website is for sale!
..Weight Loss.. Search.. Search the Web.. Buy this.. ..The first internet search engine for domain offers..
www.acsiom.org/nsr/neuro.html - 28.1k - [archived copy] - [older copies] - indexed: May 09 2004

Scrub The **Web Search** Engine
..HELP] ARE YOUR WEB PAGES SEARCH ENGINE FRIENDLY? CHECK HERE.. ..STW search engine provides quality.. ..Submit your URL to Scrub The Web today!.... ..Enter your..
www.scrubtheweb.com - 9.3k - [archived copy] - [older copies] - indexed: Apr 24 2004

Search More of the Web - SEO & Search Tips

02–01

Gigablast is not as well known as Google, but it has many interesting search result features. (Image from http://www.gigablast.com/search?k7h=552375&q=%22web+search%22.)

page was indexed (which in most cases Google does not provide) and an "older copies" link that leads to the Internet Archive, a vast repository of archived Web content gathered over a long period of time.

Gigablast has gotten some attention thus far, but not as much as I feel it might. This search engine is constantly undergoing improvement; if it indexes a lot more pages it could become a legitimate—and very independent—Google contender.

LookSmart/WiseNut--http://www.looksmart.com and http://www.wisenut.com

LookSmart and WiseNut are owned by the same company, but they're different search engines. LookSmart is a searchable subject index, while WiseNut is a full-text index.

LookSmart defaults to the Boolean AND; it is a basic keyword search with not much in the line of special syntaxes. Descriptions of sites are pretty good, but since listing in LookSmart nowadays requires money, your search results will be slanted more toward businesses and those who can afford to pay for a search engine listing.

WiseNut defaults to Boolean AND, though you can't be sure how many results you might get as it provides no count of how many pages are in its index. An advanced search (called WiseSearch) allows you to use a series of query boxes to specify allowed words, disallowed words, and phrases in the query. There's a preference page that lets you tweak how the search results display, but there's not much else in the way of advanced searching.

Because WiseNut doesn't indicate how many pages it indexes, it doesn't seem to offer much in the way of advanced searching, and because when I tried to review how to submit a page (to see if it was free or not—nonfree submission search engines have a very different index than those that allow free submissions) it timed out on me, I tend to put this one at the bottom of my searching heap. As a searcher you want to know how many pages are available in an index and how the pages get there (Are they paid for? Are the submissions free? Is the index purchased from somewhere else?), and if that information isn't available, that should send you a warning sign.

Ask Jeeves/Teoma--http://www.askjeeves.com and http://www.teoma.com

Back during the Internet boom days, Ask Jeeves was truly dynamic and innovative. And they proved it by doing things like advertising their search engine on fruit labels (this was back during the boom time, remember). What was innovative about their offerings was that they allowed a searcher to do *natural language searching*: enter a question instead of a search query ("Why is the sky blue?") and Ask Jeeves would attempt to answer the question.

However, that was then and this is now, and while Ask Jeeves does attempt to answer natural language questions, it also provides you sponsored (paid for)

Web results in addition to regular Web results. Ask it why the sky is blue and it'll tell you at the top of the page. It'll then give you a sponsored Web result (at this writing for an eBay affiliate) and from there give you results that mostly seem to come from pages that contain the words "blue" and "sky." So while you can get good answers to natural language questions (if you ask one it knows—don't ask it "Why does an elephant have a long nose?"), the relevance of its Web search results, in my opinion, leave a bit to be desired. If you really want to search an Ask Jeeves engine and you don't have a natural language question, use Teoma.

TIP

Is it always better to use the search engine that indexes the most pages? In other words, is bigger always better? In a word, no. No search engine indexes the entire Internet, and not every page indexed by a search engine is going to be relevant or useful. Your focus should be on getting the most useful results possible, not just getting the most results.

Teoma to me is much more interesting than Ask Jeeves, though also much newer. It's a full-text search engine that indexes about a billion pages.

Teoma defaults to Boolean AND, with a much more robust advanced search than WiseNut's. With the advanced search you can limit your search to the page title or URL, and limit results by domain or geographic region. You can also do limitations by date. Surprisingly enough the search `Why is the sky blue?` (no quotes) provides a reasonable result on the first page, though you also get a lot of irrelevant pages containing the phrase "blue sky."

Keeping an Eye Out for New Search Engines

Search engines are always popping up like mushrooms after a hard rain. A lot of them are "PFI" engines—Pay-for-Inclusion—that won't index your site unless you give them some money. I usually don't bother with those because I can't guarantee that the information I'm looking for will come from a site that can afford to pay to be included in every search engine that comes along. Others will index other sites, but will give preferred indexing and position to those that pay a fee. Sometimes I try those, and sometimes they work well (that is, they find the information I'm looking for) and sometimes they don't.

It's like this: Internet companies have to make a living somehow. Many search engines now charge for frequent indexing of a site and some other perks. This may become a standard way that search engines increase their revenue. So I don't want to tell you, "Don't ever use a search engine that accepts money for anything having to do with indexing." However, I will give you two hints:

1. Avoid search engines that will not include a site without payment, *unless* you're shopping. For example, if you're looking for a site that'll sell you flowers, it doesn't matter so much if you're using a search engine requiring payment, because retail sites on the Web are generally more likely to pay for

placement on a search engine. (Yahoo requires payment for listing commercial sites nowadays, but they didn't for so many years that they have a good database of sites to search. In addition, they have lots of paid surfers who will go around looking for "site of the day" candidates and other picks that aren't the type to pay to get into a directory.)

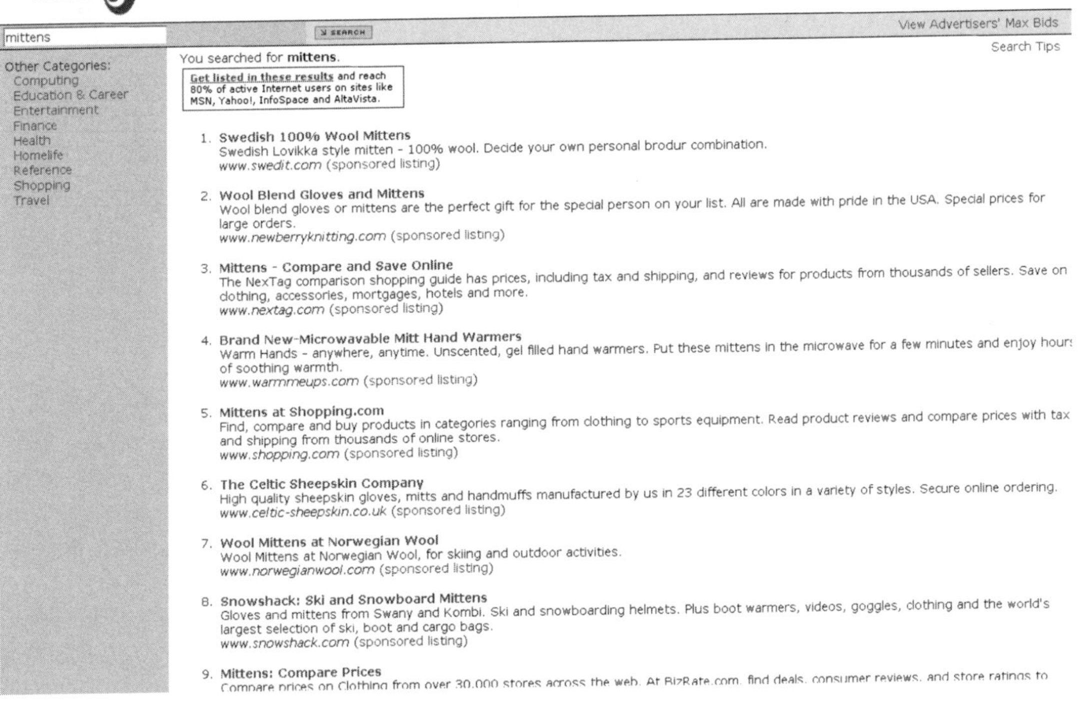

02–02

BeenShoppin'? Overture is a great engine when you want to get product information. (Image from http://www.overture.com/d/search/?type=topbar&mkt=us&lang=en_US&Keywords=mittens&sbuttonT.x=0&sbuttonT.y=0.)

2. When evaluating a site that does request money for listing, look at it what it's requesting. Is it requesting pay for any kind of placement? That's not good for your purposes. Pay for preferred placement (at the top of results)? That's okay if the listings are clearly indicated as sponsored listings (most of them are). Pay for more frequent indexing? That's fine and can actually benefit you, as more frequently indexed sites will have fresher content in the search engines. But when a search engine requests money—for any purpose other than advertising—you should always review what it's being requested for and take that into account when you use it.

Where should you look for new search engines? I have two favorite places: Yahoo's directory and Webmaster World.

Yahoo's Directory--http://directory.yahoo.com

I used to have a whole technique for searching Yahoo's directory, but I find that it doesn't work like it used to. So now I use Yahoo's latest listings instead.

Though you can't find results sorted by date on Yahoo, you can get the listings of the latest sites that Yahoo has added to its directory. These are available at http://dir.yahoo.com/new/. You'll see that Yahoo offers yesterday's additions on this page, in a categorized subject index, and you can also get archives at the bottom of the page.

For me, reviewing this set of new additions is a bit tedious but necessary, as my interests are difficult to encapsulate within one or two categories. If you can narrow your interests down to one or two categories, you might wish to monitor those categories with page monitoring software). For example, if you really like dogs, you could monitor the http://dir.yahoo.com/Science/Biology/Zoology/Animals__Insects__and_Pets/Mammals/Dogs/ page for changes and see if you can find any new search engines that way. See Chapter 11, "The Principle of the Expanding Web," for more hints on monitoring Google and Yahoo.

Webmaster World--http://www.webmasterworld.com

Webmaster World is a tremendous community for anybody interested in search engines or searching. There's a lot of information there tilted toward Webmasters (search engine optimization, site indexing, and that kind of thing) but certain forums will yield gold for researchers interested in keeping up with new resources.

The site is divided into several forums. The forums I recommend you keep up with are Alternative Search Engines, Directories, and any regional search engine forums in which you're interested (like European Search Engines).

With all the hype surrounding Google it's easy to get the idea that Google is *the* search engine and there will never be another one. The only problem with that is that there was a lot of hype surrounding Yahoo, AltaVista, and HotBot at one time! The Internet is always changing, and there are always new search engines out there. Don't get into the habit of using just one search engine. Stay out of the rut and keep your eyes open for new engines on which to experiment and hone your searching skills.

3

ONLINE TOOLS AND GADGETS: BROWSERS & MORE

If you've bought this book you know that the tool used to explore the World Wide Web is called a browser. (If you didn't know that, please take this book back and buy something a lot more basic. Thanks.)

Many people on the Internet use Windows, and many people who use Windows use Internet Explorer (because it's the browser that comes with Windows). But you don't need to use Internet Explorer; there are many other choices out there. (I use Opera, which I'll discuss in this chapter.) Even if you use Explorer and you're content with it, you can tweak it a little for security and a little for speed.

Once you've tweaked it, you can add to it. Search toolbars can be integrated into browsers and allow you to do precise search engine searching without having to visit the page. Bookmarklets—special bookmarks that contain JavaScript—allow you to do even more specific searching tasks. And there are plenty of Web-based tools and client-side tools (client-side means you install them on your computer) to help your searching. Preparing your browser and picking out a few useful programs will save you a lot of searching time down the road.

Let's start with browsers, since you use them most often.

Browsers

Browsers were very simple in the beginning, since HTML was very simple in the beginning. HTML files are basically text files formatted in a certain way. The browsers look at the formatting and, based on the formatting, present pages in a certain way.

But as the Internet has gotten older, HTML has given way to DHTML, XML, Flash, and many other ways to display information. There are still lots of HTML files around—I would guess that they're still the majority—but even they have become more complicated with the addition of JavaScript, Java, ActiveX, and other technologies. Because of all these technologies, different pages can be displayed in different ways. Keep this in mind as we discuss four well-known browsers, starting with the most popular: Internet Explorer and Netscape.

The Big Two

Internet Explorer—http://www.microsoft.com/ie/

Internet Explorer has one very good thing about it and one very bad thing. The very good thing is that it's overwhelmingly the most popular browser on the Web, and therefore most Web sites are designed to work well with it. In this chapter you're going to learn about toolbars, bookmarklets, and plugins, almost all of which work with Internet Explorer.

Unfortunately, the popularity that's the good thing is also the bad thing. Internet Explorer has had several security holes exposed throughout the years; some of them are severe enough that they can cause an intruder to be able to take over your entire computer! If you want to use Internet Explorer, that's okay. But you will need to be extra careful to keep it updated and to follow any reports of vulnerabilities.

Netscape—http://www.netscape.com

Back in the day—"the day" being 1996 or so—Netscape was a standalone company, its browser was incredibly popular, and most Web surfers were surfing via the big N.

Those days are long gone, but plenty of people still use Netscape (now a division of Time Warner). From Netscape.com you can download the browser by looking for the "Browser Central" link on the left side of the page. The Netscape browser is free.

Netscape and Internet Explorer really are the "big two"; those sites that design for browsers generally design for both Netscape and Internet Explorer (you will occasionally find a site that works only with Internet Explorer). That doesn't mean those are the only browsers available, however.

> **NOTE**
>
> You may be saying to yourself, "I don't need to worry about visiting a bad Web site that might take advantage of a security hole. I only visit safe sites. I'm very careful about where I go online." You might be incredibly cautious, but you're still at risk. Web sites get hacked. Domain names expire. And if you're doing searches on Google, can you be absolutely sure about every site you visit?

The Other Two

Mozilla—http://www.mozilla.org

Mozilla is an open-source browser developed by a team of people. Netscape's browser is partially based on Mozilla technology, but they're still different browsers. Web sites aren't as oriented toward designing for Mozilla as they are for IE or Netscape, but I find it makes a good backup to Opera. It's free.

mozilla

download products support developers about

search mozilla:

Make a donation
Join the thousands of Mozilla users who are supporting our work. We'll send you, or a friend, a Mozilla CD or t-shirt.

Mozilla CD & Store
Order all Mozilla software on CD and purchase Mozilla logo merchandise.
Order CD-ROM
Mozilla Merchandise

Latest News

17 June 2004
Mozilla 1.7 is out and includes improvements to pop-up blocking, multiple identity support in Mail, and much more. See the readme for more on "What's New in Mozilla 1.7".

16 June 2004
With a smaller download size,

Firefox 0.9

Firefox 0.9 Now Available!
Our award winning next generation browser is a sign of things to come from Mozilla. Powerful yet easy to use. Perfect for those who live on the cutting edge! Press Release, Release Notes, More Information...
download: Windows, Linux, Mac OS X or in Europe: Windows, Linux, Mac OS X (or try other download sites)

Mozilla 1.7

- For web browsing, email, HTML editing, IRC chat, and more
- Built with your privacy and security in mind
- Stop popups and junk mail
- Open multiple web pages in the same window with tabbed browsing

Free Download: Windows, Linux, Mac OS X, More... or in Europe: Windows, Linux, Mac OS X or via BitTorrent: Windows, Linux, Mac OS X
Order the CD & Guidebook

"Best browser of 2003"
— *PC World Magazine*

"Beyond Bliss"
— *Time Magazine*

Technology Preview

Mozilla 1.8 Alpha 1
This is the latest preview of the Mozilla application suite, including Navigator, Messenger, and Composer.

03–01

Mozilla actually offers several different types of browsers. (Image from http://www.mozilla.org/.)

Opera—http://www.opera.com

It's a browser, not a musical style. Opera is a browser company that's the David to Internet Explorer's Goliath. There's a free version but it's supported by advertising. The paid version costs $39 at this writing.

Why would you pay $39 for a browser when all the other ones listed here are free? I've used Opera for several years now and I love it. Without Java it's a small download, the system requirements tend to be lower than other browsers (so if you're using an older computer you may want to consider it first), and it was one of the first browsers that had multiple window capability, handy when you're constantly jumping from page to page like I am.

Other Browsers to Consider

There aren't as many browsers as there used to be back in the beginning of the Internet boom, but there are still plenty. I haven't even mentioned here iCab (browser for the Macintosh, http://www.icab.de/), or the text-only browser Lynx (http://lynx.isc.org/release/), or the default browser for the Mac OS X operating system, Safari (http://www.apple.com/safari/). You can get an extensive list of the browsers available at http://dir.yahoo.com/Computers_and_Internet/Software/Internet/World_Wide_Web/Browsers/.

Which Browser Should I Use?

You may have noticed that I'm giving you a lot of browsers to consider but I'm not telling you which one to use. It depends on what your priorities are.

If you want to make sure that your browser is compatible with as many sites as possible and you're using a fairly new computer, you want to use Internet Explorer. If your computer isn't quite as new and you still want compatibility, or you don't want to use Internet Explorer for whatever reason, try Netscape. If you have an older computer and you want to use a graphical browser with low system requirements, look into Opera. If you're the geeky type who likes tinkering with system settings and you want to support the open-source community, give Mozilla a whirl.

No matter what browser you decide to use, don't just install it and start surfing. Take the time to tweak your browser for security issues and for bandwidth issues.

Optimizing Your Browser for Security

It seems like every five minutes there's a news story about a new security vulnerability. And these things are scary; baddies can install software on your computer, read your cache, even direct your computer to other Web sites without your permission. But if you take a few moments and tweak your browser settings, you can surf a little safer.

Tweaking these settings will change your browsing experience. You'll find that some pages won't work. There will be times that you'll have to adjust your browser settings in order to play a game or view a certain type of content. I've found it doesn't happen that often and it's worth the security tradeoff.

Turn Off Scripting

Look under the Preferences for the Scripting option. For browsers besides IE there's a listing for JavaScript, but IE has several scripting options. Look under Tools -> Internet Options, and from there choose Security, and then Custom Options. Look at the listings for Active X Controls and Plug-Ins. Usually I turn all these entries to the Disable option, or at least Prompt (with the prompt option, Internet Explorer will ask you before it runs an ActiveX control).

NOTE

While these recommendations will help you surf safer, your computer connects to the Internet in other ways besides a Web browser. If you're using a broadband connection (like a cable or a DSL modem), a firewall and anti-virus software are essential. (A firewall is either hardware or software that controls communications between your computer and the Internet.) Even if you're on a much slower dialup connection, you want to consider a firewall (anti-virus software is essential no matter how you connect to the Internet). Don't use these browser security tweaks and think your computer is completely safe. It isn't.

Turn Off Java

Most browsers will have an option for turning off Java, except for text-only browsers like Lynx and the non-Java version of Opera. I've found that rarely is Java necessary to a Web site, and that turning it off usually speeds up my browsing a little bit.

NOTE

Wondering where you're going to find all these switches? It depends on your browser. Look for a Preferences option.

Turn Off Auto-Password Reminders

If you share your computer with anybody, this one's pretty important. Turn off the options to auto-remember passwords so that nobody who uses your browser after you can log in to your Web sites.

Turn Off Pop-Ups

Pop-ups are less about security risks and more about your browser getting overwhelmed. If you're running low on memory, and you hit a site that opens ten pop-up windows at once, your browser and possibly your entire computer will crash. Pop-ups are not the problem that they used to be (most major sites and search engines have abandoned them as surfers tend to really hate them), but they're still used on some sites. Some browsers (and toolbars) offer you the option to only open pop-up windows you specify—they are used legitimately on many sites.

Almost as important as optimizing your browser for security is optimizing your browser for speed. Some of you who are using broadband connections might be saying, "Aw, I don't need to read this part." You have my formal permission to skip it—but I still think these tips will come in handy if you're forced to use a dialup connection, if you're on the road away from your broadband, or there's some other crisis that takes you away from your blazing speed.

Optimizing Your Browser for Speed

NOTE

Some people absolutely cannot stand surfing with images turned off. They feel like they're missing something, or they tend to like image-heavy sites, or they don't like the way that no images messes up the formatting on some sites. So while this tip will speed up your searching a lot, you might find that you just really don't like it.

Turn Off Some Plugins

When you disable ActiveX and Java, you're both helping with the security issues and you're speeding up your browser a little bit. With Java disabled, Java programs don't start up, and with ActiveX disabled, you often don't see Flash movies (which can sometimes be quite large and require a long download). If you're still seeing Flash movies, go into the Plug-Ins part of your Preferences and turn Flash off.

Try Turning Off Images

Once you've gotten used to having all those scripting and content options turned off, try turning images off. One of the reasons I love Opera so much is that you can easily toggle images on and off; unfortunately far too many sites don't know what ALT tags are, and you'll need images at least part of the time. If you're using Mozilla you can install the

Preferences toolbar, available at http://prefbar.mozdev.org/, which allows you to toggle images, JavaScript, pop-up windows, and a variety of other preferences on and off. Once you're surfing without images you'll be amazed at how often you're *not* missing anything, and you're going a lot faster.

Just like a firewall can add security to your browsing experience, using a couple of programs external to your browser can also speed up your surfing experience.

First off, check your firewall; it can speed up your surfing too! Some firewalls, like Symantec's Norton Internet Security, have an ad block feature that strips ads of many ad networks from Web pages. (Of course, if you're surfing without images, you won't see most ads anyway.) Fewer ads means faster loading.

If you're not running a firewall that offers this feature, check the software repositories on the Internet or check in and see if your Internet service provider offers ad-filtering software.

I must confess that I give you this information with a divided mind. On one hand you should be able to make the most of a dialup connection. On the other hand Web sites can't stay in business unless they're able to generate revenue. So try to strike a balance with this one; if you're blocking all images, consider donating to sites you find very useful or subscribing to online resources you want to support.

Once you're done adjusting your browser's preferences for security and bandwidth, you're still not finished completely. You'll need to round out the power of your browser by adding some plugins.

Finding and Using Plugins and Helper Applications

What's a plugin? A plugin is a bit of software that integrates with your browser to allow it to display certain kinds of content. A helper application is a software program that allows you to display content that you might download via your browser, like a PowerPoint display you might get from a Web site.

I can't give you an exhaustive list of every kind of plugin and content on the Internet. But I can tell you the ones I come across the most frequently, and which ones you're likely to come across most frequently as well.

NOTE

Some browsers already have the ability to read some of the content formats mentioned here, so be sure to check before you download new plugins.

Absolutely Necessary Plugins

PDF—Portable Document Format

Brought to you by Adobe, this format is the standard for many government forms and online paper presentations. You can get a list of several different readers for several different operating systems (including OS/2 Warp) at http://www.adobe.com/products/acrobat/alternate.html.

Microsoft Word

Sometimes people will put up papers in Microsoft Word instead of Acrobat, either because they don't have Adobe Acrobat or because Microsoft Word is the standard in their office. If you don't have Word, or you have an older version, use the reader at http://office.microsoft.com/downloads/2000/wd97vwr32.aspx. It reads Word 97 and Word 2000 files.

Windows Media Player

Now, just because I'm mentioning all this Microsoft stuff doesn't mean that I want you to go out and buy piles of Microsoft products. It just means that a lot of people use Microsoft formats. I see that the Windows Media Format, used for video and audio, has been getting more popular lately, though just from observation I'd say that Real still has a bit of an edge. Anyway, you can get Windows Media players at http://www.microsoft.com/windows/windowsmedia/players.asp. Players are available for Windows, Mac, Solaris, Palm OS, and Pocket PC.

Apple Quicktime

Don't be fooled by the Apple in Apple Quicktime—it runs very nicely in Windows. And Mac, of course. At http://www.apple.com/quicktime/download/ you can both download this movie player (for free) and upgrade to QuickTime Pro (for $).

Real—RealAudio, RealVideo

First it was called RealAudio, then it was called RealVideo, now it's just called Real. This was one of the first streaming media players available and it's still used by an awful lot of sites.

Unfortunately Real's in the position where they're trying to make money just like everybody else, so you might get the impression when you visit their site that you have to pay for their player. They do have a player that costs, but they also have a free version. You can get to it at http://www.real.com/realoneplayer.html. Look for the link on the right that says "Download Free RealPlayer" and click on that. This download is for Windows.

Macromedia Shockwave and Macromedia Flash

You might not know Shockwave, which is used for really interactive stuff, but you probably know Flash, which is used for movies and games and ads. You can download players for several different operating systems at http://sdc.shockwave.com/shockwave/download/alternates/. And to test and see if your Flash plugin works, may I recommend the Flash version of Tom Lehrer's "The Elements Song"? It's at http://www.privatehand.com/flash/elements.html.

The players above are for content that you'll run into a lot. But there are a few more players I'd like to recommend, mostly for Microsoft Office content.

Not As Essential, but Still Very Useful

XLS—Microsoft Excel

Google indexes Microsoft Excel content, making it possible that you might find an Excel file and need to read it. You can download a reader at http://office.microsoft.com/downloads/2000/xlviewer.aspx that handles Excel 97 and Excel 2000 documents.

Microsoft PowerPoint

Like Excel, Google indexes PowerPoint documents, and unlike, say, Word, PowerPoint documents transformed into HTML can be really hard to read. Downloading the viewer at http://office.microsoft.com/downloads/2000/Ppview97.aspx will let you read PowerPoint 97, 2000, and 2002.

As I said earlier, there's no way that I can cover every potential content type on the Internet, but you don't need me to. There are other places on the Web to get information on plugin types if you find yourself confronted with some content type you've never heard of.

Places to Find More Plugins

Netscape's Plugin Directory—http://wp.netscape.com/plugins/

If you're running Netscape (and probably Mozilla, though that isn't made clear at this site) you'll want to use what's probably the granddaddy of plugin sites. From here the Netscape users can see what plugins they've got installed, get information on implementing plugins on their own sites, and browse a selection of available plugins divided by categories, including audio/video and presentations. Use the finder (http://wp.netscape.com/plugins/search_pi.html?cp=plp) to get a list of plugins by operating system or type.

Download.com—http://download.com.com/3150-2378-0.html?tag=dir

Yeah, Download.com is a general software site, but they've got a plugins section (that's what you'll get when you go to the URL above). You'll find at this writing over 60 plugins, which you can list by date added, number of downloads, and name. Some plugins are rated by users and can be sorted by that as well.

Tucows—http://www.tucows.com/internet.html

Yup, Tucows is another general-download site, but they've got an Internet section. The above URL is for Internet software for Windows machines—look for the "Web Browsers and Tools" section. The Mac page is at http://mac.tucows.com/internet.html and the Linux page is at http://linux.tucows.com/internet.html.

I know it seems like a lot of work to mess around with a browser so much even before you start searching, but it'll pay off. You'll save time, you won't bump up against unknown content types when you're hot on the trail of some research, and you won't go (as) cold every time you read a browser security alert.

Up to this point we've just talked about the browser in particular, but now we need to step back and look at more software. Some software integrates directly into the browsers—like search toolbars—while other software runs from the desktop. Let's start with search toolbars, which allow you to run searches without having to visit search engine sites.

Search Toolbars

Search toolbars are compatible mostly with Internet Explorer, though I will mention some here that work with other browsers or that are platform independent. Search toolbars integrate with your browser and allow you to search particular resources from your browser without having to visit a Web site. They'll give you other information, too—Google's toolbar, for example, allows you to see the "Page Rank" of a page, giving you an indication of how popular it is. (Page Rank is calculated by Google and has some impact on the ranking of a page within Google's search results. Google's not talking about exactly how this works.)

As you might expect, Google's popularity means that there are many versions of its search available via a toolbar. There are toolbars for other search engines available as well.

Google Toolbars

The Official Google Search Toolbar—that is, the one put out by Google—is available at http://toolbar.google.com/. You'll need Internet Explorer to install and use it. (If you get an error message when you try to install it with Internet Explorer, go into your security options and enable file download.)

Once you download the toolbar, you'll have the option to install the toolbar with the advanced features either enabled or disabled. Enabled means that Google will send anonymous information to Google about your surfing. Disabled means no information about your surfing will be sent.

Once you've installed the toolbar you'll see it appears at the top of your screen.

This search allows you to search the Web, search just the site you're browsing (those parts of it which have been indexed by Google, anyway), vote on whether or not you like a page, view a site's Page Rank, get Google-provided information about a page (cache, similar pages, backward links, etc.), and move up one level on the site you're looking at (for example, if you're browsing at http://www.example.com/levelone/, one click would move you to http://www.example.com). That's a lot to be able to do without having to visit the Google Web site.

But you're only seeing some of the toolbar options. Click on the Google logo on the far left of the toolbar for a whole slew of other options, including direct links to other Google search properties, an automatic pop-up window blocker, and an "auto-fill" button that automatically fills out basic form information (and it goes without saying that if you share your computer you shouldn't use the auto-fill feature).

If you use IE, I absolutely recommend that you use Google's official toolbar. It offers Page Rank information, and Google's been very good about frequently updating it. But if you don't use IE, you'll have to consider another Google toolbar. You have two choices.

Mozilla or Netscape—The Googlebar Project

Use Mozilla or Netscape? Check out the Googlebar project at http://googlebar.mozdev.org/. You can download the latest version of the 'bar at http://googlebar.mozdev.org/installation.html.

If you've used the "official" version of Google's toolbar with IE, the Googlebar will look really familiar. In fact, it can provide all the information that

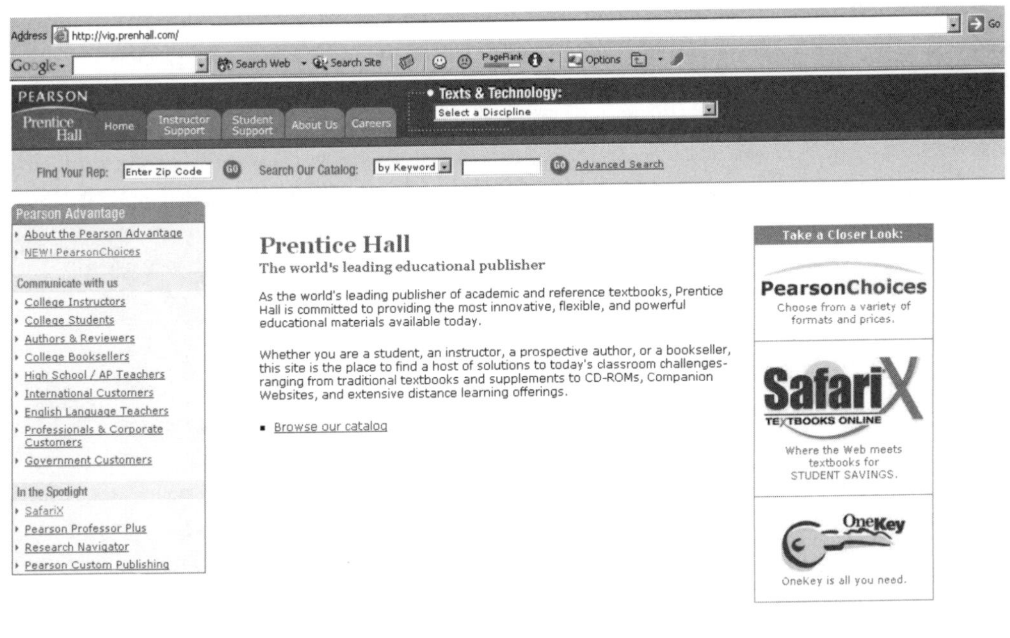

03–02

The installed Google toolbar fits right in with the IE menu.

the official version can with the exception of Page Rank. From this toolbar you can use the "I'm Feeling Lucky" function, search Google's regular searches (Google Groups, News, Directory, Catalogs, etc.), and use all the specialty searches (Uncle Sam, BSD, glossary, etc.).

You can also get page information from the toolbar (like the cache, if available), related pages, backwards links, or a one-button translation to English. Very handy. And for one-touch searching, highlight a word and click on the highlighter icon to search for that word in Google.

But maybe you don't use IE or Mozilla/Netscape. Maybe you use Opera or something else. What do you do then? Google SearchTool to the rescue!

> **NOTE**
>
> Make sure that your Software Installation is enabled (Preferences -> Advanced | Software Installation) or installing this toolbar won't work.

Google SearchTool

The Google SearchTool isn't tied in to the browser—it runs as a desktop application (a very small desktop application. Once you've downloaded it and installed it from http://www.frysianfools.com/ggsearch/, you'll have to launch it independently of your browser.

Once you do, you'll see that it sticks as a top window no matter what you do. Here you'll have the option to search several Google properties, including Web sites, news, groups, images, and stocks. If you pass your mouse underneath the query box, you'll see "Click here for options." Click there and you'll get options to set options for this site, including turning the relevance filter on and off, turning safe search on and off, and changing the number of search results you're getting. Unless you use IE, I strongly recommend you choose "Enable custom browser," because otherwise when you run a search using the SearchTool the default browser (usually IE) will open with the results. A lot of fun to use.

Of course Google isn't the only search engine option in town; Teoma and Ask Jeeves are also offering their own toolbars. You'll need IE for these.

Teoma Toolbar

You can download the Teoma toolbar at http://sp.ask.com/docs/teoma/toolbar/.

Once the Teoma toolbar has been installed, it'll appear as a toolbar under your location bar. The default install puts three items on the toolbar: a query box, a Highlight button, and a button for e-mailing a page to a friend.

The query box works as you'd expect. Enter a search query in the query box and you'll get a Teoma page full of results. Hit the Highlight key in the toolbar and instantly all the query terms on the page are highlighted. If you click the "Email this Page to a Friend" option, you'll get a pop-up box that you can use to send the title and URL of the page you're doing to an e-mail address. (It doesn't send the entire page.)

Clicking on the Teoma button at the left of the toolbar gives you the option to add one more button—check dictionary—as well as the ability to change highlight colors, change the button style, and visit the Teoma homepage. You can't do as much with this toolbar as you can with Google's, but I like the ability to e-mail pages.

Ask Jeeves Toolbar

You can download the Ask Jeeves toolbar from http://sp.ask.com/docs/toolbar/. It's also IE only, so everything I mentioned about IE and ActiveX applies to this toolbar as well.

The Ask Jeeves toolbar offers far more than the Teoma toolbar. There are only a few things on the default installation of the toolbar—query box, highlight tool, news search, a button for sending a link to a friend, and a JeevesLinks tool I'll get into in a moment. But by clicking on the Ask Jeeves logo on the right, you can get add several buttons, including search AJ Kids, search dictionary, search stocks, and the weather.

I like the toolbar better than the regular Ask Jeeves interface. I also like the Jeeves Links. This is a little bookmark manager that allows you to add bookmarks to a favorites list and then use them in a variety of ways, including sending them out by e-mail. Jeeves Links takes a little getting used to, so be sure to read the help file (available by clicking on the Jeeves logo at the left of the toolbar).

You may be used to just visiting a search engine to do your searches, but search toolbars can give you plenty of search oomph without ever leaving your browser. If you're not using IE, I heartily recommend Google SearchTool. If you use IE and you'd like to explore something beyond the official Google toolbar, give the Ask Jeeves toolbar a whirl.

Specialty Toolbars

The toolbars that are most relevant to everyone who reads this book are the search engine toolbars. But there are literally thousands of other toolbars out there. Some of them are basic search tools for one site, while others aggregate searches for a variety of sites. Let's take a few minutes to examine how you can find these specialty toolbars.

But first, a few cautionary words.

A Cautionary Word for Toolbar Users

And that word is: privacy. Before you install any toolbar, make sure you read and understand the privacy statement. Since it hooks into your browser, a non-private toolbar can do nasty things.

Are you feeling cautioned yet? Fine. Let's look for toolbars.

Finding Specialty Toolbars on the Web

You may know of a site or two that has a toolbar in which you're interested, but I found that to find toolbars that interested me I had to do a Google search. Toolbars are not ubiquitous; you may find more of one type than another one. And you'll probably have to do some search experiments.

The simplest core search is for a keyword and the word toolbar. Use very general keywords; if you're interested in medical issues, start with the keyword "medical" or "biology"; don't start with something like "aneurism."

```
toolbar biology
```

From this search you'll see some good stuff at the very top mixed in with some not so good stuff. Since this toolbar is IE-specific, you can try mixing in some IE-specific keywords:

```
toolbar biology IE
```

Yuck! That didn't help at all. Maybe a keyword that specifies that the toolbar is downloadable?

```
toolbar biology download
```

That was somewhat better. Like I said, you're going to have to do some experimenting to get to the search results you want. Try searching for `medical toolbar`, `stocks toolbar`, and `books toolbar` for more examples of how these search bars might turn out.

Search toolbars aren't the only tools that integrate directly into the browser. There's also bookmarklets. Bookmarklets are like bookmarks, but they're a little more powerful.

Bookmarklets

What's a Bookmarklet?

If you've been using the Internet for any length of time you know about bookmarks. But you may not be as familiar with bookmarklets. If you want to be a power surfer, though, it'll benefit you to get familiar with them; they can make your browsing, searching, and even site developing a lot easier.

Bookmarklets (also known as favelets) are not plain HTML links like a regular bookmark. Instead they're small bits of JavaScript code that you access from your browser just as you'd access a bookmark. There's a limit to how much JavaScript bookmarklets can contain, but they can still do all kinds of useful things: search, translate, give page information, resize windows, and even more.

Bookmarklets and Browsers

Because bookmarklets are made of JavaScript, you'll obviously have to have JavaScript enabled in your browser for them to work. You'll also find that which browser you use will make a difference as to which bookmarklets are available for you. If you use Internet Explorer, you'll find that most of the bookmarklets you come across will work. If you use Netscape, Opera, or Mozilla, however (especially the older versions), you'll find that some of the bookmarklets don't work at all. Many bookmarklet listings note which browsers aren't compatible. Some bookmarklets give you an error message when you try to use them with noncompatible browsers, while others simply do nothing.

Adding a Bookmarklet to Your Browser

Adding a bookmarklet to your browser is no big deal. It works much like adding a bookmark.

> Internet Explorer—To add a bookmarklet to Explorer, click on the link and drag it to the favorites folder of your choice; you may find you've found so many useful bookmarklets that you want to set up a separate bookmarklets folder. IE may give you a warning that the link you're going to add is not safe; that's because it contains JavaScript. Specify that you do want to continue and the bookmarklet will be added to your favorites.
>
> Mozilla—Either right-click the link and choose "Bookmark This Link" or click-and-drag the link to your personal toolbar.
>
> Opera—Right-click the link and choose "Add Link to Bookmarks," as you would normally save a bookmark.

So What?

Are you asking, "So what? Why should I care about bookmarklets?" Good. I'll tell you why.

Bookmarklets can give you a lot of search shortcuts without your having to use a toolbar or Internet Explorer. In addition, you can do some very specific search tasks with some bookmarklets that you might not find on a search toolbar. I have a bookmarklet called a "LuckyMarklet"—enter a query and it goes straight to the first result of a Google search. I use it constantly. (You can get LuckyMarklets at http://www.researchbuzz.org/archives/001414.shtml.)

Where to Find Bookmarklets

Now that you know what they are, here are some collections of cool bookmarklets that'll give a little edge to your surfing.

Bookmarklets—http://www.bookmarklets.com/—Bookmarklets.com is probably the most famous bookmarklet site on the Web. This site contains dozens of bookmarklets divided into several categories including page data, search tools, and calculators/converters.

You can find plenty of cool bookmarklets here, but start by going through the whole Search Tools section. Bookmarklets you'll find here include searches for several search engines, directories, and news searches, image searches, and even a phone book search. Be careful, though; at this writing there are bookmarklets for search engines that haven't been active for years. Test each resource before you add it to your toolbox.

Favelets—http://tantek.com/favelets/—If you do a lot of HTML authoring you'll like this collection. It allows you to automate a lot of design and validation tasks, including validation of CSS and HTML, resizing windows all the way down to iPaq size, and viewing CSS and images.

This collection of bookmarklets isn't particularly search-oriented, but do give the translation bookmarklets a try; using them you can translate French, German, Spanish, Italian, and Japanese pages to English.

Jesse's Bookmarklets Site—http://www.squarefree.com/bookmarklets/—This is an unusual collection of bookmarklets. You'll find a bookmarklet here to tip a site through Yahoo's PayDirect.com, a bookmarklet that lets you transfer cookies to another browser, and an entire category called "Zap," which lets you fix site annoyances (removing plugin activity, deleting cookies, and even translating "leet speak"!). Bookmarklets are marked by platform and some of them are customizable.

There are bookmarklets on this site good for both gathering and searching data. Check out the link bookmarklets; using them you can list all links on a page, hide visited links on a page, and open all links in a new window (warning: this will crash your browser if there are too many links on a page!), and it changes link color based on whether you've visited them or not.

Milly's Bookmarklets—http://www.imilly.com/bml.htm—This brief list of bookmarklets mostly focuses on specialized searches in Google. Searches here include searching the Microsoft Knowledge Base via Google and searching one of the Google specialty searches (Google Images, Google News, etc.). You can even search the Google Glossary. Any of these will help you in your searching since for the most part they're focused on Google.

WorldTimZone Bookmarklets—http://www.worldtimzone.com/bookmarklets/—This one-page selection of bookmarklets covers seven categories, including

Navigation, Search Engines, Religion and Christianity (find a saint, Bible lookup), and World Lookup (dictionary, thesaurus, acronyms, and more). There's a separate page of bookmarklets relevant to and useful for Open Directory Project volunteers and editors. Spend some time wandering around the general search category, but you should also look at the other categories, as you will find some specialty search help (like the bible lookup).

Bookmarklets for Opera—http://www.philburns.com/bookmarklets.html—Feeling a little left out, Opera users? This site provides bookmarklets specifically for the Opera browser. Options here include searching, code validation, and navigation (though a little warning: don't try the "Open all Links in New Windows" bookmarklet unless you're sure your browser can stand plenty of new windows opening at once!). There's a brief list of searching bookmarklets here.

Bookmarklets—http://wwwhomes.manni-heumann.de/soft/misc/bookmarklets.html—Another collection of bookmarklets, I include it here because it has some interesting and unusual bookmarklets, like checking a site's server uptime, counting the number of images on a page, and splitting frames into separate new windows. These bookmarklets are not as search-oriented—there's a searching section here but it's very small—but I wanted to include it to give you a sense of the many kinds of tasks bookmarklets can do.

Search toolbars are useful and they're integrated into your browser. Bookmarklets are useful but they too are integrated into your browser as "bookmarks on steroids." But neither of these tools are going to do you much good if you're on a very minimal browser (you're surfing from a cell phone or handheld device, for example) or you're using a computer that's not your own and doesn't have your tools integrated into it. In those cases there are other tools you can use; those are the Web-based gadgets, and boy, are there plenty of them.

Web-Based Gadgets

I differentiate between a tool and a gadget this way: a tool is something you have to download and install on your computer (like a program that sits on your desktop, a search toolbar, or a bookmarklet you put into your browser. They can be pretty hefty and can perform several tasks. Tools are Good Things.

But sometimes you don't need a tool to do what you need to do. Sometimes a tool is overkill. Maybe you just need a small item to do one thing. Sometimes you can find a Web page on the Internet that has the very thing you're looking for. I call those items "gadgets" because they don't require downloading, they're usually light, and they perform one task.

There are plenty of gadgets available online that can make your research just a bit easier, or just get your browsing off on the right foot.

Browser Sniffer—http://www.webreference.com/tools/browser/javascript.html—If you're using the latest version of Internet Explorer and you keep it constantly updated, ignore this gadget—you probably have very little problem using the Web. But if you're like me and you use Opera, you're in a minority—Web sites were not designed with our browsers in mind. If you're trying to use a site that does an automatic browser detect before it displays a page, or refuses to display at all because you're using an allegedly incompatible browser, don't tear all your hair out. Use this browser sniffer first. It'll tell you plenty of information about what kind of browser you're using—hopefully enough that you can troubleshoot any display problems when you're trying to visit a site.

Sometimes it's enough to just change the way your browser identifies itself to other Web pages (Opera can do that easily)—on the other hand, sometimes you've got to (gasp!) use another browser.

NOTE

You'll need to make sure JavaScript is enabled in your browser for many of these gadgets to work.

Word Frequency Counter—http://www.georgetown.edu/cball/webtools/web_freqs.html—This gadget is very handy if you're using a Web site that contains a lot of specialized and unfamiliar vocabulary. What you do here is paste in a chunk of text, and the tool provides you with one of three reports—you can get the most frequently used words listed first, the least frequently used words first, or the words in alphabetical order.

Running a test on the Gettysburg Address shows there are 140 unique words in the 265-word address, and the most common word is "that."

This tool cannot distinguish between single words and phrases, so its usefulness is limited. However, if you're on a page that uses a lot of unfamiliar words or jargon (like a medical article, for example), this is a good way to get a list of the most frequently used words. Use the unique ones to narrow down your research.

Calculators

When you think calculators you may think simple 2 + 2 = 4 type stuff. But there are many different types of calculators online, covering everything from cooking to scientific units.

Calculator.com—http://www.calculator.com/index.html—This is a searchable subject index of calculators. Categories include agriculture, brewing(!), and photography. There aren't many annotations; fortunately most calculators are self-explanatory. Calculator.com has a developer program, so if there's ever been a calculator you wanted desperately to develop and put online, now's your chance.

Martindale's Reference Desk: Calculator Center—http://www.martindalecenter.com/Calculators.html—There are over 17,000 calculators on this site. Seventeen thousand! I didn't even know there was that much stuff to calculate! Categories are all over the place, ranging from gambling to cameras to clothing to energy.

Resources are annotated and most are noted for their depth of coverage (very extensive, very very extensive, etc.). There's also plenty of cross-referencing. When you're looking for calculators that are on the obscure side, make this your first stop. One warning: they tend to pile a lot of resources on a single page, so your page-load time is pretty extensive.

Converters

There are so many systems of measurement in the world, is it any surprise that there are so many online converters available?

03–03

It's not all pluses and minuses. Sometimes it's oats and crop rotation. (Image from http://www.calculator.com/pantaserv/get?dbname=calcindex&sts=reg&_lt=list&header=hdlist&footer=ftcat&category=Agricultural&subcategory=Crop.)

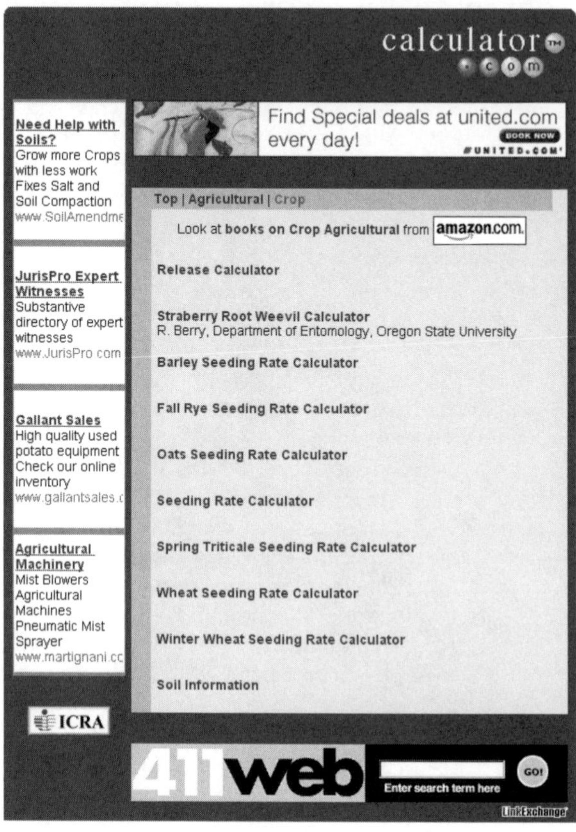

OnlineConversion.com—http://www.onlineconversion.com/—There are over 5,000 units and 50,000 conversions available. There are some calculators here, but there are also plenty of conversions—for speed, weight, cooking, and time. Annotations are good and it looks like all the converters are available on this site (no 404 errors!). If you're in need of a break, check out the fun stuff section and see how old you are in dog years.

Convert-me.com—http://www.convert-me.com/en/—Not only is this site pretty, it also has plenty of explanations and help for using their converters, though it doesn't cover as wide a range as some of the other resources I've covered here.

Categories are simple (distance, weight and mass, speed, etc.) but nicely designed and available on the site. For example, if you go to the speed category, you'll get several conversions available on one page. If you're not clear about how to use a converter, there's a general help file available. And below that there are several books (linked to Amazon) relevant to measurements and conversions.

efunda Cool Calculators—http://www.efunda.com/calculator.cfm—Warning: most of these calculators are engineering-oriented. And while the site is friendly and breezy, it's friendly and breezy in an engineering sort of way. ("OK, we all remember that an isotropic material requires only 2 elastic constants to describe its material behavior." What? Huh?)

Putting that aside, these calculators are well annotated and very thorough (check out the beam calculators and spring calculators to get an idea of what I mean). If you, like me, know next to nothing about engineering, you can investigate the financial and currency calculators at the top of the screen.

MegaConverter 2—http://www.megaconverter.com/mega2/—Putting aside the fact that MegaConverter sounds like a robot hero ("Look out, Voltron! It's MegaConverter!"), this is a useful site. You might have to get used to the interface, though.

The left side of the page is a remote control–like interface that allows you to choose from several different types of converters (including a Roman numeral converter, pressure, and wind chill). The right side of the page contains a frame with the converter.

While you're using a frame with a calculator, you can use several of the other buttons on the left frame's remote control. Pop It Up puts the converter in its own pop-up box. Converter Info gives both information on the converter and the theory behind the conversion.

Miscellaneous

I found a couple more online gadgets I really wanted to share with you but which didn't fit in any particular category.

Internet Clocks, Counters, and Countdowns—http://www.panaga.com/clocks/clocks.htm—The Internet has its share of clocks—you've heard of the Doomsday Clock? How about the Bill Gates Wealth Clock, the Environmental Clock, or the Death Clock? Some of these are just entertaining but some of them can help you look at things from a different angle. For example, try the Age Clocks; enter your birth date and find your age in relation to several different people and events.

Form Resources—http://www.formresources.com/formresources/index.html—Did you see some things in this article you'd like to have on your own site? Form Resources provides access to what looks like hundreds of different forms. There are many categories here, though only a few of them are calculators and converters. Among the calculators and converters are a mortgage calculator, a currency converter, and, um, a beer profit calculator. You'll have to poke around a bit to find the calculators and converters, but if you're looking for tools for your site, Form Resources is worth a closer look.

Up to this point most of the tools I've told you about revolve around your browser—they're for installing in your browser or using with your browser or accessing through your browser. But there's a whole other class of software you'll find useful: client-side software. Client-side software is software that installs on your computer; you don't access it through the Web or via e-mail. A browser is an example of client-side software, but there are other software programs that are also useful for research.

Client-Side Software for Internet Research

There are several kinds of software programs for Internet research. Some of them have to do directly with searching, while some of them just make the everyday tasks of sifting and directing information a lot easier.

Search Software

If you do a lot of research and you like to track your search results over time, you may want to try client-side search software. This software is installed on your desktop and goes out and gathers information from search engines. Copernic (http://www.copernic.com/en/index.html) is probably the most famous search software, though there are others. Copernic comes in everything from a free version to a professional version that costs $79.95.

While I appreciate that they can be useful, I generally don't use search software. I find that doing individual searches is more useful to me than getting an aggregate of several available engines. If you do the same kind of searching over and over, however, or you want to keep thorough records of the kinds of sites you've found, you might appreciate using a desktop-based search client.

Other Internet Connections

The Internet isn't just the Web. Sometimes you need to use FTP as well. FTP stands for "File Transfer Protocol" and as you may have guessed is a way to download files from the Internet. It isn't necessary to retrieve material via FTP as often as it used to be, but it still happens. When I have to use FTP, I find CuteFTP (http://www.cuteftp.com) a great way to do it—especially if I'm helping somebody else.

CuteFTP offers a couple of ways to add new FTP sites to your list. There's a very simple wizard that walks you through the process. If you don't care for that, there's also a simple form to fill out that gives all the information necessary to connect to an FTP site.

The thing I like most about CuteFTP, though, is its friendliness. If I'm working with someone who's having a problem using FTP, and they also use CuteFTP, it's very easy to walk through it with them over the phone because CuteFTP's interface is so easy to understand. CuteFTP's site organizer also makes it easy to quickly connect to the site you want. Friendly UI, easy-to-use—if you FTP I urge you to check this program out. And as long as you're here check out CuteZIP, a snappy Zip program, and CuteHTML, a text-editor-type HTML editor.

CuteFTP offers a free 30-day evaluation download. Purchase is $39.99 and includes a copy of CuteHTML LE, a "light" version of CuteHTML. You can find plenty more FTP programs on the Internet. Just do a Google search for "FTP Clients."

Text Programs for Writing and Processing

It's funny how finicky people are about their text editors. You'd think that Notepad would be enough, but it isn't. There are so many time-saving things you can do with a good text editor. I've found UltraEdit (http://www.ultraedit.com) to be my favorite.

I initially type most of my articles in UltraEdit (I don't type articles in Word because it's hard to make sure that I've removed all the funky non-ASCII formatting). At any one time I may have a dozen text files opened in UltraEdit, with the names of the files tabbed across the top of the page.

This is an excellent, excellent way for me to organize the stream of information that comes to me every day. Sites for one topic go in one file. Notes for another project I'm researching go in another file. Some topics have their own set of files. Collections of files are saved as "Projects," meaning I can open several files with one click.

Once I'm writing about a topic, UltraEdit makes it easy to format my writing. There's a search/replace function, obviously, and a word count, but there's also a column mode (which selects columns instead of lines—handy when you're pulling specific information from a delimited text file). There's a case change command that lets me quickly change input that's all uppercase, lowercase, capitalized, or inverted cases. (It's amazing how often this comes in handy.) There are several levels of Undo and a Revert to Saved command that's saved me a few times. And I'm not even mentioning the powerful macro function that I barely use.

UltraEdit is available for free download and evaluation for 45 days. If you like it, registration is $35. Upgrades are free for one year.

Sometimes you might not need to do any typing, but you may absolutely need to process files in some way—to count the number of occurrences of a word, for example, or to substitute some text, or even to add in some text. The program I'm going to recommend may very well be the most complicated one in the book (it's certainly the most expensive), but it's saved me way too much time for me to skip it. It's called TextPipe and you can purchase it at http://www.crystalsoftware.com.au/textpipe.html.

If you do a lot of text file manipulation, *you want this program*. Trust me. I've done global search and replace on it, I've turned text files into HTML files, I've processed survey results, I've cleaned up text files, I've processed press release summaries, I've done all kinds of stuff with this program.

TextPipe comes in several versions, but the most important for you are Pro and Standard. (An evaluation copy is available for free download.) Neither one of them is cheap—Standard is $169 and Pro is $299. I promise you, though, that TextPipe has saved me far more than $299 worth of time. If you find yourself needing to process a lot of information that you've harvested off the Internet, this is a must-have.

Other Useful Programs

I don't want to spend a lot of time talking about client software in this book, because I don't know what your setup is. I don't know what operating system you're using, I don't know how old your computer is, etc.

But I do want to address some other types of software and where you might want to get it.

Bookmark Managers

You might be thinking, "Why do I need a bookmark manager? I keep my bookmarks with my browser." Bookmark managers allow you do to a certain level of sorting that you can't do within browsers, and some bookmark managers offer bookmark monitoring. Some even offer thumbnails of Web site pages so you have more than a URL and a description to jog your memory. Search Google for "bookmark managers" or "bookmark utilities."

Spyware Checkers

Spyware sounds pretty ominous, and in some cases it really can be. Spyware, when installed on your computer, communicates with another computer providing more information about your Web site than you know about or agreed to. (For example, a program might monitor the sites you visit and then send that information back to the program's creator without telling you.) A variation of Spyware, Adware, sends you a lot of unsolicited ads and in some cases covers existing banners on Web sites with their own banners.

Spyware checkers scan your computer for known spyware applications and remove them. You can search for the words "spyware" or "scumware" in Google and find plenty of examples. *Warning:* When considering a spyware or scumware program, please consider other people's experiences and reviews (you'll learn more about this later in the book). There have been cases when a product advertised as a spyware remover was in fact spyware itself. This is a category with a lot of tricky stuff going on. Be careful.

NOTE

You'll hear Spyware called by other names—Scumware, Thiefware, etc.

Anti-Spam Software

E-mail is sometimes less important than the Web to Internet researchers, but still important! If your e-mail address is available anywhere on the Web, you've probably found that you're getting a lot of spam—and that it's increasing every day. Some e-mail programs have built-in spam filters, while sometimes your ISP will offer a spam-filtering program. If you don't have either of those options you may wish to consider a spam-filtering program to keep your e-mail more about research and less about any number of a dozen scams. Do a search for "spam filtering" or "anti-spam software."

Some General Places to Get Software

If you're not interested in any of the above categories, but you still want to see what kind of Internet software is available, try the following software repositories:

Download.com—http://www.download.com—CNET's repository of lots and lots of software. The Internet category will hook you up with the latest browsers as well as pop-up blockers and spyware detectors (look in the "online privacy" section.

Tucows.com—http://www.tucows.com—When you visit this site you'll first have to choose your operating system (Tucows archives software for several) and then choose the Internet category to get listings of software in over a hundred—seriously—subcategories. Keep an eye out for the spyware busters, the Web browsers, and the Web browser add-ons.

CWSApps—http://cws.internet.com/—Holy cow, I remember visiting this site back in the mid-90s. It's got a ton of software in a variety of Internet categories (check out "Internet Agents" for a listing of search software). The "New Releases" list keeps you up-to-date on freshly available client software.

Version Tracker—http://www.VersionTracker.com—Everything changes on the Internet constantly, and nothing changes faster than version numbers. Version Tracker to the rescue; it keeps tabs on the latest versions on a variety of software. This site ain't pretty; the main page is pretty much a listing of recently updated software programs and their version numbers. But if you want to make sure you've got the latest and greatest, check it out.

Hurry Up and Slow Down

The thought of spending time getting some software and gadgets to make your searching easier might be just as irritating as the idea of tweaking out your browser. But just as with your browser, it will pay off by saving you time and effort.

PART II
PRINCIPLES OF WEB SEARCHING

4 THE PRINCIPLE OF UNIQUE LANGUAGE

The Principle of Unique Language: For any given search there is a vocabulary, slang, or other unique word set that will make finding relevant results for that search easier.

Take a 16-year-old and a 60-year-old and spend some time talking to each of them. One thing you'll notice is that they use very different words. Take a doctor and a mechanical engineer and spend some time talking to each of them and you'll notice that they also use very different sets of words.

Several things shape our vocabulary: our age, our profession, our education, what we like to read, our hobbies, and so on. If you think about it a minute it makes sense that unique language would extend to the Web. If you think about it another minute you'll realize that you can use the fact of this very distinctive vocabulary for finding information online.

Using this principle breaks up into two parts: finding unique language for your searches and using unique language in your searches.

Understanding and Finding Unique Language for Your Searches

If you're already a doctor or a mechanical engineer or whatever, you know your unique vocabulary, and you don't have to learn from this section. But sometimes you'll need to at least be aware of a certain kind of vocabulary even if you're not an expert, in order to be able to do effective searches.

In some cases you'll need to find examples of unique language to enhance your search. We'll look at that scenario in a minute. In other cases you'll already at least know a few words, and the issue will be finding what those words mean and where to go to find related words so that you can put them together into meaningful search queries.

Here's an example: You have a family member who's just been diagnosed with hydrocephalus. You don't know anything about it. You're reasonably sure you have the right spelling of it, but that's all you know. You want to get a general sense of what it is before you start doing research. You don't know of a Web site you trust to learn about medical conditions. You'll have to start your search via a general Web search engine.

You have two clues. You know that hydrocephalus is a medical condition. And you're pretty sure you've got the spelling right. Start with that. Do a full-text search engine search for it using the word "means": `"hydrocephalus means"`.

Such a search (try using it with any technical or unique word or phrase) immediately cuts down your search results and orients them towards instructional pages. Don't visit any pages. Look only at the summaries. Certain words and phrases will pop out at you over and over again. In this case you'll see "water on the brain" and "spina bifida." You may find that there's a page in this set of search results that does indeed explain hydrocephalus and leaves you understanding it a little better.

You've done the hunt phase. Now you gather. Gather (in your mind, on a scratchpad, via cut-and-paste, whatever works for you) words that are related to hydrocephalus. "Spina bifida", "water on the brain," "neurology," whatever. If you don't find any words that jump out at you, try a search engine that suggests additional search words for you, like Teoma (look for the refine search suggestions on the right side of the page) or Yahoo (look for the related searches below the search box on a search results page). Once you've got them, start blending these words into search queries. Try searching for `hydrocephalus neurology "spina bifida"`. Or try `"water on the brain" hydrocephalus`.

You'll find you're getting "meatier" pages that are more oriented to your topic. If you're not, try restricting your search to a certain kind of site. Adding site:edu to a Google search will get more academic results. Adding site:org is dicey but can find you pages that are oriented toward support of people with medical conditions and research sites. Sometimes omitting a type of domain—like -site:com—will render useful results by getting rid of most shopping sites, book sales sites, and so on.

Doing these kinds of searches will have two effects. First you'll learn more about the condition. Second you'll get acquainted with the language of the condition. If you decide later that you want

NOTE

Why aren't you just going ahead and doing a dictionary search for the word "hydrocephalus"? Because unless you're using a medical dictionary, you're going to get a general description that might not help you narrow down your search results. If you do a Web search with the word "means," you'll get several different angles on the meaning of the word and several potential pointers to additional information.

to narrow down your search (you want to study the genetic underpinnings of hydrocephalus, for example) you'll have a core vocabulary to start.

Bottom line: you use one word to start a broader acquaintance with a larger language set.

But what happens when you don't know even one word? When you want to search a particular type of information (neurological, legal, technical, whatever), but you don't even know one place to start? That requires a slightly different tactic. You'll start with a general search, find one or two words, and then use those one or two words as a wedge to get more information, as above.

For our second example, perhaps we want to learn about custody rights. "Custody rights" isn't exactly a technical term, but we can start there. Perhaps `"custody rights" law`. That'll get you relevant initial results but a lot of them. Try to narrow down exactly what you're interested in. Are you interested in custody laws for fathers? Start there.

```
"custody rights" law fathers
```

Run an eagle eye over the search results for one unique term—one legal term, a case mention, a law name—that clearly belongs to legal vocabulary. Then take that and use it as your wedge to expand your knowledge as above.

Is this not working for you? Another option you have is to find glossaries and dictionaries related to the topic you're looking for. In that case you'll want to do a slightly different search. This kind of search will find relevant unique words quickly, but it won't give you as thorough an overview of what your topic is all about.

Back to the custody rights example. Finding glossaries and dictionaries relevant to your search is as easy as adding a couple of words to your search. Start with the words "custody rights" law and add the word "glossary" or the word "dictionary" (glossary is better to use initially; it's not a word that's used casually). See what you come up with. Are you finding FAQs and pointers to glossaries? Are you finding the glossaries themselves? If you are, you know what to do—review what you've found for more unique words relevant to your search.

If you're not finding useful sites, back up. Maybe "custody rights" is too narrow a search. Try searching for the words "legal glossary". Or "law legal dictionary". Once you've found a useful resource, you can search within that site to zero in on the topic in which you're interested.

Let's look at some Web sites relevant to specialized language sets, be they technical language, slang, or otherwise.

The Probert Encyclopedia--Slang--http://www.probertencyclopaedia.com/slang.htm

Slang changes all the time and it's different all over the world, so relying on a Web site to give you the latest and greatest definitions doesn't always work. But this site contains information on over 12,000 slang words from all over the world. You can browse alphabetically or search. Bear in mind that this slang site (and most slang sites) contains objectionable language.

MedTerms.com--http://www.medterms.com/

MedTerms provides definitions for over 10,000 terms. If you search for hydrocephalus here you'll find several different definitions, but these definitions together would give you a good overview. The definitions are somewhat technical, but not such that you can't follow along and pull out some unique words.

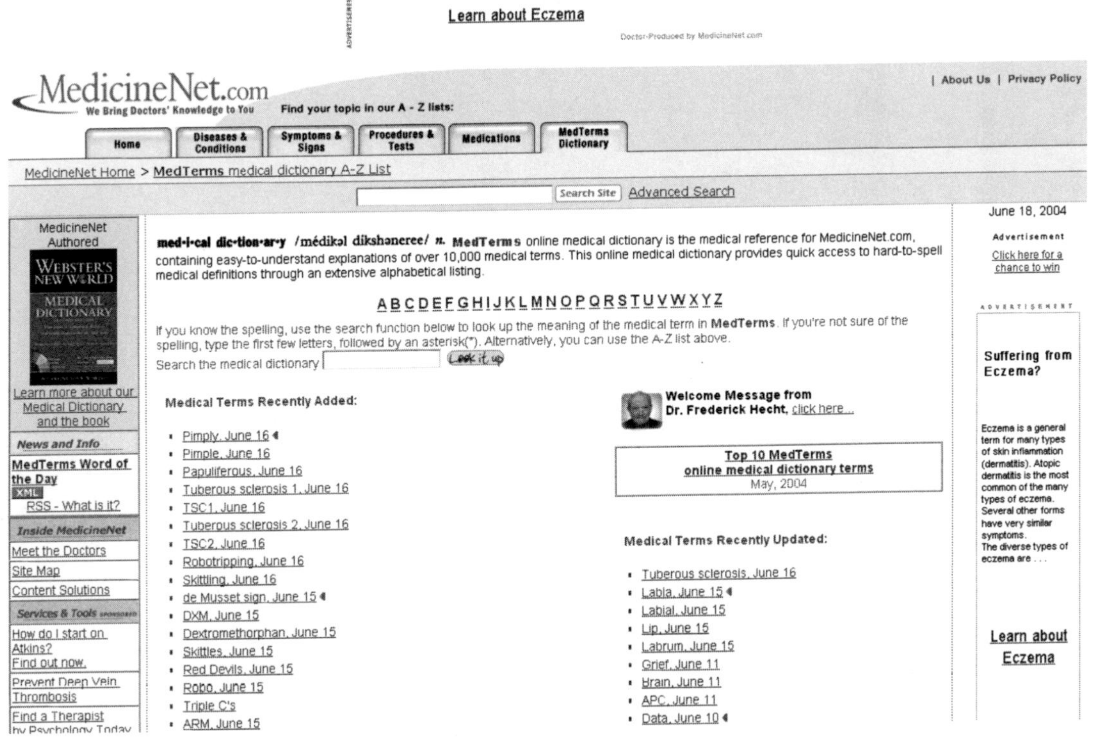

04–01

MedTerms includes recently added words as well as a full dictionary search. (Image from http://www.medterms.com.)

Law.com's Legal Dictionary--http://dictionary.law.com/lookup2.asp

Like MedTerms, you can browse alphabetically or search by keyword. And like MedTerms, searching for something as innocuous as "custody" will result in many possible definitions. Try to stick to the most simple definitions—make sure you understand what "child custody" means before you get into parens patriae.

TechWeb Encyclopedia--http://www.techweb.com/encyclopedia/

For nontechnical people, it seems like the computing world is endlessly spewing out acronyms, definitions, and technology slang. I've got a secret for you. That's almost true. It seems like there's nothing the average geek likes better than making up an acronym. The TechWeb encyclopedia offers thousands of definitions searchable by keyword. If TechWeb doesn't give you the information you need, try WhatIs (http://whatis.techtarget.com/), which allows you to both search by keyword and browse definitions by category.

The Glossarist--http://www.glossarist.com/

If you're looking for more obscure vocabulary, check here first. This site is a link collection that provides pointers to over 6,100 dictionaries and glossaries on the Web, from arts and culture to transportation. Don't try to search for definitions on this site; search for general categories of information instead. Do a search for "botany" to get a sense of what this site offers.

I've spent a lot of words telling you how to develop a sense of unique language and you may be feeling discouraged at this point. You may be thinking, "Good grief, do I have to do all this rigmarole every time I want to research something that's unfamiliar? I do not have time for this."

Trust me. It's taken a lot longer for me to explain than it will for you to do once you've gotten the hang of it. Once you've gotten the habit of looking for the unlikely word and the unusual phrase, you'll do it automatically. You'll do a couple of searches and have a nice set of words all lined up in the back of your mind ready to search for. This is a good habit to cultivate.

You've got the words. Now how do you use the words?

Using Unique Language in Your Searches

The results of any given search will have a tendency to be general. If you search for the word "cat" you will not get a page about a particular Burmese kitty or the problems with Persians. Instead you'll get a general cat page.

Specialized words and vocabulary slant the results of your search to more technical and specific results. Do a search for `cat` and see what you get. Now do a search for `cat "dew claw"`. The results become much fewer and very cat-oriented. (The phrase "dew claw" just isn't used casually.) Finally, search for `cat "dew claw" alopecia`, and suddenly you have less than ten results.

You're going to use your unique language that's relevant to your subject to slant your results to your topic. When you find your results are too general, not relevant to what you want, you're going to put your unique words in a query to bring the search back to what you want.

Let's go all the way back to the hydrocephalus example. You want to get a sense of the tests that are used to diagnose hydrocephalus and its possible side effects. You find that the simple search `hydrocephalus tests` doesn't get the results you want. So you add a word oriented toward hydrocephalus—"spina bifida." From there you can add another word—"neurological," perhaps—or swap out words. The point is to start with a basic search that encompasses what you want, and then use the unique words you've found to "salt" your search and get it more oriented to the results that you want.

3 The Principle of the Reinvented Wheel

The Principle of the Reinvented Wheel: For most given topics, interests, and hobbies, there are already at least a few people who are interested in it, and some of those people have already put up a Web site, community, or some other resource on the Internet devoted to that topic that gathers and reviews relevant links. You can make your search much easier by using these specialty resources instead of trying to build your own.

When you first start doing serious Internet research, you might think to yourself, "There are so many Web pages, and so many people on the Internet, I've got to find exactly what I want." And then after a couple of searches you may have revised that to, "There are so many Web pages, and so many people on the Internet, there is no way I'm going to find exactly what I want."

I've got good news for you. You were right the first time. There is a huge number of people and a huge number of interests represented by Web pages. You can put a huge shortcut in your searching by finding and using specialty resources like link lists and specialty subject indexes in your research.

How do you do this? You find friendly communities that discuss the topics in which you're interested. You find resource-rich Web sites that will give you clues and pointers

NOTE

Flat Wheels. I find that the technique of using others' research in finding research on specialized topics is very useful. However, you'll have to watch out for link lists that were started in 1997 and never updated, mailing lists that have been in a torpor since the turn of the century, and plain abandoned sites. So, as you're finding wheels, pay attention to whether or not they've been updated recently.

to other useful resources. And you find Weblogs and other personal sites that comment on the topic in which you're interested.

Finding Friendly Communities

The first thing you want to do is find out where the like-minded people hang out. Where are the communities friendly to your topic? There are a few large repositories of mailing lists so we're going to start from there.

Yahoo Groups--http://groups.yahoo.com

A service of Yahoo (as you might imagine), Yahoo Groups has a directory of mailing lists that looks a lot like the regular Yahoo directory. You can either search by keyword ("kitesurfing" finds 44 results) or you can browse through the mailing lists like you'd browse the Yahoo directory. Search results include a description of the list, how many people are in the directory (giving you a sense of how active it might be), and whether the archives are public or private (sometimes you just want to get a question answered; you don't necessarily want to join a list. If the archives are public, all you have to do is browse them).

When you click on the name of the list, you'll get details that will give you additional clues as to whether the list is worth delving into. You'll see when the list started, the title of the last few posts if the list archives are public, and, at the bottom of the page, an indication of how many messages were posted to the list during each month since the list's inception.

Pay attention to these numbers! If you want to join a list to ask a question of its membership, you don't want to join a list that has only a couple of messages a month. You want to find one that's more active. If all you're going to do is search the publicly accessible archives, however, it doesn't matter how busy the list is; all that matters is whether the archives contain the information you need. Note also on the details page that you can search individual archives when they're publicly available.

Topica--http://www.topica.com

Like Yahoo Groups, Topica has a directory of mailing lists. But there's one crucial difference: with Yahoo Groups, you can search for mailing lists and you can search individual archives when they're publicly available. With Topica, you can search for mailing lists and you can search the aggregated archives of all the mailing lists.

The directory of mailing lists is not as detailed as Yahoo Groups': it doesn't have as many subcategories visible on the front page. But once you start "drilling down" through the categories, you'll get extensive subcategory listings along with the number of lists per subcategory. Each listing contains several icons that note a variety of information about the list, including whether the archives are publicly available, whether the list is hosted at Topica, and whether it's a restricted list or not.

Information for individual lists is similar to Yahoo Groups but it's formatted a bit differently. You will notice that you won't see many posting details, though you will get a little bit of information (a list may be noted as having 100 members and less than one message per week, for example).

Since you can search for both lists and the messages within lists, feel free to get more specific in your searches. You don't have to search for just "windsurfing"; you can search for both the words "windsurfing" and "Hawaii." Just make sure that the pulldown menu is set on messages and not lists, so you're searching the right thing.

Yahoo Groups and Topica are two of the big mailing list archives out there, but there are other independent lists and archives available.

Google Groups 2--http://groups-beta.google.com/

Google Groups 2 is a new feature, currently in beta, from Google. While you might think of Usenet when you think of Google Groups (and you'll learn more about Usenet later in the chapter), with Google Groups 2, Google is now offering mailing lists.

This site has not been around as long as Yahoo Groups or Topica, so you may not find as many lists here. Listings show both how many members are in a group and the newest topics. You can add new topics (if you're registered; registration is free and requires a minimum of information), review active threads, and track those threads you find interesting. You may also search individual mailing lists by keywords when they are open to the public.

At the moment, Google's mailing list archive isn't nearly as impressive as Yahoo Groups, but knowing Google it will do nothing but grow.

Tile.net--http://tile.net/lists/

Tile.net is a service of SparkList, an e-mail hosting service. Unlike Yahoo Groups and Topica, there isn't a lot of detailed information about each mailing list available here. You can browse lists alphabetically by list name, description, and domain. Choose a way you'll want to browse and you'll be presented with an alphabet. Choose a letter and you'll get a list of mailing lists.

When you pick a list you'll get additional information, including list name, subscribe and unsubscribe information, the list administrator address, and (sometimes) a description of the list.

Tile.net is useful because it can lead you to smaller mailing lists that aren't hosted by one of the Big Two, or to lists hosted by a university or small organization that might be more difficult to find online. But it's still a pain to search because it offers little in the way of description and not much of a search mechanism. What do you do when the searching of a useful resource is as limited as it is with Tile.net? You take a very good searching tool—in this case, Google—and you focus it so it's concentrating just on Tile.net.

How? Site search! Let's go back to the windsurfing example. If you want to find a list relevant to windsurfing but you don't want to browse through every list looking for one that might mention windsurfing, try going to Google and searching for windsurfing site:tile.net. In this case you won't find any results; you'll get pointers to Usenet newsgroups instead (Tile.net also maintains a list of Usenet groups). Try surfing `site:tile.net` and you will get pointers to mailing lists.

How do you get rid of those pesky pointers to newsgroups? Easy; modify your Google search a little bit. If you look at the URLs for the Usenet results, you'll see that "news" is included in the URL (the URL for mailing lists has "lists" in the same place). So you'll want to use the inurl: syntax to ensure that you don't have the word "news" in any URLs that Google finds:

```
surfing site:tile.net -inurl:news
```

Do that search and you'll immediately narrow down the 11 mailing lists—and with this search result there are only mailing lists—that mention surfing.

Tile.net isn't the only potentially good resource that is helped by an external search engine. The Mail Archive has a lot to offer, but it takes Google to bring it all together.

The Mail Archive--http://www.mail-archive.com/

The Mail Archive doesn't go by provider or topic when it indexes a mailing list. Instead, to have your mailing list added you just have to add the Mail Archive 'bot to your mailing list. At the moment, over 1900 active mailing lists and over 15 million messages have been archived.

From the front page you can search for mailing lists. Your search results will include only the name of the list and no description; some of the lists have rather esoteric names. You can also choose to browse the list of available archives, and once you've found a list in which you're interested you can search that individually.

The individual searching is good when you know what mailing list you want to look at; it's always best to use a site's internal search engine before moving to an external search engine like Google. But if you want to search the entire site at once, try Google.

Searching the Mail Archive with Google is much like searching Tile.net with Google. Searching for surfing would look like this:

```
surfing site:mail-archive.com
```

What's the first thing you notice when you do this search here as opposed to searching Tile.net? You get a lot more results. That's because Mail Archive archives entire mailing lists as opposed to just listing details about mailing lists. (Kind of like the difference between full-text search engines and

NOTE

Why should you want to use an internal search engine before you go to something like Google? Because there's no guarantee that Google has indexed every page on that site. A site's own internal search engine is going to be at least as complete as Google's index and possibly more complete.

searchable subject indexes.) Since you're searching archives as opposed to just a group of available lists, you can get more specific:

```
surfing Hawaii site:mail-archive.com
```

or even very very specific:

```
surfing sand Hawaii site:mail-archive.com
```

To wrap it up: for Tile.net, you'll need to keep your searches general because you're searching an index and not content. For the Mail Archive, you can search with more specific keywords because you're searching both an index and content; if you search generally you'll get lots of results.

Are these searches not getting you the results you want? Though I don't recommend it, you *can* search a full-text search engine for mailing lists. It's not as effective as going straight to mailing list archives, but you can do it.

Finding mailing lists requires that you remember the Principle of Unique Language. In the case of mailing lists, search-specific vocabulary includes digest, list, and thread. Think of words that are relevant to mailing lists.

Let's try to find a mailing list about kitesurfing. We'll start with the general word "kitesurfing" and then narrow it down with our search-specific vocabulary:

```
kitesurfing digest thread
```


You'll get one page of results, with a couple of mailing lists right at the top. Let's try a slightly different search and see if it makes any difference:

```
kitesurfing digest message
```

Eh, you'll get a couple more potential lists but nothing to write home about. Let's try one more, using Google's title syntax and one search-specific word:

```
kitesurfing intitle:digest
```

That'll get you all of three results!

If you searched for just the keyword "kitesurfing," you'd get tens of thousands of results. By adding your search-specific vocabulary (which is discussed in Chapter 4, "The Principle of Unique Language"), you're skewing your search toward mailing lists, with a very limited number of results as you'll see here.

Now, do you have to search for just mailing lists? No, you can search for archive contents as well. Let's go from kitesurfing to Mustangs. Perhaps you've got a muffler problem with your Ford Mustang. Try this search:

```
mustang muffler digest thread
```

You'll see that instead of just mailing lists, you're getting digest messages and archives (some of them several years old!). If you're not finding the information you're looking for immediately, try narrowing down your search with more keywords:

```
mustang muffler noise digest thread
```

Using Google or some other general search engine is good to do when you want to quickly narrow down search results (more information on why you'd want to do that in a minute), but when you want to browse mailing lists, do general mailing list searches, or get a sense of what communities are available, you're going to have to visit one of the mailing list hosts or one of the resources that index mailing lists. You can also blend the use of mailing list archives and Google, as you'll see a little later on in this chapter.

No matter what mailing list archive you're searching, there are some general tips you can follow to ensure that you're getting the most optimal search results possible.

Tips for Searching Mailing Lists

1. Search Like You Talk

When someone puts together a Web site, they're aware that they're making a one-to-many communication, and because of this their sites tend to be a little formal. But a mailing list is an ongoing conversation; slang, sentence fragments, and so on is the order of the day. People do not talk like dictionaries and grammar handbooks, so relax your searching a little bit and search for incomplete sentences, slang, and the other ways that people talk.

2. Search in the Form of a Question

Because mailing lists are ongoing conversations, people ask questions. Searching for a question (`Where can I buy a Ford Pinto?`) without quotes works well in Web searching but works especially well in mailing lists, where there tend to be a lot more questions asked and answered.

> **NOTE**
>
> Why search for a question without quotes? What's the point in searching for a question if you're not going to gather it into a phrase? Because Google counts word order when giving search results. So even when you're not using quotes, Google will give greater weight to a search result that matches the word order on your search.

3. Don't Be Afraid to Introduce Typos

If you're not finding the information you need with a regular search, try introducing some typos. This is especially important when you're searching a mailing list that might be using an unusual vocabulary. For example, you might be searching in a mailing list archive to support people who have a particular illness. The people on the list are probably not medical professionals, but they will use medical vocabulary in the course of their discussions. This is the perfect place to try misspelling a couple of the medical vocabulary words to see if it makes any difference to your search.

Google Web Images Groups News Froogle more »
"ford mustung" Search Advanced Search Preferences

Web Results **1 - 27** of about **36** for **"ford mustung"**. (**0.31** seconds)

Did you mean: "ford ***mustang***"

1970 **ford mustung**
... sites. You searched for: 1970 **ford mustung**. Results 1 - 25 of at least
203 -- ranked by score. ... Hot Rod Search for: 1970 **ford mustung**. Perform ...
www.hotrodders.com/terms/1970-**ford-mustung**.html - 23k - Supplemental Result - Cached - Similar pages

www.hotrodders.com/terms/ford-mustung.html
Supplemental Result - Similar pages
[More results from www.hotrodders.com]

Carrera James Bond Goldfinger DB5 Slot Racing "Scalextric" Set ...
... the thrills from this memorable "Goldfinger" sequence as you manoeuvre the classic
Aston Martin DB5 driven by James Bond and the **Ford Mustung** Convertible with ...
www.goldstarstockists.com/bond-jamesbond/ james-bond-carrera-goldfinger.htm - 47k - Cached - Similar pages

□□□□□□□□□□□□ □□□ ...
... □□□ 1.72MB □□ Mustang Screensaver C1 MustangsMustangs.com
Ford Mustung□□□□□□□□□□□□□□□□□□ ...
www.screensaver.co3.jp/pages/menu14-14.html - 13k - Jun 17, 2004 - Cached - Similar pages

saeedamen.com
... Thunderbird. Although not as famous as the **Ford Mustung**, the Thunderbird
still remains one of America's most popular sports cars. ...
www.hadbai.co.uk/samen/images/7.htm - 6k - Cached - Similar pages

JOHNNY LIGHTNING
... 261-00, Sunbeam Alpine, □(□□□), Dr.No. 261-00, **Ford Mustung**, □(□
□□), Goldfinger. ... 261-00, **Ford Mustung** Mach-1, □(□□□), Diamonds Are
Forever. ...
homepage1.nifty.com/yoshinori/ handbook/johnny/johnny.html - 8k - Cached - Similar pages

Jiggle.de - suche 71 `cuda cabriolet - [Translate this page]
... Beiträge: 5.798. Und wer hat für mich einen 1968'er **Ford Mustung** zu verschenken.
_______________ Dieser Beitrag ist urheberrechtlich geschützt. ...
www.jiggle.de/vb/showthread.php?t=11714 - 80k - Cached - Similar pages

05–01

Even a misspelled search can produce useful results. (Image from http://www.google.com/search?q=%22ford+mustung%22&sourceid=opera&num=100&ie=utf-8&oe=utf-8.)

4. Follow That Thread

With Web pages you can usually count on finding your answer on one page or one site. But, again, mailing lists are conversations. If you find a thread that answers your questions in one message, follow the thread to see if there's any other information you can pull out of it. You might find additional information. You might find an argument against the first bit of information you found. Or you might find additional information that leads you down a variety of paths. Don't settle for one message. Follow that thread!

5. Use "Buzzwords"

With mailing lists it can be tough to search by date, though you can try it if you search for different date formats (more about that in a minute). You can try to narrow down your searches, though, if you search for places, people, or even words associated with a certain era. For example, if you are searching a Chicago Bears mailing list archive and you're particularly interested in the 1985 season, try including the keywords "Superbowl Shuffle" in your search. Remember that different keywords can invoke different eras, and that this works especially well on mailing lists since people talk a lot about events and happenings.

6. Try Different Date Formats

Usenet is organized very well by date, as you'll discover in a minute, and because of that it's very useful when you're looking for date-based information. With mailing lists it's a little tougher to search by date, but you can if you pay attention to search results you find initially.

Let's say you're searching Mail Archive via Google and you want to limit your search to the year 2003. Run a search:

```
surfing Hawaii site:mail-archive.com
```

and take a look at the first couple of results. Note the date.

Yes, there's a date. Let's take an example of this first message, and we'll see that the date is "Date: Fri, 29 Aug 2003."

Say you want to search for those messages that occur in August 2003. You'll want to replace the day and the date—the Fri and the 29—with full-word wildcards, and leave the Aug and 2003. Your final date search, integrated into the keyword search, would look like this:

```
surfing Hawaii "date: * * aug 2003" site:mail-
                archive.com
```

This will limit your search results to both those messages that appeared in August and those messages quoting other messages that appear in the month of August. You may find that the other messages you want to search by date have other formats. That's fine; the important thing is that you find a typical message with a date on it, and then emulate that date in your search, like we do above.

Mailing lists are hosted by literally hundreds of different sites all over the Web and that's good in one way and bad in another way. The good thing is that it means there are millions of mailing lists on literally hundreds of thousands of topics all over the Internet. The bad thing is that different mailing lists are archived in different ways, and it's difficult to search across a wide range of mailing list resources across a wide date range.

Usenet, on the other hand, has one primary repository of data that stretches back over 20 years, in the form of Google Groups. While Usenet doesn't offer as many different forums as mailing lists do, and sometimes the noise (of spam) on mailing lists outweighs the signal, Usenet is a lot easier to search in toto and across a range of dates. If you want to do a date-based search for items of interest to popular culture, Usenet should be your first choice. As a place to find communities, it's secondary (I find that mailing lists are generally more spam-free and have a better "signal to noise" ratio), but it's still a useful search.

Searching Usenet

What is Usenet? Usenet is a set of discussion groups, organized into a hierarchy. Instead of the discussion groups being distributed by e-mail, they're either hosted by news servers (which will require that you have special news readers to read the discussion groups) or maintained on Web sites.

There are various places all over the Web that host mailing lists; your ISP, in fact, may have a news server. But for the purpose of this book, we're going to focus on Google Groups.

Google Groups is a Web-based archive of Usenet that goes back over twenty years and contains tens of millions of messages. Its search, as you might expect, is extremely thorough; you can do some serious searching using Google Groups. But before we get into how the search interface works, let's talk about how Usenet is organized.

The Usenet Hierarchy

The Usenet hierarchy is organized into eight major hierarchies and countless minor hierarchies. The major hierarchies are divided into many subhierarchies; for example, there's the comp hierarchy, then comp.os beneath that, then comp.os.windows, and on and on and on. Here are the major ones you'll need to be acquainted with.

ALT—Covers just about any topic; alt newsgroups include everything from alt.abraham-lincoln to alt.zima.

BIZ—The advertising-friendly section of the Usenet hierarchy; groups are for the most part business-oriented and include biz.entrepreneurs, biz.jobs, and biz.mlm.

COMP—This one's my personal favorite. Comp stands for computing and the newsgroups here cover all aspects of computing, both hardware and software.

MISC—"And the rest!" Covers everything from activism to legal and technical issues to writing to for sale ads.

NEWS—Devoted to news and announcements about a variety of topics. This hierarchy includes news about software, electronics, and Internet information (Frequently Asked Questions, or FAQs).

REC—Rec is short for recreation. As you might expect, this hierarchy includes sports, games, hobbies, and other diversions from everyday life.

SCI—Sci is short for science, and this hierarchy covers hard science, soft science—even the "dismal science" of economics.

SOC—Short for social, soc is for covering cultural and lifestyle issues. Newsgroups here include soc.veterans, soc.adoption, and soc.culture.

There are many other hierarchies—those based on region or very specialized discussion groups—but these are the major ones. It's important that you be acquainted with this list so you understand how to use these hierarchies to narrow down your search. Google Groups allows you to browse the groups, and even read the messages in them, without doing any searching at all. Before you get into some serious searching, take some time to browse through some groups and get acquainted with how groups and message threads are laid out.

Searching Usenet Resources with Google Groups

Google Groups is searchable in a couple of ways. There's a quick search by keyword that works much the way that the regular Google search does, and then there's the advanced search, available at http://groups.google.com/advanced_group_search?hl=en.

The advanced search for Google Groups looks a lot like the advanced search for Google, but there are some important differences. The first important difference is the fact that you can specify which newsgroup(s) you want to search. Knowing the hierarchies, you can quickly narrow down the scope of the newsgroups being searched. For example, if you want to search just for computer-related issues, you can search in the comp hierarchy (you would do that by entering `comp*` in the "Return only messages from the newsgroup" box). If you want to search only operating system–related messages, you can search for `comp.os.*`; there's a whole set of operating system newsgroups under the comp.os subhierarchy.

You don't have to use wildcards at just the beginning of the newsgroup name; you can use them in the end and the middle of the group name too. If you want to search every newsgroup that has anything to do with football, put `*football*` in the newsgroups box. If you want to search for everything related to computers and games, search for `comp*games*`. Now you understand why knowing the hierarchies is so important!

Once you've narrowed down what you want to search, look at the message dates option toward the bottom of the screen and figure out when you want to search. It's extremely difficult to search Web pages by creation date, but since Google maintains the huge collection of Usenet messages in one place and indexes their date information along with everything else, they're easy to search by creation date. The option to search by creation date is very valuable; with the millions and millions of messages available, you've got to narrow them down in any way possible.

For example? Let's consider the 1998 Olympics. You want to read discussions on the skiing in the 1998 Olympics. You can narrow down your search to the rec* newsgroups (remember, "rec" stands for "recreation"), but you can also narrow down your search by date. So let's say you search for the keywords "skiing" and "Olympics," in the rec* newsgroups, in January and February of 1998.

You'll see that even though you've narrowed this search to just two months, your results will include over 1,100 messages. Narrow down your search a little bit more (perhaps by adding the keyword "downhill") and you'll get a manageable number of results.

Some events will excite a lot of comment on Usenet; some won't. Start with a couple of general keywords about the event/trend/fad, and do a search in the general time range. (If you want to do a search related to something that happened during the summer of 1983, for example, search from April to September 1983. You want to leave enough space on both ends of the time span to pick up on early mentions of the event/trend/fad and to pick up any straggling mentions and conversations.) If you find that you're getting too many results, you know the drill: add more keywords to narrow down your search until you get a reasonable number of results. If it's at all relevant, though, use the date range search to narrow down your results first.

Tips for Searching Usenet

The tips for searching Usenet are very much like the ones for searching mailing lists, with a few extra things for you to keep in mind.

1. Use the Newsgroup Hierarchy

Yes, I know; I won't be quiet about that hierarchy of the way Usenet Groups are organized. But choosing the right newsgroup or range of newsgroups is the fastest way to narrow down your search results on Usenet and zoom in on what you want. So make sure you're limiting your search result to a newsgroup if at all possible.

2. Use the Date Range Search

If the fastest way to narrow down results is to search specific newsgroup(s), the second fastest way is to specify a date range to search. If you're searching for anything related to an event, a trend, a fad, or anything else that can be tied to a date range search, then use the date range search.

I want to mention something else about searching a Usenet date range. Usenet predates the Web by years; Google Groups' search goes back to 1981. If you want contemporary commentary on events—like the Challenger disaster, for example—Usenet is a much easier resource to search than the Web.

3. Don't Believe Everything You Read

Mailing lists tend to be smaller communities than Usenet lists. Because they're not built around a central hierarchy like Usenet, they can remain tucked away in obscure Web sites, not reaching a large number of people and maintaining the integrity of small, private communities.

Usenet is more open. In fact, it's so open that it's easy for people to swoop in on a list and leave spam, start pointless arguments, try to spin out hoaxes, and do other nonsense that makes it hard to punch through the noise of public discourse and get to the heart of the information you need. To view everything skeptically is an excellent bit of advice for the Internet in general, but it goes triple for Usenet.

Once you've found communities, you'll see a lot of dialogue, pointers to new resources, and discussions of other available resources that communities might find of interest. However, you might find you want more resources to fill out your research. In that case your next step would be to go to the Web and find specialty link lists and directories.

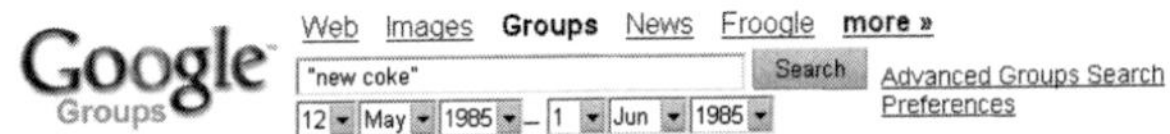

Groups

Results **1 - 10** of about **51** from **May 12, 1985** to **Jun 1, 1985** for "**new coke**". (**0.10** seconds)

Sort by relevance **Sorted by date**

Related groups: net.followup
net.flame

Re: New Coke Blegh!!
Gee, Arash, I can't make the comparison you did because I don't have the same eclectic taste you do, but orange crush over here is fairly good. ...
net.followup - May 31, 1985 by R.GRANTGES - View Thread (5 articles)

Re: The New COKE (actually sugar prices)
As a result, cane (and probably beet) sugar is currently a glut on the world market. Here in Hawaii the sugar cane plantations are gradually closing down. ...
net.followup - May 31, 1985 by Brian Gordon - View Thread (3 articles)

Re: Old Coke loses blind tasting
... Old Coke was much less preferred than **New Coke**. Only two people out of eleven rated it as better or much better than **New Coke**, and one thought it was the same. ...
net.followup - May 31, 1985 by Erik Mintz - View Thread (4 articles)

Re: the new COKE
... which is more expensive). Now I can't get any of the old COKE to compare the ingredients against the **new COKE**. So will someone in ...
net.followup - May 30, 1985 by Barry Margolin - View Thread (23 articles)

Re: What is "capitalism"?
... Anacin. Are you? (But I don't like the **new Coke** -- I know that) I don't WANT to make every decision and take every risk in my life. A ...
net.politics.theory - May 29, 1985 by Tony Wuersch - View Thread (32 articles)

RE: The new COKE
I like OLD Coke > Pepsi > Coffee >= Tea > Water >= **NEW Coke**. The main reason I drink **new Coke** is that I get it free anytime I eat ...
net.flame - May 29, 1985 by Steven Schultz - View Thread (1 article)

Re: The "New" Coke
... (I must reveal my bias: I hate the **new coke** so much that I will not drink it and am currently exploring Royal Crown as a substitute. ...
net.flame - May 28, 1985 by Christopher F. Harrison - View Thread (17 articles)

05–02

Remember the New Coke controversy? (Image from http://groups.google.com/groups?q=+%22new+coke%22&hl=en&lr=&ie=UTF-8&c2coff=1&as_drrb=b&as_mind=12&as_minm=5&as_miny=1985&as_maxd=1&as_maxm=6&as_maxy=1985&scoring=d.)

Finding Specialty Link Lists and Directories

Specialty link lists and directories, as you might infer from the name, are those directories and link lists that are concentrated on a single topic. They don't try to have the sweeping scope of Google or Yahoo, and for that reason they're usually more in-depth about one particular topic than Google or Yahoo.

Strangely enough, the first best way for finding specialty link lists and directories is to use DMOZ or Yahoo.

Searching DMOZ and Yahoo

In the rest of this book I'll tell you to search as specifically as possible, to get as narrow as you can, and then work your way more generally.

Here I won't. Here I'm going to tell you to think generally and then use that general search to find the categories that encompass your topic of interest.

Let's start with an example. Say you want information on dogs—specifically Jack Russell terriers. Go to http://directory.yahoo.com or http://www.dmoz.org. There's a difference between general searching and way too general searching, so don't start searching for dogs. Instead, search for `Jack Russell`.

Look at the top of the results and you'll see that there are directories related to your categories. One of the directories is for Jack Russell terriers. Click on that category and you'll see some subcategories and pages related to Jack Russell. Bingo! You've just started your collection of specialized knowledge.

Perhaps it's not that easy. Perhaps you're searching for information on the Frisbee-Fetching Puggle breed. But the directory does not have a category for that breed. In that case you should get more general and try searching for dogs. When you search for dogs, look for a subcategory called "Directories" or "Web Directories." This category will contain the sites that link to other sites on the Web, and here you might find references to the elusive Frisbee-Fetching Puggle.

But what if even that doesn't lead you to directories devoted to the Frisbee-Fetching Puggle? Then you need to do your specialty directory search via Google or some other full-text engine.

Using Google to Find Specialty Resources

Finding specialized resources on Google or any other full-text engine is sort of like using the Principle of Unique Language. You want to use words that are specific to specialized search engines and directories. These words include:

links
directory
resources
"what's new"

Let's try another example. You might want directories of links dedicated to roses. You liked what you found on Yahoo but you want more. Start at Google and do the following search:

```
roses links directory
```

At this writing you'll get over 183,000 results, and you'll find that Open Directory results pop up first, so you know that you're on the right track. But you're also getting inappropriate results (links for Guns N' Roses), so you know you've got to narrow things down some. So add a couple more garden-oriented keywords:

```
roses garden flower links directory
```

Bingo! Now you've got a lot of results, but they're all oriented toward flower roses, and not heavy metal roses. From here you can tweak your keywords and do some more searching as you gather these information-rich resources.

> **TIP**
>
> You might find that you're getting Open Directory results from several different sites. This is because the Open Directory makes its content free for anyone who cares to download it. To make sure that you don't get any Open Directory content in your search, add this to your query: `-"Help build the largest human-edited"`. That's a phrase from the Open Directory content that will weed out any sites using Open Directory listings.

Finding Voices

Finding communities and conversations is useful, and finding collections of links is useful. But it is also often useful to find the leaders in a community, those folks whose commentary is respected and passed along. They have double value: first as pointers to valuable information and second as credibility indicators.

If you read the writings of a community voice long enough and you come to trust them, you can gauge the merits of resources by how that voice views them. What do they think of the latest hot directory? Do they barely mention it at all? Do they give a thumbs-down? Do they support it enthusiastically? This is especially useful when you're doing research in a field you have very little knowledge of. If I were researching diabetes, for example, I would not feel knowledgeable enough to evaluate all the information I came across. However, I would trust the assessments of Rick Mendosa, who runs a frequently updated diabetes resource at http://www.mendosa.com/diabetes.htm.

When I'm looking for leading commentators, I generally look in Weblogs. And that leads me to two resources: one for finding Weblogs and one for checking how widely they're known.

Voices in Weblogs

If you don't know what Weblogs are, let me give you a quick overview. Weblogs are Web sites that are usually maintained by one person or a few people, usually updated fairly often (at least that's the intention), and usually have some kind of personal slant. As you might expect from that definition, there's a lot of "gray area" for defining a Weblog and a lot of argument over what is and isn't a Weblog. But we'll stick with that definition.

To find Weblogs that line up with your sphere of research, start at Feedster.

Feedster—http://www.feedster.com

Feedster searches RSS feeds, which are special kinds of files that give information about Weblog posts, including date, content, author, and sometimes even details such as language and location. These RSS feeds include a lot of Weblogs. Start here with a plain search. Say you're searching for diabetes. Start with a single-word search: `diabetes`. Feedster's default is set to sort results by date; leave it that way to get the most recently updated sites on top.

Your search results will be a little different from a regular search engine result. You'll see the title of the entry that appeared in the result (Feedster indexes individual Weblog entries from the RSS feeds, not entire pages), the URL, when it was published, and the name of the Weblog that published it.

What you're looking for is the name of the Weblog. Sometimes the name of the Weblog will show you that it's exactly something you'd be interested in ("Datamonitor: Healthcare") and sometimes it doesn't help at all! ("Fingertips"?).

Click on an ambiguous Weblog title. You'll go straight to that Weblog. Spend a few minutes perusing the entries. Glancing at the content for a bit should give you an idea of whether you want to explore it more deeply.

Look for the following things:

1. How relevant is it to your topic?
2. How often is it updated? (Even if it's spot on target, it's not going to be helpful in your quest to aggregate new resources if it's only updated once every four months.)
3. Can you get any feeling for the author's credibility from what they're writing?
4. Is it mostly stuff copied from other blogs or is there a lot of original content?

Ideally a Weblog that you plumb for information, specialty link lists, and directories would be right on target, updated frequently, and written by either a professional involved in the field in which you're interested or a savvy layperson (either a doctor who works with many diabetics, for example, or a diabetic who has spent a long time researching the condition and steers his or her own treatment). That's not going to happen often, so go for updated and on-target. Credibility (or its lack) will become clear as you gather resources from other places in the Web.

Determining Credibility in Other Ways

There are other ways that you can determine the credibility and popularity of a writer. (We'll get into this issue more deeply in Chapter 13, "The Principle of Salt Grains.") One way is to track what other people are saying about them and how popular their Weblog is. You can do that with a tool called Technorati.

Technorati—http://www.technorati.com

Many tools search by keyword, but Technorati searches by URL. On the front page of the site, you'll find a query box. In the query box enter the URL of a site in which you're interested.

Example time. Say you're interested in researching cutting-edge consumer electronics. You've looked around and decided you want to track the Weblog Gizmodo, but first you want to see how popular it is. You go to Technorati and plug in `http://www.gizmodo.com`.

The first thing you'll notice is that there are well over 1,000 links to this particular blog, so it's pretty popular. From there you can look at the kind of blogs that link to Gizmodo, see if any of them should be browsed through, and go on and on ...

... which you could do pretty much indefinitely. What I'm describing for you here is a very thorough method of gleaning information. If you're trying to get every last scrap of information or buzz or linkage or whatever, you could follow these resources for possibly days. Adjust your degree of intensity depending on how deep you want to go. No matter how much work you do, though, enjoy the fact that you're getting more work done because you're following the Principle of the Reinvented Wheel, and you're finding more stuff because other people found it first!

6 THE PRINCIPLE OF ONIONS

The Principle of Onions: When searching, it's better to start with very specific search queries and then get more and more general. If you start with more general queries you will tend to get overwhelmed with results.

Google indexes over four billion Web pages but admits that they don't index the entire Internet. The Internet Archive, a collection of older copies of Web site pages, is by itself well over ten billion pages. And the Internet is getting larger, not smaller.

It's crucial that you start your Internet search right by structuring a query such that you get a limited number of results—otherwise you're going to get overwhelmed with information. If the very narrow query doesn't work, you should slowly get more and more general, until you achieve a good balance of useful—but not overwhelming—information. That's what the Principle of Onions is all about.

Of course, different types of search engines have different levels of information. What is just narrow enough on a full-text engine is impossibly narrow on a searchable subject index. That's because a full-text engine indexes an entire Web page, making searches on obscure keywords possible. Searchable subject indexes include only the title, URL, and description of a site, leaving little room for narrow search results.

How does this apply to the Principle of Onions? Let's take a look at four search scenarios and see how "narrow" means different things to the two different search engines. For these scenarios we'll use Google as our full-text engine and Yahoo as our searchable subject index.

Searching for Lyrics

Are there really lyrics to that song you're listening to or is the singer just saying "Ugga oomp blat argh"? Now you can find out by searching for the lyrics online. Though the lyrics transcriptions provided by any given Web site are not guaranteed to be accurate, they'll get you a lot further than "ugga oomp."

Full-Text Engines

For full-text engines the onion is simple. Search for the name of the artist, if you know it, and one line of lyrics that you're absolutely sure of, the more unique the better. If you're not sure of a single word within a line, use the full word wildcard. A nice narrow search therefore might look like this:

```
"they might be giants" "dot or is he a speck""
```

Google Web Images Groups News Froogle more »

"they might be giants" "dot or is he a speck" Search Advanced Search Preferences

Web Results **1** - **100** of about **191** for **"they might be giants" "dot or is he a speck""**. (**1.33** seconds)

They Might Be Giants - Particle Man Lyrics
... **Giants** Album: Flood Particle man, particle man Doing the things a particle can What's he like? It's not important Particle man Is he a **dot, or is he a speck**? ...
www.lyricsdepot.com/ **they-might-be-giants**/particle-man.html - 7k - Cached - Similar pages

They Might Be Giants - Schoolchildren Singing "Particle Man" ...
... Artist: **They Might Be Giants** Album: Then-The Earlier Years ... It's not important Particle man Is he a **dot, or is he a speck**? When he's underwater does he get wet? ...
www.lyricsdepot.com/**they-might-be-giants**/ schoolchildren-singing-particle-man.html - 8k - Cached - Similar pages

Particle Man - **They Might Be Giants** (Lyrics and Chords)
ARTIST: **They Might Be Giants** TITLE: Particle Man Lyrics and Chords Particle Man, Particle Man ... E - / D - A - / A - / Is he a **dot, or is he a speck** When he's ...
www.guntheranderson.com/v/data/particle.htm - 3k - Cached - Similar pages

They Might Be Giants - Particle Man lyrics
... Artist(Band):**They Might Be Giants** (Print the Lyrics) Particle man, particle man Doing the things ... It's not important Particle man Is he a **dot, or is he a speck**? ...
www.sing365.com/music/lyric.nsf/ Particle-Man-lyrics-They-Might-Be-Giants/10BB2D2D34A352A3482568B10025E7E1 - 24k - Supplemental Result - Cached - Similar pages

THEY MIGHT BE GIANTS – (Particle Man Lyrics)
... Particle man, particle man Doing the things a particle can What's he like? it's not important Particle man Is he a **dot, or is he a speck**? ...
www.lyricsfreak.com/t/**they-might-be-giants**/136387.html - 12k - Cached - Similar pages

They Might Be Giants Lyrics » (Schoolchildren Singing & Quot ...
... it's not important Particle man Is he a **dot, or is he a speck**? When he's underwater does he get wet? Or does the water get him instead? ...
www.lyricsfreak.com/t/**they-might-be-giants**/136458.html - 12k - Supplemental Result - Cached - Similar pages

Lyrics By XVR27 - **They Might Be Giants** - Particle Man
... It's not important Particle man Is he a **dot, or is he a speck** When he's underwater does he get wet Or does the ... It is an original song by **They Might Be Giants**. ...
www.com-www.com/musiclyrics/ theymightbegiants-particleman.html - 3k - Cached - Similar pages

Compare Prices and Read Reviews on Flood - **They Might Be Giants** at ...
... Particle man. Is he a **dot, or is he a speck**? When he's underwater does he get wet? ... There's

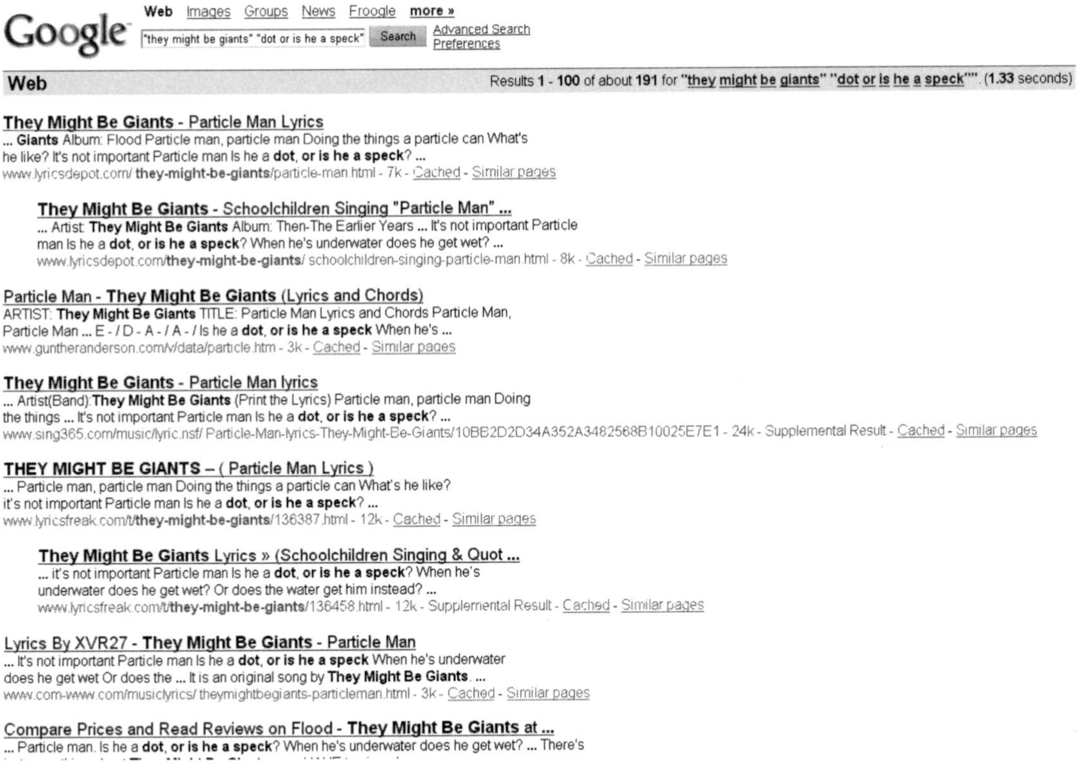

06–01

A simple search still gets a lot of lyric results. (Image from http://www.google.com/search?q=%22they+might+be+giants%22+%22dot+or+is+he+a+speck%22%22&sourceid=opera&num=100&ie=utf-8&oe=utf-8.)

This search will get you results. But if it doesn't, start by removing the line of lyrics (you might be absolutely certain that you have the right lyrics, but you might be wrong) and substitute the name of the song:

```
"they might be giants" "particle man"
```

If that still doesn't work, use the band name and the words "lyric" and "search"—remove the song title. If you're lucky you'll land on a lyrics search engine.

Do you see how you're moving from more specific to more general with just a few searches?

Searchable Subject Indexes

Searchable subject indexes are lousy for searching for the lyrics for one song. Instead, you'll want to use them to search for lyrics collections. Search for the name of the band and the word "lyrics":

```
"they might be giants" lyrics
```

Not only will that get you results, but you'll also discover that there's a category for that band, which will lead you to other resources if you want them.

The two techniques above will work for any band that's halfway well-known. But you may be interested in a band that has only a regional following. In that case you'll have to realize that "as specific as possible" is not going to be very specific. You may have to go to Google and just search for the band name and the word "lyrics."

Searching for Technical Help

Whether you need a walkthrough for a game or help getting your video card to work right, you'll find that the Principle of Onions can make your search a lot easier. (We'll discuss the topic of finding technical help in greater depth later in Chapter 25, "Getting Technical Support—Drivers, Cheats, Walkthroughs, and More.")

Full-Text Engines

When I'm using a full-text engine for technical help, I try to start by simply expressing the problem that I'm having:

```
My screen is flickering. I think it's my BadBrand
video card.
```

From that simple expression extract the relevant concepts—screen, flickering, BadBrand video card—and turn that into a search. Usually I add the word "problem," which seems to focus the results:

```
screen flickering BadBrand "video card" problem
```

If that doesn't do the trick, keep the brand name and what the item is and the word "problem," but shuffle the descriptive words around. You may say "screen" and someone else may say "monitor." Someone might say "flicker" instead of "flickering."

After trying that, cut the search down to just the brand name, item, and the word "problem." If you still can't get results, try the brand name, item, and the word "support" or "FAQ."

Searchable Subject Indexes

You're not going to find specific technical answers on Yahoo unless the problem is extremely popular and therefore extremely well documented (the computer equivalent of a car with an exploding gas tank). The best you're going to find are support sites for whatever you're interested in. So you might search for `BadBrand "video card" support` or even just `BadBrand support`. This is an option best suited for when you have a problem but you're not exactly sure how to describe it, or you're having a problem with a computer that could come from one of many components, and you're trying to find support for the computer itself.

NOTE

Usually general search engines aren't the best place to find support information. I recommend you use Google Groups for finding technical support instead of Google's Web search. The cool thing is that the Principle of Onions works as well on Google Groups as it does on Google's general Web search.

Searching for Dog Breed Information

Can you tell a Chihuahua from a collie? If you can't you might need a little help from the Internet. But whether Google or Yahoo is better for this kind of search depends on what you're looking for.

Full-Text Engines

You might think that a search like `dog breed chihuahua` is a narrow enough query if you're searching Google. It's not. Go run that search in Google. I'll stay here. Did you run it? Did you get over 100,000 results? Right. For this kind of onion searching you want to search full-text only if you have a question about a particular breed. For example, you may want to know about hip problems in elderly German Shepherds:

```
hip aging "German Shepherds"
```

That gives you a reasonable number of results. If you don't find what you want here you could expand out a little bit:

NOTE

Technical support includes viruses, and full-text engines are useful in searching for virus information. If you get something you think is a virus, extract an unusual line from the virus e-mail and search for it with the word "virus" (`"this is a very excite game" virus`). Unless the virus is brand new, this'll pop up some information.

```
hip "German Shepherds"
```

but no way can you get more general than that if you're searching a full-text engine. You'll just get too many results!

Searchable Subject Indexes

If you're just searching for general information about a breed, using a searchable subject index is a much better way to go. Just search for the name of the breed. In most cases, except when it's an incredibly obscure breed or one your friend made up to play with your mind, you'll find a Yahoo category for them that you can work from.

Searching for Biographical Information for a Term Paper

Biographical information is tricky. On one hand you want enough data that you can learn about the person for your term paper. On the other hand, you want credible data in limited, usable qualities.

The Principle of Onions will apply a little differently here. Instead of trying to use very specific query words, you'll try to use special syntaxes so you're narrowing your query down to credible data.

Full-Text Engines

Let's search for Sally Ride, first woman in space. `"Sally Ride" biography` is actually a pretty narrow query, but you can narrow the search even more by excluding .com sites:

```
"Sally Ride" biography -site:com
```

When you do that you'll get a lot of Sally Ride material, and a lot of it is more oriented toward credible sources (NASA, ThinkQuest, etc.). And you're not finding ads for Sally Ride memorial plates or whatever.

The more famous the person is, the more you may find yourself having to get narrow (perhaps this is the Principle of Famous Onions). For example, if you search for George Washington:

```
"George Washington" biography -site:com
```

you will still get over 60,000 results. Relevant ones will pop right up, but you may decide that you want more detailed information. In that case, you may want to add a few more words that reflect what you're looking for:

```
"George Washington" president "cherry tree" -site:com
```

While these query words don't narrow your search in an appreciable way—they're too general—they will bring a different set of search results to the top. You can rotate the query words, bringing in different keywords that coincide with popular ideas about George Washington's life, and see how the results change.

Searchable Subject Indexes

When you're searching for a very famous person, searching for them in a searchable subject index is absolutely the way to go. In this case you don't need to make much of an onion at all. Just search for the name and the word "biography":

```
"George Washington" biography
```

You'll see that George Washington has his own category with all the information you could use.

Sometimes it's hard to get the idea that you should immediately narrow down your query as much as possible in the hope of getting good results. You might be worried that you won't find all the information you're looking for. And you might not want to spend a lot of time trying to map out the perfect query.

Trust me, it will save you time in the end. The time you spend now to specify a narrow query will limit the amount of time you'll have to spend slogging through result pages. Furthermore, the Web is only going to get bigger. The habits you learn now to narrow down your search results are going to help you when you have to worry about slogging through twenty billion Web pages instead of only four billion.

7 THE PRINCIPLE OF NICKNAMES

The Principle of Nicknames: Most things, unfortunately, have nicknames. New York can be NY, Street can be St., Jennifer can be Jen or Jenny, etc. Nicknames must be accommodated in searching.

Wouldn't it be nice if there was only one way to say something and people had only one possible name? Thomas would only be Thomas; there would be no possibility of Tommy, Tom, or Tomster. Los Angeles would only be Los Angeles, it would not be L.A. or, in the case of some Web pages, LosAngeles.

If that were the case then Web searching would be so much easier. But it's not that way. If you do any searching for proper nouns—people, places, or things—then you've already run up against the Principle of Nicknames. There are so *many* different ways to say something that it's hard to search in a way that includes them all!

Don't worry. The first thing to discard is the idea that you *can* find every single possible iteration of a name or a place. That having been said, you can also make an effort to do your searches in a way that finds as many matches as possible. Different kinds of nouns—person names, place names, and people names—have different techniques for getting the most out of a search. Let's start with people.

People

Not only can names be difficult to search when you're doing your research, but different institutions will express names in different ways. Library card catalog listings, for example, might list an author with their last name first, as will many bibliography formats. Court papers and other formal items of record might list someone's full name—first, middle, and last—even if they rarely use their full names themselves.

Treat the formatting of this kind as a variant of the Principle of Unique Language. If you format your search in the way that it's used in a certain kind of resource, then you'll get more results that are like that resource.

Let's take an example: Stephen Hawking wrote *A Brief History of Time*. If you do a Google search for "Stephen Hawking" you will find Professor Hawking's official Web page and similar resources. But now do a search for "Hawking, Stephen" (Google will not pick up the comma; I'm just formatting the search as you might see in a library's card catalog). What did you find? Aha! You still got the official Stephen Hawking page, but you also got library and book listings. Let's take it one step further: "Hawking, Stephen W." You'll see more bookselling listings with this version. Finally, let's try "Hawking, Stephen William." With the use of his entire name we'll see listings for Professor Hawking in source documents like encyclopedias.

So when you're doing person research, try various iterations of their names to see what kind of results you get. Sometimes, though, this won't help. I have a couple of hints for you.

The Mystery of the Middle Name

Sometimes you're looking for a name listing and you don't know if the middle name will be used or not (or, in the case of married women, you don't know if they're using their maiden name as their middle name). Use Google's full-word wildcard to search for the first and last name with any word in the middle:

```
"stephen * hawking"
```

If you're not sure about the middle name to the extent that you don't know if it's one word or two, or you want to pick up on very unusual name variants (like Stephen "Utterly Brilliant" Hawking), you can use two wildcards in a row:

```
"stephen * * hawking"
```

For Very Unusual Names

For unique names, try just searching for the first and last name without using quote marks.

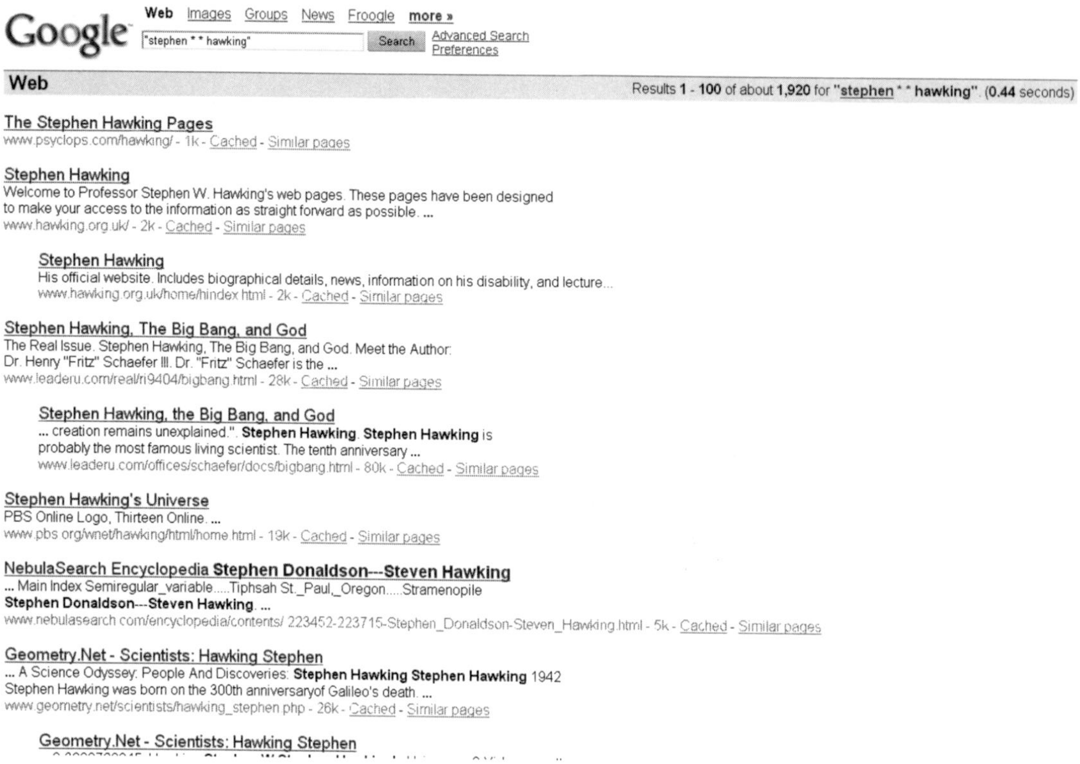

Google Web Images Groups News Froogle more »
"stephen * * hawking" Search Advanced Search Preferences

Web Results 1 - 100 of about 1,920 for "stephen * * hawking". (0.44 seconds)

The Stephen Hawking Pages
www.psyclops.com/hawking/ - 1k - Cached - Similar pages

Stephen Hawking
Welcome to Professor Stephen W. Hawking's web pages. These pages have been designed to make your access to the information as straight forward as possible. ...
www.hawking.org.uk/ - 2k - Cached - Similar pages

Stephen Hawking
His official website. Includes biographical details, news, information on his disability, and lecture...
www.hawking.org.uk/home/hindex.html - 2k - Cached - Similar pages

Stephen Hawking, The Big Bang, and God
The Real Issue. Stephen Hawking, The Big Bang, and God. Meet the Author: Dr. Henry "Fritz" Schaefer III. Dr. "Fritz" Schaefer is the ...
www.leaderu.com/real/ri9404/bigbang.html - 28k - Cached - Similar pages

Stephen Hawking, the Big Bang, and God
... creation remains unexplained.". **Stephen Hawking**. **Stephen Hawking** is probably the most famous living scientist. The tenth anniversary ...
www.leaderu.com/offices/schaefer/docs/bigbang.html - 80k - Cached - Similar pages

Stephen Hawking's Universe
PBS Online Logo, Thirteen Online. ...
www.pbs.org/wnet/hawking/html/home.html - 19k - Cached - Similar pages

NebulaSearch Encyclopedia **Stephen Donaldson---Steven Hawking**
... Main Index Semiregular_variable.....Tiphsah St._Paul,_Oregon.....Stramenopile **Stephen Donaldson---Steven Hawking**. ...
www.nebulasearch.com/encyclopedia/contents/ 223452-223715-Stephen_Donaldson-Steven_Hawking.html - 5k - Cached - Similar pages

Geometry.Net - Scientists: Hawking Stephen
... A Science Odyssey: People And Discoveries: **Stephen Hawking Stephen Hawking** 1942 Stephen Hawking was born on the 300th anniversaryof Galileo's death. ...
www.geometry.net/scientists/hawking_stephen.php - 26k - Cached - Similar pages

Geometry.Net - Scientists: Hawking Stephen

07–01

The many name formats for Stephen Hawking. (Image from http://www.google.com/search?q=%22stephen++*+hawking%22&sourceid=opera&num=100&ie=utf-8&oe=utf-8.)*

For Very Common Names

For very common names (George Bush) try either including words that put the person in a context ("president") or in a particular place ("DC" or "Texas"). You also have to do this with famous people who have the same name. There are Levi Strauss jeans and then there's Levi Strauss the French social anthropologist. You probably don't want to mix them up on your anthropology paper.

For historical figures, if you've tried all these tricks and they're not helping, try including the year of birth and death in your search (though not as a phrase). This will weed out the false positives and the marginal mentions.

Places

Places are, in a way, even more confusing than names. After all, people can expect to be listed by their first and last names. But there's no telling how a place might be listed! A city and state might be listed (but will it be Oklahoma or OK?).

A city alone might be listed, especially for very local businesses (but are they going to list the nearest big city or the small town that they're actually in?). And sometimes a locally understood area might be listed, but no city name at all (North Carolina's "Triad" area covers several different cities).

Tearing your hair out yet? Dodge a lot of this confusion by assuming that there's some existing organization. If you're searching for a place, and you have its full address and a zip code, try searching for just the name of the place and the zip code. Or the name of the place and its area code. Or the name of the place and the city. The point is that you can use the existing organization structures under which it's already listed (zip code, area code) to find it.

When you search for entire addresses you'll notice something very similar to using very formal name types. You'll find that your search results tend to bring back listings of businesses and other places. Let's take an example: say, the Burger King in Walla Walla, Washington. Here's its address according to a Google phone number search:

```
1748 East Isaacs Avenue, Walla Walla, WA 99362
```

Where can that address be shortened or otherwise changed? The words "East" (which could be E or East) or "Avenue" (which could be Av, Ave, or Avenue) or "WA" (which could be Washington or WA). So replace those with Google full-word wildcards:

```
"1748 * Isaacs *, Walla Walla, * 99362"
```


Now what did you find? In this case you found that there's only one result for this search, but it's for restaurants in the 509 area code (in other words, right on target). And that's generally what you'll find when you use entire addresses: lists of other addresses. Also sometimes you'll find newspaper accounts that refer to that address.

As you'll see in Chapter 16, "Finding Local Information on the Web," you can also search for just a business name and a zip code, or a business type and a zip code (nursing homes, for example). That will generally not give you exact results for one place, but instead a list of places.

Another trick you can try is searching for just the phone number. Let's go back to the Burger King in Walla Walla again. Searching for its phone number—(509) 525-0843—gives you about half a dozen results, including listings of restaurants in Walla Walla, commercial real estate, etc. Here's another thing to try. Search for the business name and the phone number without the area code:

```
"Burger King" "525-0843"
```

Sometimes that will get you more results, though in this case it didn't. Local Web pages don't always use the area code when they're listing phone numbers.

We've talked about people and places. Now let's talk about things—landmarks and other well-known places—and searching for them in context.

Things

When I say "things" I don't mean just any old noun like a hairbrush or an egg timer. I mean a landmark, or some other place that might not be best searched for as a place.

The Eiffel Tower. That's a place, but I have no idea of its address; do you? How about its phone number? No clue. But you can search for "Eiffel Tower" and get any number of search results. How do you get additional information?

Start by adding the word "official" to your search:

```
"Eiffel Tower" official
```

Any site that exists at least marginally as a tourist attraction is very likely to have a Web site. Take advantage of that. In this case we'll be directed to the official site of the Eiffel Tower. There you can get additional information on the tower (who the engineers were, how tall it is, contact phone numbers, etc.) that you can use to build more specific queries and winnow out just mentions of the tower in Web pages.

You can use the "things" technique with any place that doesn't have a well-known address: parks, forests, bodies of water, etc. You can even use it for (famous) imaginary places like Santa's North Pole, though you might find yourself getting plenty of results for North Pole, Alaska. When you don't have an address or a phone number, and no recourse for getting an address or a phone number, try using the word "official" with the name of the place and gathering information from there.

Knowing that there are many different ways to express names and addresses can be really, really frustrating. But try these tips and see if they don't help you get a few more results for your searches.

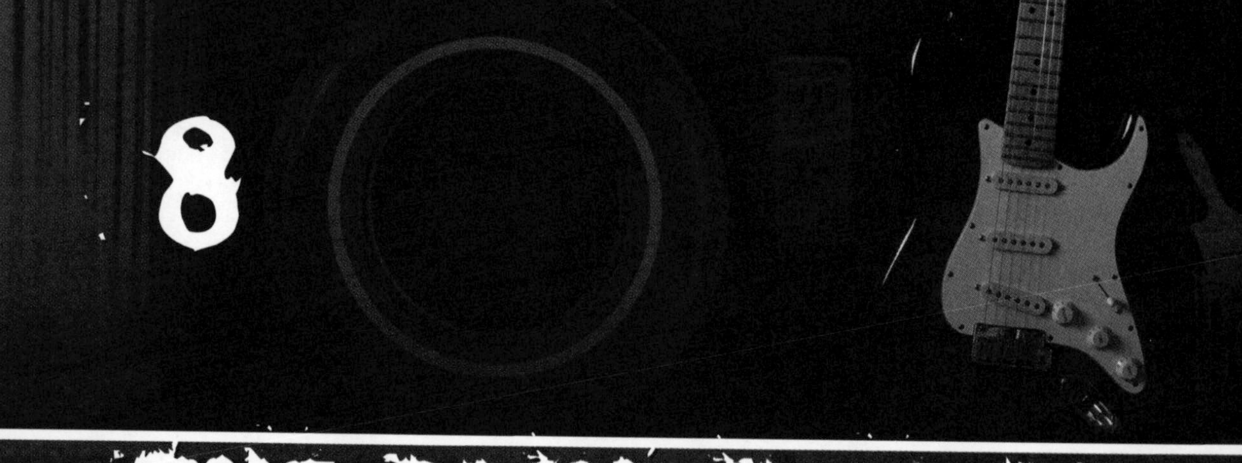

8 THE PRINCIPLE OF EVERY SCRAP

The Principle of Every Scrap: You never know what information will be the useful bit that brings all your research together. So keep your eyes out; watch for every scrap of information that might potentially bring all your research together.

Don't you wish all Internet research was like a game of Clue? "It was Colonel Mustard, in the drawing room, with the candlestick!" All you'd have to know is what the primary impetus and main parts of all your research was, and you'd get squared away quickly.

But unless you're looking for one absolute bit of information—like a song lyric, birth date, or some other kind of reference information—it won't work that way. The most offbeat, weird bit of information may be the thing that breaks your research into what you're looking for. Thus the Principle of Every Scrap: you should save every scrap of information you find with the expectation that what you save now may be what helps you bring all your research together later.

That doesn't mean just taking the content of the Web page. It also means looking at the characteristics of the Web page itself for clues (the title, URL, etc.). It means organizing your scraps so you can go back and look at them later. And sometimes it means putting scraps on "to simmer"—taking interesting bits of information and monitoring them with the expectations that those interesting bits could lead to other searches later on.

Now, if most of your searches are pretty basic—the song lyric and birth date type—you are probably staring at this and thinking, "Every time I want to check on the lyrics to 'Boogie Shoes' she's going to make me write a term paper?"

No! I know it might sound that way, but it's not what I want. Instead, I want to give you a foundation for gathering information when you have long-term research to do—whether you're looking for historical information or medical conditions or whatever. The Principle of Every Scrap absolutely doesn't apply when you're just looking for a quick factoid.

So let's start with an example—a long-term project where you'll be wanting to research a lot of sites. Let's use a medical example—Asperger's Syndrome.

Your First Search and Your Next Searches

Obviously your first search is going to depend on the amount of information you have, as we've discussed in previous principles. For here let's start with Asperger's Syndrome, searched for as a phrase:

```
"Asperger's Syndrome"
```

Once you do the search, look at the results on three levels. The first level is the search results, the second level is page characteristics, and the third is page content.

First Level: Search Results

Run your eyes over the first hundred results and see if anything pops out at you. There will be several things you can notice with this first viewing:

1. Sometimes it's called "Asperger Syndrome."
2. It was discovered by Hans Asperger.
3. It's related to autism.
4. Tony Attwood is a noted Asperger Syndrome author.
5. It has its own Yahoo Directory (which tells you that it is not a rare disorder and that there are at least a fair number of resources available).
6. There are several books available about it (which, again, indicates that it is not a rare or little-known disorder).

Note all this information wherever you want to note it (more on that later). On to the second level.

You'll notice that the information you're gathering together is kind of like the information you gathered together when you were exploring the Principle of Unique Language, when you gathered vocabulary unique to your topic and used it to steer your search. It's true; the idea is similar. However, in this case you're going beyond vocabulary and into concepts (like autism) and people (Hans Asperger and Tony Attwood).

Second Level: Page Characteristics

Run your eyes over the search results again, this time paying attention to the page title and page URLs. Does anything jump to your attention now?

1. There are lots of edu and org results.

2. In many page titles autism and Asperger's are mentioned together.
3. There are an unusually small number of .com results—most of the results are .edu, .org, or country codes like .uk and .au.

Some of these kinds of scraps you won't notice when you start your observation. It'll take many bouts of research before you recognize an unusual amount of top-level domain results. But gather what you can from here and move on to the third level: page content.

Third Level: Page Content

How far you go—that is, how many pages you review—with the third level is entirely up to you. You may go over ten pages. You may go over fifty. Some people will patiently go over hundreds of results. It depends on how deeply you want to research and how important a thorough answer is for you.

Regardless of how many pages you want to go over, keep an eye out for the following things:

1. Unique words (a la the Principle of Unique Language) .
2. Names—Are the same ones coming up over and over again? Note people names and organization names.
3. Dates.
4. Places and addresses, if they come up more than a couple of times.
5. Facts associated with your topic. If all widgets are pale green, note that. If all gadgets are exactly 37 centimeters wide because of a European declaration in 1964, note that. Of course you will not know which facts are true and which are not (we'll get into that more in Chapter 13, "The Principle of Salt Grains"), but when you see a fact repeated more than a few times, you'll know it's a pointer to more information about the topic.

You'll notice I didn't mention opinions here. Most of the time opinions are couched in such a way that they're not unique and not searchable. If someone "loves widgets" or "hates widgets," that doesn't give you much to go on to change your search. If someone "loves widgets because they're light blue" or "hates gizmos because they cost 14 times as much as widgets," then those might be facts that you can add to your scrap pile.

As you gather scraps, you'll need to organize them in some way. You can organize scraps in your head, but you run the risk of missing something or misremembering something. I find that there are two general ways to organize scraps—via bookmarks or text files.

Organizing Your Scraps

You want to keep this information as you continue your search, and you can do it either by gathering a set of bookmarks or keeping information in text files. Both situations have their drawbacks.

Scraps to Bookmarks

I have a prejudice about bookmarks that I might as well admit right now: I hate them. I find them cumbersome, useless, and annoying. And they tend to take over your browser like kudzu. But I will use them on occasion, especially when I'm doing long-range research.

I could have a folder, for example, on Asperger's. Within it I could have separate folders for autism, mental health, support groups, coping strategies, disability, and so on. Opera allows me to make comments for each bookmark so in the comments section I could pull out the information I found most useful.

The benefit to this way of saving information is that it's in a standard format that on most browsers can be exported. The disadvantage, in my experience, is that it's difficult to look at a bookmarks file and have the information it contains "gel" into additional paths or searches that you might try. When I use text files, I find the information is easier for me to scan and reassemble into other data.

Scraps to Text Files

When I'm researching something using text files, I just dump things as I find them into a text file. I'll include the URL and a quote from the URL, copy-and-pasted into the text file.

It's harder to consolidate this way; you don't have your information organized into neat little folders. On the other hand I find that having my information in this format allows me to read all of it, think about it, and then add more information as I do additional searching. If I must have my scraps in a format that I can shuffle and pass along, I'll do my research, and then go through my scraps and drop them into a simple Excel file (of course you can use any kind of spreadsheet).

Why am I quoting instead of summarizing what I find? So if I ever need to find that page again—it changes URLs or vanishes off the current Web—I can search for that specific phrase in Google or in a place like the Internet Archive, which archives old copies of Web sites.

You've done some searches, and you've got lots of scraps. You've organized them. Now what? Do you let your scraps shape your search, or do you turn them into some final form?

Scraps to More Search?

The answer to that depends on what you're trying to do with your search. Your research my lead to some kind of offline endeavor—contacting a support group, buying a program, getting a new job, moving to a new city. Or your research may lead you to narrow your focus to just one thing—you may want to search for information on one specific cancer drug instead of a certain kind of cancer.

In that case you pull out what you need—the name of the drug, the place to which you'd like to relocate, the job title you want to get more information on—and go on with your research, striking out in that new direction.

You may want to keep going in the direction you started—more information on a history of a country, or a movement in art history, or a particular species of dinosaur. In that case I would periodically narrow my pile of scraps, taking the best information and writing an informal report, and discarding the rest.

You should also let the scraps adjust your search. I wish I could say "do this, then do that, then take your scraps and do the other," but I can't. Unfortunately things are not that linear when you're doing online research. Any category of research can develop dozens if not hundreds of lines of inquiry (as I have discovered, to my chagrin, over and over again). The best I can tell you is that if you organize the materials you find initially, it'll be easier for you to delineate categories of searches that you might want to pursue later. Don't try to do everything at once; follow one thread at a time.

I do want to address something that might come up for you no matter where you decide to search: the idea of letting your scraps simmer.

Putting Scraps on to Simmer

During the course of your search you may come across an item or a topic that you want to track, but which doesn't have immediate interest as a research topic. For example, you may be researching Western literature and want to get ongoing information about Elmer Kelton while not really wanting to pursue him as a research topic.

In that case you'll want to put that scrap of information on to simmer; in other words, you'll want to monitor the topic without putting time into researching it. This works best in the case of proper names. Use one of the monitoring services, like Google Alert or Google News, and enter your scrap there. That way you'll be assured of getting pointers to additional information on that topic without having to revisit it all the time.

The notion of tracking and extracting all relevant information from a Web search can be intimidating, but don't let it deter you. You can never tell which bit of information is going to be the one that makes it a successful search.

9 The Principle of Mass Similar

The Principle of Mass Similar: The more kinds of proper nouns describing item X you search for, the more your search results will be slanted toward the topic of X.

The Principle of Mass Similar is much like the Principle of Unique Language, with two differences. The first difference is that you're not trying to gather up all the unique vocabulary that you can; you're just trying to find proper nouns that are relevant to your topic. The second difference is that you can apply this principle where it would be difficult to apply the Principle of Unique Language.

Let's take an example: candy bars. You want to find Web sites that deal heavily with candy bars. You can try to search for the phrase "candy bars" but you'll get a lot of irrelevant results. You can try using the Principle of Unique Language and search for `"candy bar" nougat caramel`, but you might find that your results are too slanted towards trade industry sites.

Using Brand Names to Narrow Your Search

Enter the Principle of Mass Similar. Try using *brand names*. Use at least three, preferably more, and don't use brand names that are associated with other things. (For example, I wouldn't use the candy bar Mounds because it by itself is a noun. Snickers can be a verb, but both it and Three Musketeers are sufficiently associated with candy that I feel safe using them.)

```
"almond joy" snickers "three
    musketeers" hershey
```

Do that search and you'll see that not only do you get a limited number of results, but they're all oriented toward candy bars. In fact some pages may be too oriented—they're shopping pages. Try another search to get rid of those pages. How about removing the word "shopping"?

```
"almond joy" snickers "three musketeers"
          hershey -shopping
```

That helped some.

Will this give you every kind of page oriented toward candy bars? No, because you're not using every possible candy bar brand name. You could run this search for a long time, trying every combination of four or five candy bar names. Try this one:

```
"tootsie roll" "baby ruth" "butterfinger"
          hershey -shopping
```

(Are you getting hungry, reading this?)

As you can see, various combinations will bring about various results. But perhaps you don't eat a lot of candy bars, and you don't recognize any of the brand names I'm using here. In that case your question right now is probably, "How the heck do I find all those brand names in the first place?"

Good question. You've got a few options, depending on how many proper names you know in the first place.

TIP

By saying "use brand names," am I saying that you can only use the names of consumer items when using this principle? No; you only have to use the proper names for items. If I were looking for Web sites dealing with hawks, I might search for "red tailed," "red shouldered," "sharp shinned," etc. These are different kinds of hawks—hawk "brand names."

Finding Brand Names in the First Place

Go to Google Labs (http://labs.google.com) and choose Google Sets at http://labs.google.com/sets. Here you should enter all the different types that you know of and choose a result set: small or large. Then if you've given Google enough information it'll pull together a list of related items, and if you're lucky you'll get enough information to build queries using the Principle of Mass Similar.

Let's use the candy bar example. Try entering Twix, Snickers, and Butterfinger in the Google Sets slots and click Enter. You'll get a long list of candy items that you can use in building your queries.

The Google Sets tool is great to use when there are enough types of an item to build a list. But sometimes there isn't enough information to give Google Sets to build a query. Consider ferrets, for example.

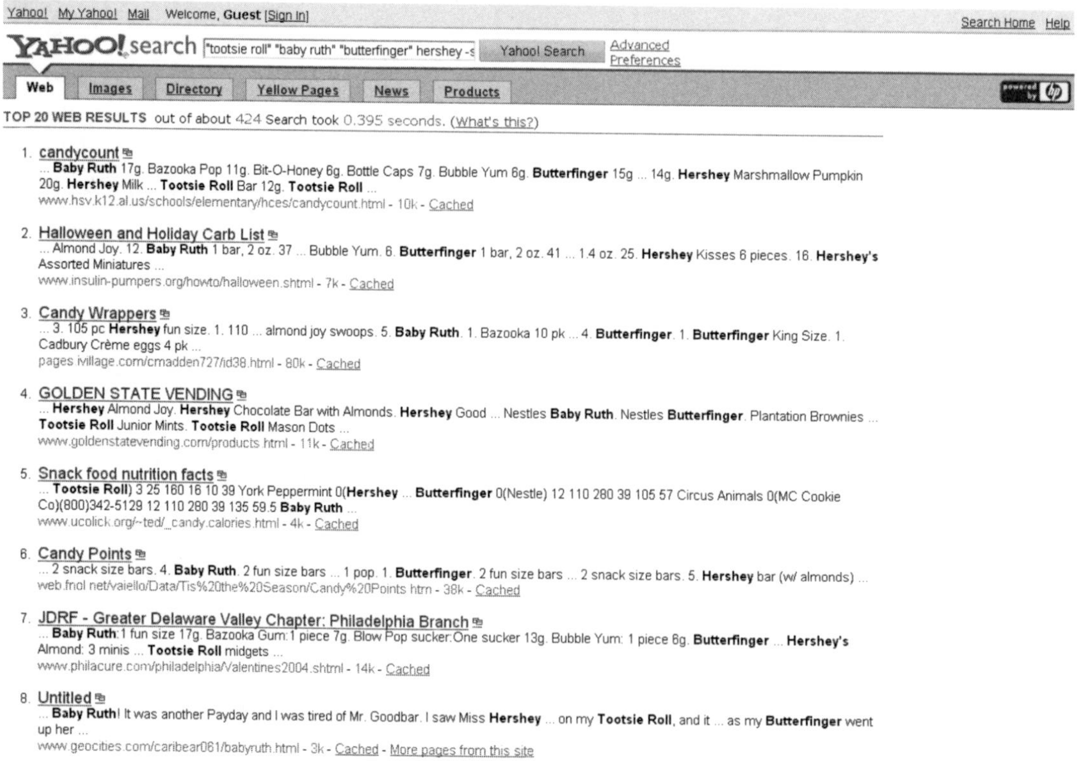

Yahoo! My Yahoo! Mail Welcome, **Guest** [Sign In] Search Home Help

YAHOO! search "tootsie roll" "baby ruth" "butterfinger" hershey -s Yahoo! Search Advanced Preferences

Web Images Directory Yellow Pages News Products

TOP 20 WEB RESULTS out of about 424 Search took 0.395 seconds. (What's this?)

1. candycount
... **Baby Ruth** 17g. Bazooka Pop 11g. Bit-O-Honey 6g. Bottle Caps 7g. Bubble Yum 6g. **Butterfinger** 15g ... 14g. **Hershey** Marshmallow Pumpkin 20g. **Hershey** Milk ... **Tootsie Roll** Bar 12g. **Tootsie Roll** ...
www.hsv.k12.al.us/schools/elementary/hces/candycount.html - 10k - Cached

2. Halloween and Holiday Carb List
... Almond Joy. 12. **Baby Ruth** 1 bar, 2 oz. 37 ... Bubble Yum. 6. **Butterfinger** 1 bar, 2 oz. 41 ... 1.4 oz. 25. **Hershey** Kisses 6 pieces. 16. **Hershey's** Assorted Miniatures ...
www.insulin-pumpers.org/howto/halloween.shtml - 7k - Cached

3. Candy Wrappers
... 3. 105 pc **Hershey** fun size. 1. 110 ... almond joy swoops. 5. **Baby Ruth**. 1. Bazooka 10 pk ... 4. **Butterfinger**. 1. **Butterfinger** King Size. 1. Cadbury Crème eggs 4 pk ...
pages.ivillage.com/cmadden727/id38.html - 80k - Cached

4. GOLDEN STATE VENDING
... **Hershey** Almond Joy. **Hershey** Chocolate Bar with Almonds. **Hershey** Good ... Nestles **Baby Ruth**. Nestles **Butterfinger**. Plantation Brownies ... **Tootsie Roll** Junior Mints. **Tootsie Roll** Mason Dots ...
www.goldenstatevending.com/products.html - 11k - Cached

5. Snack food nutrition facts
... **Tootsie Roll**) 3 25 160 16 10 39 York Peppermint 0(**Hershey** ... **Butterfinger** 0(Nestle) 12 110 280 39 105 57 Circus Animals 0(MC Cookie Co)(800)342-5129 12 110 280 39 135 59.5 **Baby Ruth** ...
www.ucolick.org/~ted/_candy.calories.html - 4k - Cached

6. Candy Points
... 2 snack size bars. 4. **Baby Ruth**. 2 fun size bars ... 1 pop. 1. **Butterfinger**. 2 fun size bars ... 2 snack size bars. 5. **Hershey** bar (w/ almonds) ...
web.fnol.net/vaiello/Data/Tis%20the%20Season/Candy%20Points.htm - 38k - Cached

7. JDRF - Greater Delaware Valley Chapter: Philadelphia Branch
... **Baby Ruth**:1 fun size 17g. Bazooka Gum:1 piece 7g. Blow Pop sucker:One sucker 13g. Bubble Yum: 1 piece 6g. **Butterfinger** ... **Hershey's** Almond: 3 minis ... **Tootsie Roll** midgets ...
www.philacure.com/philadelphia/Valentines2004.shtml - 14k - Cached

8. Untitled
... **Baby Ruth**! It was another Payday and I was tired of Mr. Goodbar. I saw Miss **Hershey** ... on my **Tootsie Roll**, and it ... as my **Butterfinger** went up her ...
www.geocities.com/caribear061/babyruth.html - 3k - Cached - More pages from this site

09–01

Pardon me while I step out for dessert. (Image from http://search.yahoo.com/search?fr=fp-pull-web-t&p=%22tootsie+roll%22+%22baby+ruth%22+%22butterfinger%22+hershey+-shopping.)

Using Google Search to Build Lists of Names

I know ferrets are skinny, and people keep them as pets, and sometimes they bite. Thus endeth my font of ferret knowledge.

Except for one thing. I know from a *Mystery Science Theatre 3000* sketch that there are black-footed ferrets. I can use that little bit of knowledge to build on.

Putting "black-footed ferrets" into Google Sets doesn't provide additional types of ferrets. But by using the Google search engine carefully you can find additional types. Try these phrases:

"compared to X"—Where X is the name of one item. Example: `"Compared to Snickers"`.

"X vs."—Where X is the name of one item. Sometimes this search type finds you a lot of sports type results and sometimes DJ results, depending on the kind of item you're searching for. If that happens change your search to "X versus." Example: `"Twizzlers vs."` (and, of course, `"vs. Twizzlers"`).

"types of Y" X—Where Y is the type of item you're looking for and X is the name of one of the item types. Example: `"types of ferrets" "black-footed"`.

Getting Lists of Names When You Don't Even Have One

If you don't know the names of any of the things you're researching—you know you want information on candy bars, for example, but know nothing about candy bars—you can just try "types of Y":

```
"types of candy bars"
```

Now, candy bars are open-ended. If you sat ten people down and asked them each to name twenty candy bars, they'd all have different lists. But if you're researching something more specific, you can build even more specific queries.

For example, collies. Run the query

```
"there are * types of collies"
```

and see what you get. Or:

```
"there are * types of pine trees"
```


Or:

```
"there are * types of hawks"
```

Basically, anything that can be scientifically classified can be searched for with this query. If you're having trouble finding search results using this query, substitute the word "varieties" or "kinds" for the word "types."

Anything that you can divide into a group of proper names, be it animals, candy bars, flora, or even computer games, is fair game for this search principle.

10

THE PRINCIPLE OF THE WORLD BEYOND

The Principle of the World Beyond: When doing your research online it's essential to remember that there's a world beyond the Internet. Web pages are generated by people, and sometimes people are the most valuable search resources you can find.

I have had many successful searches where I didn't find my search result on a Web page at all. Instead, I found a Web site that contained contact information for a person who could answer my question. Sometimes, instead of an answer in glorious HTML, that's all you need.

Where you'll find an expert varies. Sometimes when you're searching you'll stumble upon a Web page of someone who might know the answer to a complicated or possibly ambiguous question. Once I was helping a friend with a paper she was writing on the subsonic communications of elephants. She had a complex question about subsonic elephant communication research, and we were having a difficult time answering it until we found the Web page of a professor of zoology who had done such research. She answered the question, the paper was completed, and the A grade obtained.

Other times you might want to deliberately search for an expert. There are two ways you can do this: you can find associations (which often have representatives who can answer questions), or you can use one of the many online indexes of experts. If you have a very obscure field of research, you can also resort to a full-text search engine, but I would do that only as a last resort.

Before I point out some resources, though, I want to remind you of your responsibility as a questioner. Follow these five rules for contacting an expert.

The Commandments for the Questioner

1. Thou shalt be polite—It should go without saying but often doesn't. Don't demand; request. Be sure to address the person politely. E-mail them using the contact information they request. Be sure to use their title if they're a professor, doctor, etc. And if they say on their Web site that they can't answer e-mailed questions, don't ask! Sometimes folks are just really busy.
2. Thou shalt make it clear what you want—You should be polite, but you don't have to be obscure. If you're looking for a particular fact, say so: "I'm trying to find out who kicked the longest field goal in NCAA football history." If you're trying to get more information on a particular point, describe it clearly: "I'm trying to understand how subsonic communications between elephants were discovered in the first place. Since we can't hear them, how did we become aware they existed?" Make sure the expert knows what you're asking for.

Be sure to make your subject line meaningful to your question, or else your question may languish unanswered at the bottom of a spam pile.

3. Thou shalt give a reasonable amount of time for an answer—Part of courtesy is giving the expert plenty of time to answer your question. Try to give them three or four days. Sometimes it might take longer. Don't e-mail them and say you have to have the answer in an hour (well, feel free to say that, but don't expect a response). On the other hand, if you have a deadline say so, so the expert knows you need to hear back from them within a certain time frame.
4. Thou shalt not ask the expert to do thy homework—If you write to an expert on Shakespeare with a request like, "Please send me 500 words on the underlying themes in *Romeo and Juliet*," don't be surprised if you get no response. It's one thing to ask for help; it's another thing to ask someone to do your work for you. I've found in my research that an expert is a lot more willing to help if you describe what you've done already, where you've tried to get the answer, and why you're contacting them.
5. Thou shalt not get in a twist if the expert does not answer—Sometimes people get busy, or tired, or their computer breaks, or they can't get their e-mail, or they get carpal tunnel syndrome. Sometimes you won't get an answer. Don't take it personally! People have lives and those lives don't (usually) revolve around making sure their e-mail gets answered. If you want to, send one follow-up e-mail—sometimes legitimate e-mail gets caught in a spam filter or otherwise undelivered—but then leave it alone.

If you follow all these rules, I'd say there's a better than even chance that your mail will get answered. Most experts who don't mind being contacted by e-mail are happy to help folks who ask politely and who show that they've already tried to help themselves.

Now that you know *how* to ask, *who* do you ask?

Experts in Associations

Occasionally I'll need industry knowledge. How many red cars are manufactured in the United States each year? When are the most popular times of year for guacamole? If I can't find the statistics I'm looking for via a Web search, I can always go to the American Automobile Manufacturers' Association or the California Avocado Commission. But first you'll have to know where to find the association.

Finding Associations

TIP

If these links don't have the association you're looking for, try searching for a general keyword and the word "association." It's not surefire, but it helps. This is also a good way to find regional or lesser-known groups; try a Google search for `blueberry association` and see how many trade groups pop up in your results.

Gateway to Associations—http://info.asaenet.org/gateway/OnlineAssocSlist.html

The American Society of Association Executives has a gateway to over 6,500 associations available online. You can search by keyword, by topic (from Accounting to Youth Organization), by city, or by state. Instead of listing information about each organization, this search gives you a list of results, each of which links to that association's Web site.

Scholarly Societies Project—http://www.lib.uwaterloo.ca/society/

If your research is more on the academic side, you'll want to visit this site first. This site lists over 3,800 scholarly societies in a variety of categories, from Arts and Humanities (Academy of Stanislas) to Miscellaneous (Society for College and University Planning). These associations are gathered from all over the world, so non-English sites are noted, as is the "URL-stability" for each site (i.e., the likelihood that the domain name will change at some point).

IPL Association Directory—http://www.ipl.org/div/aon/

IPL stands for the Internet Public Library. The IPL Association Directory is a list of available associations on the Web divided out by categories that look like Yahoo top-level categories, including Arts and Humanities, Science and Technology, and even Reference. Unlike the other association listings, the associations covered here have extensive annotation, handy when you're wondering what the heck the Svenska Läkaresällskapet is.

The Virtual Community of Associations—http://www.vcanet.org/index.htm

The VCA isn't fancy, but it does have a database of associations that's searchable either by name or keyword. You may also browse alphabetically.

The listings on this site have no annotations; they're just direct pointers to Web sites. But this is a pretty huge list, going from the Accrediting Commission of Career Schools and Colleges of Technology to the Workgroup for Electronic Data Interchange.

Finding Associations Using Business.com

Sometimes the association listings above don't help, usually because you're looking for some fairly obscure trade-oriented association, like the association of left-handed spray paint can manufacturers or suchlike. In that case you can try your luck at the business directory Business.com.

For example, say you're looking for information on full-service restaurants (as opposed to fast-food restaurants). You'd move from Food & Beverage on the main menu at http://www.business.com, to Restaurants & Food Service, to Associations . . .

. . . aaand you'll get a big ol' list of associations down the page. The annotations vary in their thoroughness, so you might have to do some exploring to find an association that looks useful.

Associations usually have representatives available to answer questions. If they don't, e-mail them directly and tell them what you're looking for.

Sometimes you don't need associations as much as you need single experts. Experts are a little more difficult to find than associations, and you have to be sure you're using a credible source.

The two resources I'm showing you in this section cover a variety of expert types. If you're looking for more specific experts, check out Google's Directory listing of Ask an Expert sites: http://directory.google.com/Top/Reference/Ask_an_Expert/.

Expert Lists

Why would someone set themselves up as an expert and invite everyone in the world who's doing homework to send them e-mail? Sometimes it's with the idea of helping K–12 Internet users, sometimes it's to get publicity for a cause or company, and sometimes it's because the person really loves what they do and wants to share. It can be any number of things. But the upshot is that there are a lot of places on the Web where you can ask an expert a question. Let me give you two broad places.

TIP

The expert services here are free, but sometimes they can't answer your question. In that case, if you have a few bucks, you might want to try a for-fee answering service, where you pay a fee and (hopefully) get a useful answer to your question. Google Answers (http://answers.google.com) allows you to provide a question and a price you're willing to pay, and have people provide both answers and comments. Of course there's no guarantee that even with the fee you'll get your question answered or answered by a professional, but Google Answers does offer a money-back guarantee and an archive of previously answered questions.

Pitsco's Ask an Expert--http://www.askanexpert.com/

This resource is aimed at the K–12 crowd, but there is a variety of experts here covering categories that include science and technology, health, and trade/repair ("Ask the Corvette Specialist"). Questions are submitted through a form, on which you must specify if you are a student, teacher, parent, or "other."

All Experts--http://www.allexperts.com/

All Experts is a free service, offering experts in a variety of categories who will answer questions. The cool thing about this service is that experts are rated, so you can get a sense of how good the experts are and what "prestige" they have built up. The other cool thing is that this service has an archive of answered questions that is browsable by topic. So you might not even need to ask an expert!

Finding Experts Using Google

Sometimes the ask-an-expert listings can't help you find experts. Usually it's because you're looking for something fairly obscure—there's more call for "ask the biologist" than there is for "ask the specialist in freshwater ichthyology." In that case you can do a Google search. I don't recommend this unless you are really searching for something obscure. (Don't do this looking for experts in medicine, for example, because it won't work.)

What I do when I need to find an expert this way is, basically, look for professors. So let's say I'm looking for an expert in chimpanzee anthropology. I have had no luck at the expert sites, and I want to find a professor who studies this stuff who might be willing to answer my questions. So I first create the frame of a query that will tend to limit my results to professors:

```
professor site:edu
```

Search for the keyword "professor" from a university site. Simple enough, isn't it? Then I'll add the keywords of what I'm interested in:


```
chimpanzee anthropology professor site:edu
```

When I tried this I got as my first result a professor of biological anthropology who's done a lot of fieldwork concerning chimpanzees. Your search results won't always be this neat; sometimes you'll have to get much more detailed, and sometimes you'll have to shuffle your keywords around a bit. But if you've got a question and you really do need to find an expert to assist you, doing a specialty search in Google is a last-ditch option.

11

The Principle of the Expanding Web

The Principle of the Expanding Web: The Web is always expanding, always changing, always (unfortunately) breaking down, and always rebuilding. If you're planning to do ongoing research, it's imperative to have a strategy to keep up with new sites and resources in your field of interest.

The Internet changes. Constantly. And what seems impervious to change is often the first thing to change. If that weren't true we'd all be using Netscape Navigator as our browser and WebCrawler or AltaVista as our search engine. Your favorite resource may go off the air tomorrow. You can't anticipate that, but you can plan for it by not getting yourself into a rut and by keeping yourself abreast of the new resources that are available on the Web.

Broadly speaking, there are three kinds of places on the Web that you'll need to monitor to get pointers to new resources: news sites, search engines, and specialty pages (if there are any for your topic of interest).

News Sites

News sites? Like, for newspapers and other dead tree material? I know, it's hard to believe, but I often find a lot of great stuff via news monitoring. Thanks to Google News Alerts and Yahoo News Alerts, news monitoring doesn't have to be painful or time-intensive.

Start with Google News (http://news.google.com) and run a couple of queries. For the purpose of this chapter let's say I'm interested in butterfly Web sites. Try a test query of the word "butterflies" by itself. Ugh—several thousand results. That won't work. You want to take the Principle of Unique Language and orient your query more toward Web results. A couple of simple queries might accomplish that. Let's try:

```
butterfly "web site"
```

Hmm, quite a bit better, but several off-topic results. Let's tweak the query a bit:

```
butterflies "web site" science
```

That really narrows down your search results. (Sometimes when you're having trouble narrowing down results, using the plural of a noun instead of the singular can really help.) There are other Web-oriented keywords you can try as well:

```
butterflies Internet science
butterflies online
butterfly exhibit online
```

What you're looking for is a search that gives you a useful, but manageable, number of results. You can have more than one search that does this, as long as their results don't overlap too much. Google News allows you up to fifty news alerts per e-mail address. Once you've found some queries that work for your topic, set them up as news alerts and move on to Yahoo News.

Yahoo News (http://news.yahoo.com) requires that you be registered on their site. Once you are, you can set up news queries to be monitored with results sent to you by e-mail, much like Google News. As with Google News, you're looking for searches that show a manageable number of results, but don't assume that what worked in Google News will work in Yahoo News. Be sure also to use Yahoo's advanced search, which allows you to restrict your search to categories. If you can restrict your search for butterflies to science and local (local to pick up those regional newspaper stories about new online museum exhibits and such), you'll get a far better class of results.

Yahoo News and Google News are two major news search engines that it behooves you to monitor. But

TIP

In addition to searching news for Web sites and resources of interest, you can also search Weblogs. When searching Weblogs, however, you'll probably have the option of an RSS feed of results instead of e-mail notification. (You'll remember we discussed RSS feeds in Chapter 5.) I find the best Weblog search engine is Feedster (http://www.feedster.com.) You'll have to do a lot of experimental searching before you decide on your search terms. Webloggers use less formal language than journalists, and good queries will be a matter of guessing. Also, sometimes you'll see someone mention a good site, then fifteen more people will mention it in quick succession, so expect some repetition. If you find you like RSS feeds for getting news alerts, try RocketNews.com, which monitors more traditional news sources and also offers RSS feeds.

a lot of news sites offer their own keyword alerts. CNN, for example, offers keyword alerts—you can learn more about them at http://audience.cnn.com/services/cnn/alerts/createAlert.jsp. So the next time you find a news source you really like, check and see if it offers an e-mail alert service.

When you monitor two sets of news search engines like this, you will get overlap. That's fine. If I get a little bit of overlap in my ongoing searches, I know I'm getting most of the relevant news stories out there. (I don't aim for 100% on the Internet because I don't like tearing all my hair out.) When you get too much overlap—75% of the stories from one source match another—drop one of them. In my experience there's enough difference in sources that that doesn't happen often.

Search Engines

Monitoring search engines is similar to monitoring news sites. Use Google Alert (http://www.googlealert.com) to set up monitoring queries after you've tested them in Google. When I'm monitoring for new sites I use the special syntaxes a lot. For butterflies I might try:

```
intitle:butterfly archive
intitle:butterfly encyclopedia
butterfly butterflies -"madame butterfly"
```


The archive and encyclopedia keywords are to slant the results toward more content-dense pages. You don't want to merely get alerts of all pages added or respidered by Google containing "butterfly" or any other common words. It's too much. You'd drown. If you have a more unusual word or phrase, perhaps you can just monitor for that. Check and see what kind of results you get.

Google, as a full-text index, is a full-text search engine and is fairly easy to monitor. Yahoo and the Open Directory Project are a little more difficult. I've found your best bet is the categories.

Yahoo

As you know, Yahoo is divided up into categories. If you search Yahoo's directory for "butterflies," you'll see that there's one subcategory under Science called Butterflies and Moths. There are only a few subcategories beneath it. If you wanted to use page-monitoring software, or a service, to keep up with the butterfly-related sites added to Yahoo in this way, you could.

Unfortunately you may be like me and have a more pervasive interest. You may be interested in online archives of any type. In that case it won't be as neat as just monitoring one or two categories. In that case you have a couple of choices.

You can choose to do a search—like for "online archive"—and monitor the results. If you use the advanced search interface at http://search.yahoo.com/search/options, you can choose to return only those sites updated by Yahoo within the last three months, and you can choose to get a hundred results per page. You could then monitor that page with page-monitoring software or a service.

Another option with Yahoo is to view their "What's New" URL, where you can see everything they've added to their site for the last week. Unfortunately you can't bookmark the page that shows the new daily additions to Yahoo: the URL changes every day. But you can visit this page and either review the top categories that have had interesting items added to them, or review the entire new additions list on a regular basis. Neither one of these options sounds appealing to me. I think I'd stick with directory or search result monitoring if at all possible.

Open Directory Project

The Open Directory Project lacks a "What's New" section, though you can find categories (as described above with Yahoo) and monitor them. You can also monitor pages of search results. You have another option as well, a tool that's not available for Yahoo.

xmlhub.com offers two RSS feed generators for the Open Directory Project, and they're both available at http://www.xmlhub.com/odp_feed.php. The first feed generator takes an ODP query of your choice and translates it into an RSS feed, which you can then monitor for changes. The second feed generator lets you specify an ODP category and get an RSS feed of just that category, which you can, again, monitor for changes. Either one of these methods is a bit neater than monitoring a Web page; you won't get as many false-positive page changes.

Specialty Pages

Specialty Web sites and directories can be very useful in finding new resources; it's easier for a specialty site to keep up with new kinds of pages in a certain area than it is for a general search engine. A specialty web site will be more oriented towards those kinds of resources, more knowledgeable about what to look for, and, depending on the popularity of the site, people are more likely to submit sites on that topic directly to them.

Most searchable subject indexes have a "What's New" page, and most Web sites have some kind of "What's New" or "News" pages. Monitor those for changes. What you'll get and what you'll find useful will change a lot. For example, I want to monitor for new online information collections—archives, databases, etc.—from credible sources. To that end I monitor the home pages of universities (from university libraries if they have "What's New" pages), the front pages of official state sites, the front pages of historical societies that have caught my attention, the home pages for national libraries, etc. For all of these I use monitoring software: if I didn't I wouldn't have time to keep an eye on these several hundred pages.

YAHOO! search directory

Directory Home - Yahoo! - Help

What's New
Home > What's New for Tuesday May 18, 2004

Search [ ] ○ the Web ● the Directory [Search] Advanced Search | Suggest a Site

email this page to a friend

NEW & NOTABLE SITES

Hawaiian Punch - refreshingly old school. (in Soft Drinks > Brand Names)
Tec Labs - for what itches you. (in Skin Care Products)
Relic Lures - featuring a great cast of characters. (in Fishing Tackle > Lures)

DIRECTORY ADDITIONS FOR TUESDAY MAY 18, 2004

Business & Economy *(52)*	**Regional** *(84)*
Computers & Internet *(1)*	**Society & Culture** *(18)*
News & Media *(0)*	Education *(0)*
Entertainment *(27)*	**Arts & Humanities** *(5)*
Recreation & Sports *(10)*	**Science** *(2)*
Health *(2)*	Social Science *(0)*
Government *(1)*	**Reference** *(2)*

Complete list of sites added May 18, 2004

ARCHIVES

Mon May 17 - **Sun May 16** - **Sat May 15** - **Fri May 14** - **Thu May 13** - **Wed May 12** - **Tue May 11**

YAHOO! PICKS
Canto do Brasil - a love poem of photos, words, and music.
read review - more picks

ASK YAHOO!
What is the average salary in the U.S.?
more

SUBSCRIPTIONS
Ask Yahoo!
Daily Wire
Yahoo! Picks

11–01

One day's worth of additions at Yahoo, in searchable subject index format. (Image from http://dir.yahoo.com/new/20040518.html.)

What Do You Do When You've Got 'Em?

Once you've got the Web source, you've got to decide what to do with it. I generally do a quick evaluation (see Chapter 13, "The Principle of Salt Grains"), and, if it's something I think is good, I'll cover it in my newsletter or drop it in a text file of sites to review later. Sometimes I'll find a site that's so awesome I start using it a lot. When that happens I generally pick another site to either stop using or drop in priority. When I discovered Feedster I began using that more often and dropped Daypop in my priority. Sometimes I'll find a site that I'll use often with an eye on using it more in the future, like Gigablast. If you keep an eye out for new sites related to your research interest, I bet you'll find yourself in a natural groove of adding and removing sites that you use.

I don't want you to get the idea that just because a site is old it's not worth using anymore (Google's over five years old), or just because a site's new that it's the best available option. But if you keep track of what new sites are being added out there, you'll find your resource usage evolving and you'll be less likely to get in a rut of using the same old sites over and over.

12 The Principle of Applied Power

The Principle of Applied Power: Using the special syntaxes of any given Web site will increase the power of your searches tremendously. Mixing the special syntaxes will increase the power of your searches even more. But caution is urged.

There is nothing more frustrating than spending hours and hours and days and days teaching people how to do special searches, how to implement syntaxes and use carefully chosen keywords, and then watching them plunk general keywords into search engines like they were feeding dimes into a parking meter. It's like, I imagine, being a piano teacher, and spending your days teaching the finer points of beautiful concertos, only to discover that your students prefer playing "Chopsticks." Over and over and over again.

But I persevere. I believe that once you understand how much better using special syntaxes—and mixing special syntaxes—is than straight searching, I'll have you hooked. Though special syntaxes seem difficult at first, they're really not. You just need to keep an eye out for the different kinds of syntaxes you can get from different engines, and understand how they may be mixed.

A Recap: What Are Special Syntaxes?

Special syntaxes are called that because they allow you to do searching beyond simple keyword searching. Special syntaxes can allow you to search within page titles, within page URLs, within pages indexed by the search engines on a certain date, and other very specific kinds of searching. Some examples of special syntaxes, for Google, are intitle (find keywords in title), site (find results on a certain domain or top-level domain), and inurl (find keywords in page URLs).

Why Do Special Syntaxes Work So Well?

Special syntaxes work well when searching because when you're using them, you're searching a much narrower number of keywords. Say the average page title has ten words and the average Web page has 100 words. When you restrict your search to the title only, you're searching a much smaller group of words and will therefore get a much smaller number of results. Of course, you have to bear in mind that you *are* searching a much smaller number of words; you're not generally going to find song lyrics in page titles.

Using special syntaxes works well when you're trying to narrow your search results, but you're getting a lot of useless results. For example, you might want something on zoos in Houston, but a plain search for Houston zoos will bring you too much searchgunk. Make one or both your keywords a title query and your results will narrow appropriately:

```
intitle:houston zoo
```

Both full-text search engines and searchable subject indexes have special syntaxes, but as you might expect the searchable subject index syntaxes are somewhat more limited.

TIP

Recall the Principle of Onions, which instructed you to use the most narrow search words possible, and then get progressively more general. That same principle applies when you're using syntax. However, you must use the most narrow search words *that are appropriate to the syntax*. When you're searching just page titles, which is a much, much, much smaller group of words than page titles and page content, your search words won't be as narrow. You'll probably have to experiment some to determine how narrow is too narrow.

Special Syntaxes on Full-Text Engines

The special syntaxes offered by any given full-text engine may vary. Some may offer none. Some may offer a few. Some may offer an exhaustive list. Here's an overview of what sites might offer, and how it can help your search.

Title Syntax

Title syntax facilitates searching in titles.

GOOD FOR: Narrowing down searches without using deeply specific queries, eliminating "noise" searches.

This is an overview of what full-text search engines may offer, not what individual search engines do offer. Therefore, these won't be exact syntaxes, only what you might expect to find.

BEWARE: Getting too specific in the title searches—titles are usually comparatively brief. Also be aware that not all Webmasters use page titles in more than the briefest of ways ("Home Page," "Search Page," etc.)

TIP

Don't forget the search shortcuts! Both Yahoo and Google have ways to find very specific types of information—dictionary definitions, encyclopedia entries, even (in Yahoo's case) cheap gas prices. While they're not really special syntaxes, they can help you a lot when you're searching for certain kinds of information.

Domain/Site Syntaxes

Domain/site syntaxes limit a search to a top-level domain (com, org, uk, etc.) or a domain name (geocities.com, yahoo.com).

GOOD FOR: Top-level domain searches are great for limiting searches thematically. Searches limited to .edu domains are far different than general searches. When you're getting a lot of commercial search noise (ads, affiliate sites, etc.), removing the .com top-level domains from the search results can do a lot to eliminate that noise. Individual site searches are best only when you have a good sense of the site and when the site is a fairly good size.

BEWARE: Just because a site is listed under the top-level-domain for a particular country doesn't mean that its content has anything to do with that country. Furthermore, the .com top-level domain represents Web sites from all over the world.

Date Syntaxes

Date syntaxes limit the search to the date a page was indexed by the search engine. (Note that this is not the date on which the page was created, but the date when the page was included in the search engine's index!)

GOOD FOR: Current event and other date-based searching.

BEWARE: Page index date doesn't equal when the content was actually created. Sometimes the page will change just enough (a copyright disclaimer added, a template changed) that the page will be re-indexed. Use this syntax with extreme caution.

URL Syntaxes

URL syntaxes find words within a page's URL.

GOOD FOR: Last-ditch efforts at narrowing down search results. Very specific kinds of searching for words that are associated with Web sites (archives, pages, etc.).

BEWARE: This is a very difficult syntax to use. Finding Web pages that use entire guessable words in their URLs is hit-or-miss at best. It's best to stick to this syntax only when the words or strings are commonly used (like "lib" or "library" for library, archives, "dir" for directory, etc.).

Link Syntaxes

Link syntaxes find pages that link to a specified URL.

GOOD FOR: Finding similar pages, seeing what other sites are saying about a specified page, Webmasters doing link popularity checks.

BEWARE: At least one search engine (Google) doesn't allow link syntax to be used with any other syntax. Finding a link to the front page of a site won't find all the links to a site's internal pages. Use with caution.

TIP

As you wander around the Web looking at other search engines, you'll find a variety of other kinds of syntaxes—a syntax for finding Java on a page, or finding words within text links to other pages, and so on—but you can consider those the equivalent of that weird tool at the bottom of your toolbox that rarely makes it out into the light of day. They can be used to winkle out information, but you won't find them useful very often.

Special Syntaxes on Searchable Subject Indexes

As you might expect, the special syntaxes for searchable subject indexes are much more limited, since they don't index all of a Web site or even a Web page. In fact there are pretty much only two: for title and URL.

The same caveats that apply to the full-text engine syntax apply to the searchable subject index syntax, only more so. Titles are used for sites, not individual pages, so your search terms must be fairly general. Furthermore, a subject index editor may not use a site's actual title, but more of a descriptive title, something the editor came up with to describe the site. This is another argument for general search terms. When it comes to URLs, it's the same case. Site URLs are included instead of page URLs, for the most part, and only the most general search terms are going to be easily found with a URL search. I tend to restrict my URL searches in searchable subject indexes to when I want to confirm that a particular site is listed in a directory. I'd look for their domain name in the URL. This is also useful when you want to see if a single domain has been indexed in multiple places within a searchable subject index.

Special syntaxes are extremely powerful. They narrow your search down a *lot*. If used with too narrow search queries, they'll narrow down your search to nothing at all.

Using Two or More Syntaxes

You might be thinking, "If one special syntax is good, two or more special syntaxes are better, right?" In some cases that's true. But in all cases you'll need to be even more careful about using the syntax. Mixing syntax works well when you need to find something very specific and you want to slant the result a particular way. For example, you may want to do a medical search that slants to academic search results. Using Google, you could try a search like:

```
intitle:hydrocephalus site:edu
```

Or you're looking for information on organizational theory with results slanted towards military sites:

```
intitle:"organization theory" site:mil
```

Title and site syntaxes work very well together. Here's a trickier one that uses a URL syntax. It's a Google example of trying to find new book listings on library sites:

```
library books intitle:new inurl:lib
```

And you can go one step further by restricting these results to college and higher education libraries only:

```
library books intitle:new inurl:lib site:edu
```

As you can see, you're not restricted to using only two special syntaxes or even special syntaxes without keywords. The thing you've got to remember, though, is that the more special syntax you use in a query the more you're narrowing down what's being searched, and therefore the more careful you have to be about your query words. But used carefully, special syntax can cut right through search clutter to what you're looking for. Keep them in your toolbox!

13 THE PRINCIPLE OF SALT GRAINS

The Principle of Salt Grains: You should take every page on the Internet with a grain of salt.

Too many people take anything on the Internet as gospel because someone went to the trouble of putting it up on the Web. But there's a lot of stuff on the Web that's satirical, proselytizing, or just plain wrong. One of the first rules of Internet searching is *trust nothing*.

Well, that doesn't help. Where are you going to get your information?

As you do a lot of Internet research, you will get a better sense of what's legitimate, what's not, what smells funny, and so on. But if you're new to the Internet, or you haven't spent a lot of time searching, you might want some initial guidance to decide how you should go about your evaluation. Glad you asked.

Whenever you're evaluating sites and statements on sites, you need to ask several questions.

Questions to Ask About a Web Page

1. Where does this page reside?

You can get a lot of information just based on where the page resides. If the side resides on an .edu domain, you can generally give it a little more credibility. Same for a .gov or .mil domain. The .us domains used to have a lot of instant credibility, but now they're open to registration by anybody and you can't rely on them like you used to.

You also need to consider whether the site resides on its own domain or not. I tend to automatically give a little bit more credibility to a site that has its own domain rather than a site hosted on a free Web service like Geocities or that uses the free Web space provided by an ISP. I suspect I do this because a) it's meaningful if someone has invested their time and money to register a domain name, and b) it's easier to find out a bit more about the person, which is critical in question #2.

2. Who made the statement?

When a site is on its own domain, you can get some additional information about the author by looking to see who registered the domain (you can do domain register lookups at http://www.domainsearch.com/). Sometimes you'll see that the domain name is registered anonymously, which removes a little credibility for me. Sometimes you'll see someone has registered a domain with obviously false information. That, as you might imagine, removes a lot of credibility for me.

Sometimes the domain registration won't tell you a whole lot. In that case, look for an "About This Site" or "About Us" page on the Web site. Whether you will find this will vary a lot—large sites, especially corporate or retail sites, are much more likely to have this kind of information than a Weblog focused on a silly topic or something personal. (The people who put up the "Johnson Family Wedding Pictures Web Site" will probably assume that if you're at all interested in viewing it, you know who the Johnson family is!)

3. Why are they making this statement?

If you're reviewing the statements on a site, consider why they're being made. Are they being made to sell something? To get you to support a cause? To reinforce an argument? To teach you something? Consider why the statement is being made; it may be that a truth is being twisted (or something's being fabricated) to either get you to make a purchase or accept an argument.

4. What are they doing to establish the truth of the statement?

Generally speaking, the more "out there" a statement is the more I'm going to look to some kind of sourcing for it. If a site says the sky is blue, fine. If a site says the sky over a particular part of the western U.S. turns bright pink for 45 minutes every three days,

The other question you have to ask is, "Is this person who they say they are?" You can generally determine that by reviewing external links to the site as well as site registration. Wil Wheaton, from *Star Trek: the Next Generation*, has his own Weblog. If you wondered if it really was Wil Wheaton, you could search news archive sites and see many, many mentions of his Weblog. There have been enough news sources corroborating the existence of his Weblog that I believe it's Wil Wheaton. I become suspicious of people's claims in the following instances: a) they're trying to raise money, b) they're making some really crazy claims that don't make any sense, or c) they're selling very expensive things that require that identity—autographed items, etc.

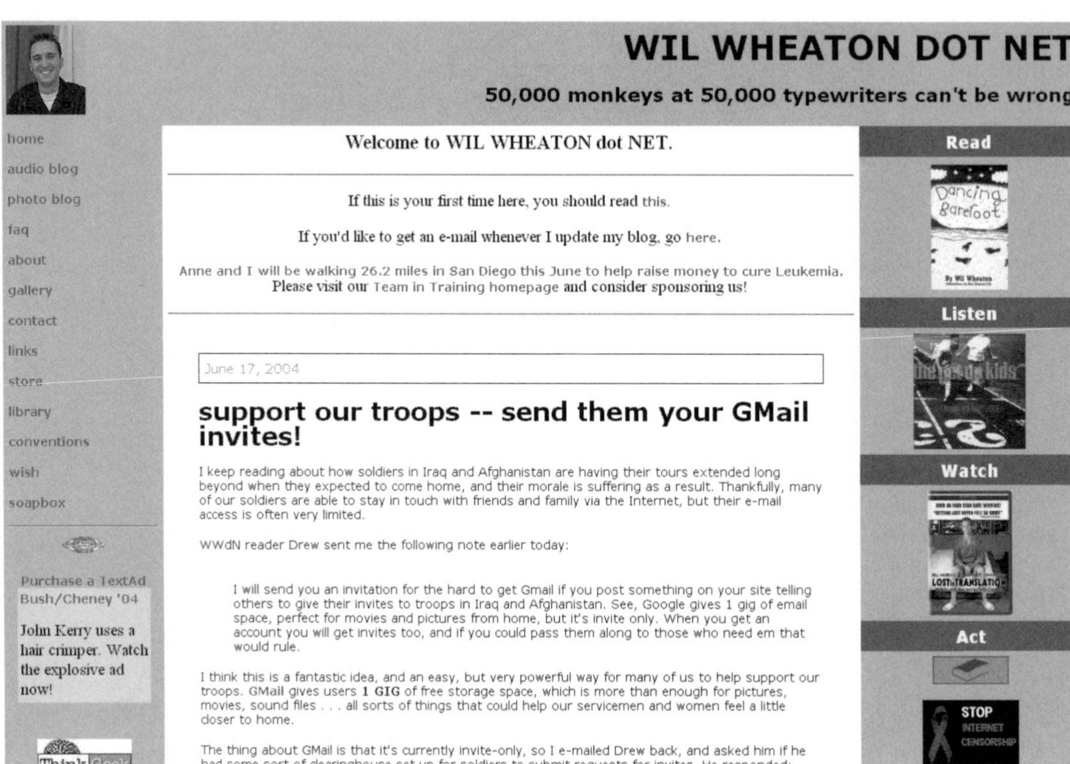

13–01

Wil Wheaton: Real guy, nice guy, real nice guy. (Image from http://www.wilwheaton.net/.)

I want pointers to news stories, scientific studies, and other data to substantiate that fact.

Of course, sources vary in *their* credibility. A Geocities Web site is less inherently credible than a news story. A news story from CNN is more credible than one from The Weekly Gee Whiz. When you see a citation or a source, go look it up. Citations can be made up just like anything else, so don't assume that just because you see a citation it's legit.

5. How long have they been online?

How long has the site been online? Was it thrown up twelve minutes ago in response to a current trend, or has it been up for several years? You can get some of this information from the domain registration information. Sometimes sites date their content, or have a "last update" note on their site, which can also give you some information.

I will also draw a certain amount of credibility data based on how often a site is updated. If a site has been sitting dormant for months (and in some cases, years), I will tend to give it less credibility. Sometimes data goes online and requires no updating—like old digitized books, for example—but often there can be some kind of activity on a site. A redesign will be implemented. Another book could be added. Questions can be answered, and so on. Activity on a site gives you some indication that someone is around who cares about the content.

6. What are other sites saying about them?

What are news stories saying about the site? What are other sites saying about the site? Do a link check in a full-text search engine and see who is linking to the site and what they're saying. If no one's linking to a site, it might be very new, so don't take that as a knock against it. But do pay attention to news stories (especially very credible institutions) and what they say about the site.

In addition to asking these questions, there are Web sites you can refer to that will help you discover the credibility of a site. Some of these debunk popular myths rolling around the Web, while others will give you tips and pointers to evaluate information sources.

TIP

Sometimes news organizations fall down, though. There have been cases where news organizations, nonprofits, and other sites have seriously quoted The Onion, a well-known online satirical newspaper. So don't take something as gospel just because an online entity that looks like a newspaper cites it, especially if it sounds outrageous to you. In the case of The Onion, checking the external links would have made it clear very quickly that it is a satirical newspaper.

Checking Out "Internet Facts"

I call them "Internet facts" because they're things that float around the Internet. They're not necessarily true. They're distributed via both the Web and e-mail. There are a couple of resources that are invaluable for checking out these sites, but in addition to these resources there are three e-mail characteristics that should raise a red flag for you:

1. You're asked to forward the e-mail to everyone you know.
2. The e-mail describes a problem—like a particularly horrible virus—that if it were legitimate would be on every cable channel as an emergency news flash, including the Golf Channel.
3. The e-mail promises you some kind of reward for forwarding/replicating the mail.

Snopes--http://www.snopes.com

Snopes is the first site I go to when I want to check out something that someone has sent me. It's never let me down. You can do a simple keyword search or you can browse through a variety of topics, including Disney, movies, love, and even an entire category devoted to Coca-Cola. Generally you can take a short snippet from an e-mail you've gotten, plug it into the keyword search, and get relevant results.

Vmyths--http://www.vmyths.com

You may be getting a lot of well-meaning pointers to virus warnings and other such information. In that case I recommend you run them through Vmyths.com. This site has been tracking virus myths for years, and busts them up with both plenty of information and a sense of humor (which comes in handy if you've just gotten your 10,000th warning for the "jdbgmgr.exe" virus).

Snopes and Vmyths are both useful if there's a specific thing you're trying to get more information on or refute. But there's a whole other class of credibility Web sites: those that provide guidance on evaluating resources.

Evaluating Information Found on the Internet--http://www.library.jhu.edu/elp/useit/evaluate/

This is a much more thorough look at information credibility online, outlining several questions you can ask as well as pointers to some external information and coverage of specific types of misleading sites, like hate sites.

Information Evaluation Form--http://www.lib.berkeley.edu/TeachingLib/Guides/Internet/EvalForm.pdf

This handy printable PDF file gives you a checklist to use when you're thoroughly evaluating a Web source.

As you might imagine, site evaluation is a big topic for the constant researcher. You'll find several more resources for evaluating Web site credibility at http://www.dmoz.org/Reference/Education/Instructional_Technology/Evaluation/Web_Site_Evaluation/.

With all these resources, am I telling you that you'll have to spend 20 minutes ticking off a checklist every time you want to visit a Web site? Of course not. But if you're going to cite a page, or use facts on a page to develop a strategy, or use them for anything but leisure and entertainment (and sometimes even then!), you've got to have a sense of how credible they are.

PART III
SEARCHING THE WEB

14 News Searching

When search engines first started appearing on the Web, they had very long delays for indexing new materials. It might take four to six weeks—and possibly longer—for a Web page to be added to a site's index.

That's no longer the case. Now a new page might be added to a search engine within days and sometimes hours. That means two things: first, the pages you find in a search engine tend to be fresher, and second, you can do a certain amount of current events searching by finding recent news articles.

Then, too, there are the news search engines. These are search engines that index only news articles. Many of them offer better date-based searching than a general search engine can, as well as the ability to limit a search by source. There are times when you'll want to use a general search engine to search for news articles, and times when using the specialty engines is your best option.

Web Searching for News Articles

Let's start with Web searching, since you'll want to use some of these guidelines when you move on to the news search engines.

Start by employing the Principle of Onions: try a very specific search and then slowly get more general. In the case of news searches, that means searching for place names and people names (this works really well). Use proper nouns before you use regular nouns. Why? Because if you're looking for information on a fire in Evansville, Indiana, Evansville is Evansville (and newspaper stories often spell out a state name at least once, leaving you less vulnerable to the Principle of Nicknames.) But a fire might be a fire, a conflagration, a blaze, or even an early morning haze of smoke and flames. I exaggerate slightly, but you get the idea. If you must use a noun, use a simple one. Fire is better than conflagration for searching purposes.

Once you've found some results, use the Principle of Every Scrap. Gather names of people quoted, unusual locations (was the fire in a boat-building warehouse?), and any other usefully unusual words and phrases. You might get a pocket of several dozen results that are all exactly the same—this happens when a syndicated news story (from the Associated Press or some other news syndication service) is distributed to many different sites. To remove those duplicates choose an unusual phrase from the oft-duplicated story and remove it from your query:

```
+fire +Evansville -"boat supply warehouse was engulfed
                    in flames"
```

Keep in mind that you may have to change your keywords if you're tracking a story via a Web search over time. Suspects are named, places change, people come into or drop out of the story. Don't develop one set of keywords for a news story and decide you're finished. Any story that's going to be covered over time is going to have relevant keywords change.

Using News Search Engines

Finding news stories in general search engines is useful when you're covering a very major story that's extended over several months, or sometimes (rarely) when you're covering a very minor story that is only covered by small newspapers that aren't indexed by the news search engines. They're also good for covering technical or industry-oriented stories that you'll find in sources that for the most part are not indexed by news search engines.

But for general news, or for news that has a short lifetime, or news that gets a reasonable amount of national coverage, the news search engines work better. You can sort your results by date, view news that was indexed within a certain date range, and eliminate a lot of false positives that you might get for general Web searching. For news searching I can recommend five different searches.

Google News--http://news.google.com

PROS: Over 4,500 sources, several international versions (look at the bottom of the page for links to international versions; more are being added all the time); a good advanced search that allows you to restrict your search by date range, by source, and by all sources in a particular country or U.S. state.

CONS: Only 30 days' worth of news is archived. A full source list is not provided.

YOUR STRATEGY: Since Google News only indexes recent news, do not use it to search for news stories that have evolved over a period of months. Do not use general search words; there are far too many sources here and you'll be overwhelmed. If the date isn't important, be sure to allow the results to be sorted by relevance (that's the default) as that "clusters" similar stories into groups. Take advantage of the advanced search if your news research is oriented toward one country or U.S. city.

TIP

Google is also in the process of indexing a lot of magazine and print content and putting it in its general search, and not its news search. If you're doing general searches you may never bump into that content, but try searching for a keyword and `inurl:print.google.com`. That'll find you both book excerpts and magazine articles containing the keyword for which you seek.

Yahoo News--http://dailynews.yahoo.com

PROS: A pretty good advanced search that allows you to search summaries and headlines as well as keywords. A good date range search. In addition to text searches you may also search photos and audio/video. All sources are listed.

CONS: Only 30 days' worth of archives. Limited sources.

YOUR STRATEGY: Since you can see the source list, use that to your advantage. If you find yourself getting an overwhelming number of results, exclude those sources that issue a large number of stories (like press wires). If you do that you can do more general searches since you have such a fine control of how many sources are searched.

RocketNews--http://www.rocketnews.com

RocketNews has the interesting quality of being a news search engine that's not affiliated with a larger search engine. Instead it's a standalone free service with a for-fee desktop application.

PROS: Searches news only and offers a desktop application that searches over 9,000 news sources and 45,000 Weblogs.

CONS: The desktop application costs money. The basic search on the Web site offers only a week's worth of searching and allows you to search the news for only one continent at a time. No sources.

YOUR STRATEGY: Frankly there are only a couple of situations in which I would start with RocketNews. First if I were getting way too many hits anywhere else and couldn't narrow down my search sources any more. Second if I were using their desktop application, which has far more sources. The desktop application is good (and does have a free trial if you want to give it a try), but the Web-based search is fairly limited.

TIP

Both Google and Yahoo News offer the ability to get news alerts by e-mail. Google requires only an e-mail address while you must be a registered Yahoo user to get news alerts. If you're doing constant research on a particular topic, getting e-mail alerts of new stories can save you a lot of time. For example, I have e-mail alerts at Google to alert me to "new search engines," "online databases," and "online archives" that are mentioned in the news.

FindArticles--http://www.findarticles.com

FindArticles is brought to you by LookSmart, which as I have mentioned is one of the minor search engines. For a long time, FindArticles drove me *crazy*. It was a huge database of articles that you might have a hard time finding online, but its search options were awful! You couldn't search by date, and you couldn't list your results by order of date. That's all changed. Now there's a date sort and date search, as well as a source list for materials in the database. There are over 2.8 million articles from over 500 sources here, so the fact that they have a far-older-than-30-days archive makes it a must-add to your toolbox.

PROS: Archive that goes back further than 30 days. Option to search by source.

CONS: Source list is small compared to other engines.

YOUR STRATEGY: Use FindArticles as a complement to other news search engines. Its deeper database will bring you different types of results, especially if you want to go back more than 30 days.

HINT.

What is an RSS feed? Here's the thumbnail explanation: An RSS feed is a kind of XML document. The content in XML documents is much more structured and defined than the content in HTML documents. That means you can potentially do much more precise searching of RSS feeds than you can of HTML—ordinary Web—pages. You'll see more about this in a moment.

Feedster--http://www.feedster.com

Feedster searches RSS feeds. Unlike some other RSS engines, it has implemented searching to make RSS feed searching very precise. It can also list search results by order of date as well as relevance, making it easier to get new results.

PROS: Huge number of sources, everything from Moreover (standard news) to esoteric Weblogs. Easy to sort by date. An image search is available, with filters to help guard against adult content.

CONS: When you're looking for pure news, this site will get you a lot of noise—Weblog rants, etc. Since it's indexing RSS feeds, it doesn't always index the full content of Web sites. The number of pure news sources is limited.

YOUR STRATEGY: I use Feedster as a tool for inspiration. When I'm trying to figure out how to approach a story, if I know very little and I want to get different points of view, or if I'm looking for op-ed information (not factual), I go here first. Sometimes the Weblog entries have pointers to articles and information that I don't find via the news engines. Be prepared to do a lot of sifting, and remember the Principle of Salt Grains: just because you read it doesn't mean that it's so.

Other Places to Search News

I've listed some of the major news search aggregates above, but they're not the only ones. Some sites, such as CNN and News.com, have their own internal search engines that cover a lot of ground. If you're looking for very old news, some libraries have digitized old newspaper collections. The Brooklyn Public Library's *Brooklyn Eagle* collection, at http://www.brooklynpubliclibrary.org/eagle/index.htm, is an excellent example. Check out http://www.researchbuzz.org/archives/cat_publicationsarchives.shtml for a roundup of pointers to publication archives, http://www.ibiblio.org/slanews/internet/intarchives.htm for pointers to newspaper archives online, or http://dir.yahoo.com/News_and_Media/ for pointers to publications and sometimes publication archives.

When you're looking for a news overview, news search engines should be the first place you go. But you may find that all of your research is leading you to the same sources over and over. In that case, you should see if those sources have their own archive search engines, because those engines usually have deeper archives than the 30 days of many news search engines.

13 JOB SEARCHING

Remember the boom times of the late 1990s? It seemed that there was a job on every corner and all you had to do to get a salary, stock options, and benefits was to show up to an interview on time and have a pulse. Those days are long, long gone.

Despite that, the Internet remains an excellent resource for job hunting. Not only job hunting, but getting career guidance and finding out what jobs are hot (so you don't proceed into that career as buggy tire repairman without knowing what you're getting into).

There are many commercials on television about job resource sites. The commercials give you a great impression: visit a site, plug in a couple of search terms, and blammo! You'll instantly find the job of your dreams. That would be pleasant, wouldn't it? Usually it requires a bit more work than that. And hey, why limit yourself to a job search engine? Working with a regular search engine will often get you some good results. If you really want to use job-oriented resources, there's a series of steps you should consider.

1. Job resource sites
2. Local classified ads
3. State sites
4. Federal sites
5. Job search engines

You can do all these steps or none, in any order. But note that job search engines are only one out of five! There are lots of career resources on the Internet.

Let's start, though, with visiting individual sites and plain old search engines.

Using Plain Search Engines and Company Sites

You may have no idea what you want to be when you grow up and that's fine. Skip this section.

On the other hand, you may have had a long-time dream. You may know exactly who you want to work for and exactly what you want to be. In that case, please don't go to a job search engine. Go to that company's Web site (you can often find company Web sites by just typing in their name at Google) and see if they have a jobs section. Most of the time they do. Look for "jobs" or "we're hiring!" Even Google itself has a jobs section, even though from what I hear working at Google is so cool nobody would ever leave.

If you have a specific job in mind and a specific company in mind, visit their Web site first. (I feel silly even suggesting this, but you'd be amazed how often people go straight to the job search engines!) And I don't want to turn this into Zen and the Art of Career Advisory, but if there's an e-mail contact, use it. Remember, the Internet at its core is people. Don't be intimidated by the Web site; unless it says something like, "Please do not send us direct e-mail; please communicate only via this form," make an effort to get in touch with the people behind the site.

If you know exactly what you want to be and exactly who you want to work for, you're in great shape and my hat's off to you. If you don't, consider starting at step one: career resources.

Career Resources

Career Voyages—http://www.careervoyages.gov

Career Voyages is an effort by the Department of Labor and the Department of Education to link the educational community with the world of work.

You'll find plenty of interesting resources here if you're trying to figure out what job you want to be trained for or where you might want to look for a job. You can "Chart Your Course": choose an industry and see both the projected job growth for a variety of careers in that industry and see the median U.S. wage for that industry over several different education levels. Click on a job title and you can get more detailed information; after you click on a title, pick a state and you'll get information about the median wages for that job in that state, a description of the job, and much more detailed job growth statistics. (Click on the TV icon beside a job title to get a short video describing the job and giving a little information on training.)

You can also see what's hot: overall either jobs that don't require a four-year degree, or jobs that require a four-year degree or better. Or if you want to concentrate on a state, you can get a list of the hottest occupations by state. Check out the menu on the right for answers to frequently asked career questions, and check out the tools to use for a list of relevant education and training links.

Quintessential Careers—http://www.quintcareers.com/
You'll learn as you go through these sites that it's sometimes hard to separate job listings and career advice. At Quintessential Careers you can search for jobs in addition to getting career information in a bunch of different categories. The site includes a career resources toolkit (checklists for job seekers, tests and quizzes, career assessment resources, etc.), lots of education resources, and an "Ask the Career Doctor" column you can browse.

This site also has a free e-zine and a full Web search of its almost 2,000 (at this writing) pages of materials. There's a lot of material to absorb here (and on any career resource site), so set some time aside.

Get That Gig—http://www.getthatgig.com/
Most Web sites focus on common but standard jobs, like accountants and teachers. Get That Gig provides "Day in the Life" articles about "cooler" jobs, like zookeeper, *Sports Illustrated* photographer, and skydiving instructor. The site also has forums for job hunters and a job search. The content is a bit thin, but I'm hoping you get inspired by the offbeat jobs.

There are literally thousands of career assessment and job guidance sites out there; you can get a substantial list of them by going to http://directory.yahoo.com and searching for "career" or by searching Google for free `"career assessment"` or `career job tools articles advice`.

NOTE

I resign! I wanted to give you a fun link as you're considering the very serious business of the work you might perform for 30 or 40 years. It's called I-Resign and it's available at http://www.i-resign.com/uk/home/. Here you'll find a gallery of funny resignation letters, a "Big Quitters" hall of fame, and some full-of-attitude-but-still-useful articles and viewpoints. If you're exiting one job and getting ready to start looking for a new one, read this site for a good laugh before getting down to work.

Local Resources (Newspaper Classifieds)

You know what you want to be, and you know where you want to work. Maybe you're happy enough to find a job in your hometown, or maybe you want to move across the country.

Try local resources first—namely, newspaper classifieds. They hold a wealth of jobs, and you can focus on finding the job you want instead of having to artificially narrow your search by area as you would have to with nationwide job searches.

If you're living where you want to work, you're in gravy; you probably know the URL of your local paper. If you don't, or if you want to find work in another town, try either a newspaper-specific resource or Yahoo to find publications in the town in which you're interested. If the city you're looking at is fairly major, search for that city name in Yahoo Directory.

Major cities usually have categories in Yahoo, and subcategories for News and Media in those cities. There you can find newspapers.

If the city in which you're interested doesn't have a category in Yahoo, try NewsLink at http://newslink.org/. There you can browse newspapers by state, and then by city.

Let's make an example. Say I want to move to Omaha, Nebraska, and get a job. I don't know what I want to do; I just know I want to work in Omaha. I start at Yahoo Directory and search the directory for Omaha. I find a Nebraska -> Omaha category and browse that for news and media, and then newspapers. I find the *Omaha World Herald* at http://www.omaha.com/.

I'm feeling very thorough so I go to NewsLink and see if there are any other newspapers in Omaha. I find a business publication and an "alternative" paper; I'll look at those if I want to expand my searching.

But for now I'll just go to the *Omaha World Herald*. I see a couple of prospective links on the left: there's Careers and there's Classifieds. As it happens, either of those will work: Careers lets me search for jobs by keyword and Classifieds

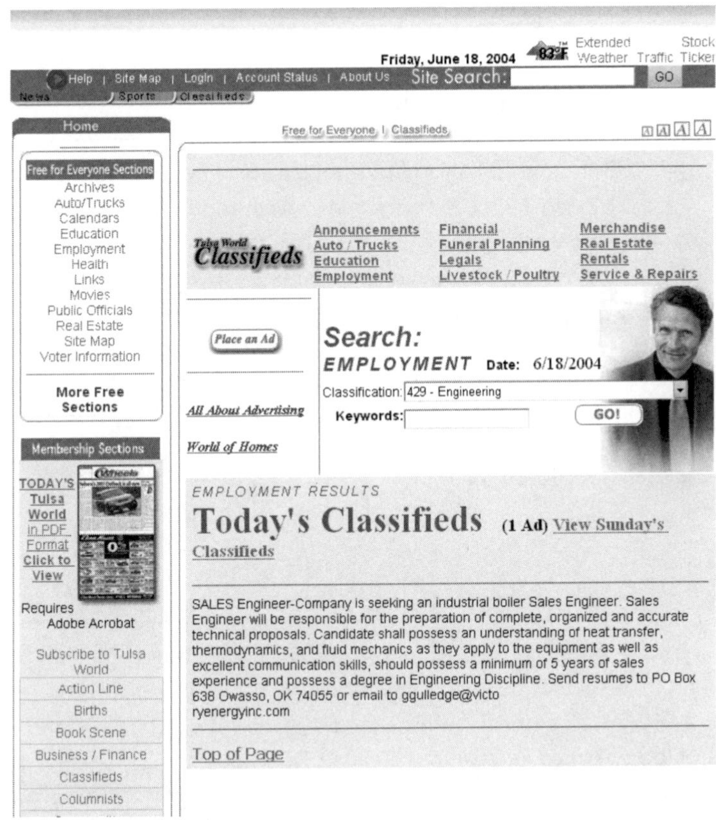

15–01

Searching for engineering jobs in Tulsa, Oklahoma. (Image from http://www.tulsaworld.com/ClassifiedsSearch/ClassifiedsEmployment.asp?Department=Employment.)

has an employment section. There is no standard that I'm familiar with for finding job listings on a newspaper site, but often you can find listings under the word "classifieds." Also look for banner ads and large graphic links saying, "Find a job at —!"

I want to be an engineer in Omaha, Nebraska. At Careers I search for "engineer" and find 24 results. There's an advanced search if I want to get specific (and select the kinds of jobs I want to find as well as date range). In the classified section I search the employment listings for "engineer" and get a busy message. Oh well. Good thing there's also a careers section.

The kind of options you'll find here are similar to the options you'll get in many newspaper search sites. Since you already have your options narrowed down considerably (by location), keep your searches general at first, and then get more specific. If you're searching for a category-specific job (like retail, for example), use the categories available.

For many people, this will be enough. They can stop right here and start the far more onerous process of printing out their résumés and making phone calls. But if this isn't sufficient—either because you don't want to limit yourself to one city or because you haven't found sufficient jobs—the next step is to look at the state level.

State-Level Job Finders

For state-level job finders you have two options. You can go to an independent state information site; for example, try Kentucky.com. These sites are usually media-based or partnered with media and they have job listings.

The second option is to go to the state government site; for example, Kentucky.gov. Often these kinds of sites will have job information on the front page, but if they don't, search the site for "job," "job bank," or "employment."

What do you do if state-level isn't enough? That's right, go to federal level.

NOTE

Don't know the home page of the state in which you're interested? Google search it for "State of [state in which you're interested]" and the word "official"—for example `"State of Oklahoma" official`.

National-Level Job Finders

Sure the government wants us all to be employed. We pay better taxes then, right? Links to several federal job resources are available at http://www.dol. gov/dol/jobs.htm (that's the Department of Labor). Note that only a couple of the links are federal in the sense that they exclusively offer government jobs; the other ones are federal in the sense that they're in some way connected to the government.

Another place to start is America's Job Bank, which is available at http://www.ajb.org/. As you can see, in addition to job listings here, there are career tools, assessments, and information on the labor market. The job search allows you to search by state (and some territories not in the U.S.) as well as within a 50-mile radius of a given zip code. You can browse by job category or search by keyword.

If you register with the site, you also have the option of setting up a job scout that will e-mail you when jobs are posted that mention your keyword. Since I'm an essentially lazy person, I like automating my searches whenever possible. Take advantage of automated searches!

Job Search Engines

Maybe you've gone all the way through this chapter, muttering to yourself, "The job search engines ... the job search engines! WHERE ARE THE JOB SEARCH ENGINES!?" All right, all right! We'll polish off this chapter with job search engines. But first I have to give you a lecture.

Tara's Brief Job Search Lecture

I know there's a lot of stress when you're searching for a job, and the pressure sometimes gives you tunnel vision—you have got to get the job and that's all you're focusing on.

But please think a little bit as you're focusing. If you get contacted by an employer and it sounds really good, you may be eager to get going. But if they start asking you for a lot of personal information—social security number, mother's maiden name, etc.—alarms should go off. There are identity theft scams on job search engines just like there are anywhere else online.

For that matter, be careful what you put in an online resume. You don't need to put in your Social Security number. I'd even be careful about putting in my age or a home address. Just provide the minimum amount necessary to get the application into the search engine. Sure you want to work, but you want to protect yourself too.

Monster.com--http://www.monster.com/

"You the monster!" Once upon a time the Monster.com commercials were all over the place. You may not see their commercials as much but they've still got an extensive Web site.

One of the first things you'll notice is that this site requires registration. You can't just start searching the jobs. Registration is free but does require some personal information (address, e-mail, etc.). After you're logged in, you'll have the option to search by keyword or by category as well as to specify a location. You can list your search results by date or by relevance; if you plan to do a lot of visiting to this site, get your results by date.

Your search results, in the brief format, include the date the job was posted, the job title, company, and location. Click on the job name for an extensive description of the job with the option to see all jobs from that company. Like the search results but don't quite see one that grabs your eye? Set up a search scout that'll search jobs in up to ten different locations and in up to ten different categories (and you can specify keywords, too, of course). You can receive alerts as often as daily or as rarely as monthly. Again, take advantage of the automated searching that's available and let the new jobs come to you! Be sure to do lots of experimenting with your search words, and get specific enough that you don't get overwhelmed with available jobs but general enough that you do get some results.

FlipDog--http://www.flipdog.com/

If you're a visual searcher, you'll like FlipDog. It allows you to "drill down" through a map of the U.S. to get to just the jobs you want.

FlipDog doesn't require that you be logged in. So go ahead and start your search. First you'll be presented with a map of the U.S. Pick a state. Then you'll be asked to select a city, and from there a job category. (You can search multiple cities and multiple job categories.) Finally you can specify keywords. As you specify categories, FlipDog will keep a count for you of how many jobs are available. FlipDog will show you a list of employers that match what you're looking for. Click on a company name in which you're interested and choose "Get Results" to see the job description and information.

Note that FlipDog "scrapes" help-wanted information from all over the Web. Therefore they have no standard format of information, which means you'll never be quite sure what you'll get when you look at a job description.

While you're visiting FlipDog, be sure to check out their Resource Center, which gives profiles for different employers and a bunch of different employment-related links, including training and résumé writing.

TIP

If you find yourself unable to use this site, check your browser; I was able to get FlipDog to work only with Internet Explorer.

Yahoo HotJobs--http://hotjobs.yahoo.com/

Yahoo offers everything else, why not a job search? HotJobs has a fairly standard search on its front page—keywords, job category, city, and state—but if you want real search options check out the advanced search. Here you can restrict your search to job title, build complex keyword queries, specify salary level and training level, and even specify from where the job should come (direct employers, staffing firms, or both).

I have not forgotten my dream of becoming an engineer in Omaha, Nebraska. My search at Yahoo HotJobs gets me about two dozen results. Notice that not all search results give you a salary range, but that doesn't seem to hurt your search results. Specifying that you want to see only search results with salary information does hurt your search results, though—I went from over two dozen results to just two in a click.

If you remember that the Internet has over four billion pages, the idea of using it to find a job can be pretty intimidating. But don't let it be; the resources in this chapter let you narrow down your search results quickly to find the job of your dreams.

16 FINDING LOCAL INFORMATION ON THE WEB

Just because the Internet is worldwide doesn't mean that you can't get local resources. From a zip code to a country, there are plenty of places on the Internet that provide information on local businesses, events, and government resources. In this chapter we're going to focus on government resources, but we'll also focus on useful nongovernment sites.

The smallest potential unit of an area would be, I suppose, a house, street, or neighborhood. And while I'm sure that there are plenty of neighborhood (or even street!) Web sites out there, they're not common enough (yet) to devote a section to. So let's start with zip codes.

Zip Code

Ah, the humble zip code. A five-digit number (in its shortest form) but there's so much you can do with it. Why? Because it's a unique identifier that's used by hundreds of millions of people. If you want to make sure your mail gets through, you've got to use it. It's both ubiquitous and unique.

Try this simple exercise: Pick a zip code and the city in which the zip code is located. For example, let's try Mershon, Georgia, with its zip code of 31551. Search for the word "Mershon" and the number 31551 in Google.

> **TIP**
>
> Why not search for the state? Because you don't know if it's going to be GA or Georgia, and besides, the word "Georgia" might not appear at all. Just a city name is a much better bet.

What have you found? At this writing, you would have found almost 200 results. They range from the weather in Mershon to moving companies to rest homes to a list of zip codes for all of Georgia. It's a manageable number of results, very targeted, from two small query words! That's the power of a zip code.

If you tried this trick with another city—say, Beverly Hills and their famous 90210—you might find that you get far more than 200 results. In that case it's time to start adding more specific keywords. `"Beverly Hills" 90210` might get you tens of thousands of results, but `"Beverly Hills" 90210 "tennis club"` gets you far fewer.

Of course, I'm not the only one who's realized all the interesting things you can do with a zip code. Here are five fun resources for making the most of zip code lookups.

Five Fun Things to Do with a Zip Code

Yahoo Get Local—http://local.yahoo.com

Since Yahoo aggregates a lot of material, it makes sense that it would have that material searchable by zip code. You can also browse by city and state, but who wants to do that?

Let's try Pasadena, MD 21122. You'll see when you search for that zip code that you get information on Baltimore, powered by CitySearch, as well as a search for the Pasadena Yellow Pages, maps, and pointers to Pasadena sites in the Yahoo directory. Get Local is a good resource when you're unfamiliar with an area and you need a "quick hit" of available resources—or you're just wondering for which area a zip code is!

Find a Neighborhood—
http://www.realtor.com/FindNeig/default.asp?poe=realtor

Wondering about that place you're planning to move? Want to see how safe the neighborhood is? Try this site. Enter in a zip code and it'll give you aggregated information about a neighborhood including average home value, average home age, and lot size. It'll also give you a pointer to school information and provide demographics about the folks who live in the area. For additional information in a tabled format, visit Yahoo's real estate page at http://list.realestate.yahoo.com/re/neighborhood/main.html. That information includes a crime index and some data about the weather in the area.

HomeTownLocator—http://Gazetteer.HomeTownLocator.com

This is a gazetteer of census information, searchable by a variety of factors including zip code. When I searched here for 21122 I discovered that according to the 2000 census, 57,533 people live there and that it contains 21,188 housing units. In addition to some other census data, there are also links to photographs of the area from TerraServer.com.

Who's Your Rep?—http://www.house.gov/writerep/

Ready to participate in the democracy? If you don't know who your representative is you can find out by visiting the House of Representatives site. Enter your zip code and state and you'll get a form to contact your state representative. Jack Kingston represents Mershon, Georgia.

And the Rest from Langenberg—http://zip.langenberg.com/

If you didn't find anything of interest in the four examples above, visit Langenberg.com. Here you'll find search forms for several different zip code utilities, including surrounding zip codes, distance between zip codes, post office locations, and zip code maps.

And if you still can't find a zip code lookup you're interested in, try searching Google for a keyword and the phrase "zip code." For example, try `"nursing homes" "zip code"`. Believe it or not, you'll get over 47,000 results for that search, and many of the ones on the first page will be search forms for nursing homes! Narrow it down by either adding a keyword to your first keyword (`rehabilitation "nursing home" "zip code"`) or by adding a state name.

With zip codes, there are plenty of nongovernment information providers out there, and most of them provide useful information. For city information, though, I find it's useful to go to the official government site first, and then visit nongovernment city sites. First you need to know how to find your city site.

City Sites

Quick! What's the Web site for your state? You probably know, or at least have a vague idea. Now quick! What's the Web site for your city? You might not have any idea.

The only reason I know the Web site for my city is because they're very good about posting the holiday schedule for trash pickup. It may be a pedantic reason but it saves me a lot of time. The Internet isn't always flash-bang, you know; there's a lot of mundane but useful information being passed around.

TIP

How do I know that it's the official Web site of Omaha? The big clue is that it's located at a site that ends in ne.us—the state of Nebraska Web site. If you're not lucky enough to get a clue like that, look for the words "official site," contact phone numbers on the front page, or the presence of a privacy policy.

If you don't know your city's Web site, try searching Google for it. Try "city of cityname"; for example `"city of Mershon"`. If that doesn't work (and in this case it doesn't), try the name of the city, the name of the state, and the word "official." In this case, a search for `Mershon Georgia official` finds a list of links to official city sites for Georgia, and Mershon is not hyperlinked.

In the cases where a city does not have an official site (and there are many that still don't, usually smaller ones), try searching for the site of a larger nearby city, or look on the official state Web site to see if there's a list of official city sites.

I wish I could be a little more definitive, but unfortunately city and state Web sites are very different, and what you find on one you won't find on another. I can, however, give you a general idea of what you might find.

Let's go back to Omaha. Searching Google for "City of Omaha" gives the official city of Omaha Web site as its first result.

What will you find on the Omaha site? You'll find Mayor and City Council information, at this moment a bulletin about yard waste, and links for the city among many other things. Keep an eye out for a link called "Services" or "City Services." As e-commerce gets more popular you'll see more and more cities offering online services.

Wondering what the official site is for the city of Washington, DC? It's http://www.dc.gov/.

Such as? Well, at the Omaha Services page you can (among other things) order accident reports, get building permit forms, register an intrusion alarm, and pay for a pet license. You can also get information on various Omaha offerings including their skate park and landmarks.

City Web sites are most useful when you either live in a city and you need to check up on a service (especially on a weekend when nobody's available at city administration offices) or when you're thinking about moving to a place and you want to get a sense of what it offers.

Nongovernment sites do not usually offer the services and the city infrastructure information that government sites do. On the other hand, nongovernment city sites usually have more information on attractions, events, and shopping, so the two types of sites often complement each other. You can look at portals for city sites, but if you want to find nongovernment city sites I recommend you use Yahoo over Google.

Yahooing for Nongovernment City Sites

Trying to find nongovernment city sites is a little trickier than trying to find government ones. You can't search for "official site." On the other hand, you can't exclude the word "official" because the site might include some wording like, "this is not the official site of Omaha."

For that reason it's better to limit your nongovernment city site search to a smaller database than Google's; namely, the Yahoo directory (http://directory.yahoo.com). Do a search for "Omaha" and you'll find categories for Omaha and Omaha Metro. When it's available, always choose the Metro category, because it links you to Yahoo Get Local and to cities and counties in the surrounding area.

For city portals, look for Communities, and then for Guides. The descriptions of the sites will give you an idea of the kind of information listed—events, shopping, lodging, community resources, and so on. Omaha.org is a nongovernment Omaha site and offers a set of links on a number of Omaha-focused topics, including work, play, and worship.

If you can't find your city on Yahoo, and you don't even get useful information from Yahoo Get Local, you can try using Google, but I'd use it only as a last resort. Search for the city name and the words "guide" and "city." If that doesn't work, try searching for the city name, the word "city," and the words "shopping" and "events." It's inexact—if the city's of any size you'll get lots of results—but if you don't find city information any other way, this can get you some pointers.

In addition to specific city sites there are also some portal sites that link to many cities.

City Site Portals

I've already mentioned Yahoo Get Local, but I don't really consider that a portal site since it aggregates a limited amount of information. Instead try these sites.

Yahoo's U.S. Metros Category—http://dir.yahoo.com/Regional/U_S__Metros/
This is also Yahoo's property but links to hundreds of separate city sites. If you're looking for in-depth information, this is a better bet than Yahoo Get Local.

CitySearch—http://www.citysearch.com/?choose=1&cslink=cs_other_cities
CitySearch provides both a list of the most popular sites and the option to view all available city guides by state. There isn't a huge number of city guides here, but what is lacking in quantity is more than made up for in quality. There's an extensive event calendar as well as listings of all sorts. Don't forget to check out the restaurant listings, which have both visitor ratings and editorial reviews.

DigitalCity—http://www.digitalcity.com/
DigitalCity starts with a pretty bare Web page; you can specify a zip code or select from a list of states. Once you've selected a city, you'll see content that might remind you of CitySearch. Be sure to check out the "Best" section on the lower right side of the page. Who knew that the best Chinese food in Baltimore (according to DigitalCity, anyway) is at Cafe Zen?

AllPlaces—http://www.allplaces.us/
AllPlaces doesn't have the extensive editorial content or the many business listings of DigitalCity or CitySearch, but an interesting variety of information is gathered here. Once you've supplied a zip code or chosen a city, you'll get both city information (area code, latitude and longitude, links to local resources, and links to several sources of offsite information) and state data (including state motto, official flower, tree, bird, song, etc., and some demographic data). If I had a slow connection or I needed information very quickly, I'd come here first.

StateChamp—http://www.statechamp.com/
StateChamp doesn't so much contain a lot of content as it does a lot of external links. Specify a zip code here and you'll get a list of external links in a variety of categories including newspapers, tourism, sports, and TV and radio stations. Generally the larger the city the more links in more categories. If you're looking for relevant links to your city and Yahoo Directory's not helping you out, look here.

City Web sites are still evolving, and differ greatly in what they offer. On the other hand, state Web sites have gotten more consistent in what they have to offer, but it's not as easy to find them as it used to be. Let me tell you about them, and about my secret search weapon for finding them.

State Sites

Long ago when the Internet was a lot simpler, there was a simple trick to finding official state Web sites. You simply used the URL:

```
http://www.state.xx.us
```

where xx was the two-letter abbreviation of the state in which you were interested—CA for California, for example. And for the most part that trick still works; http://www.state.ar.us still gets you the official state of Arkansas Web site. But at the same time many state sites are moving to more easily remembered domains; the official Web site for California, for example, is http://www.ca.gov.

There are tens of thousands of cities in the U.S., but only 50 states. And there's a quick trick to finding the Web site for each of those 50 states. So it's not important that I give you a bunch of search engine tricks to narrow down that search in Google. You may, however, want to learn how to find specific information within state sites. To do that you'll want to search within Google—but you're going to do some fancy inurl: searching.

What's .gov? It's the top-level domain for government Web sites. In a way it's more authoritative than the .us domain—while the .us domain was once restricted to U.S. entities, nowadays anybody can register a .us domain. The .gov domain is restricted to government entities only and thus has some "instant credibility" that the .us domain no longer has.

Finding Deep State Resources in Google

What will you find at state sites? It varies. You'll always find information on the state's governor (occasionally with a front page picture or even a video greeting) and some general information about the state itself, but after that it varies. New York offers a "Do Not Call" registry for citizens fed up with telemarketers; Wyoming offers a list of upcoming events on the front page and road and travel information, and Hawaii offers lookups of people who hold professional licenses in that state.

The problem with state sites is that they can hold so much information within their main sites and subsites (subsites can be anything in the state.xx.us domain). North Carolina, for example, has 100 counties and hundreds more cities and towns. Each of those entities could potentially have its own Web page within the North Carolina Web site. And that doesn't even count the state-level information like vital records, land management, etc.

Most state sites I've looked at have their own search engines, but if you're doing browser-level searching—you want to get an idea of what's available—then it's a good idea to either check for a site map or visit Google.

State Web site URLs are standard enough that you can get a lot of use out of Google's inurl: special syntax. The inurl: syntax, you may remember, searches for character strings inside a URL. There are three levels of state URLs that I've found useful to search using the url: syntax:

```
inurl:www.co.*.xx.us
```

TIP

Beware of putting an http:// in an inurl search in Google. If you do a search like `inurl: http://www.example.com`, Google will not look for http://www.example.com in the URL of the Web page results. Instead, Google will look for it in the body of the Web page.

Replace xx with the postal code of a state and you'll get page listings for counties in the state. Putting the query `inurl:www.co.*.ca.us` into Google gives you over 389,000 results for pages relating to states in California's counties.

```
inurl:www.*.state.xx.us
```

Replace xx with the postal code of a state and you'll find pages related to state-level information—governmental bodies, vital records, etc. The query `url:www.*.state.mo.us` finds over 620,000 results of state-level pages in Missouri.

```
inurl:www.ci.*.xx.us
```

Replace xx with the postal code of a state and you'll find pages related to specific cities. The query `url:www.ci.*.az.us` finds over 47,600 pages related to city information in Arizona.

Knowing these special searches to find specific types of state-level government information is all very nice, but it doesn't help if you're trying to narrow down your search results. You can use these syntaxes to do general surveys of information or find information in specific areas.

Say you're interested in gambling issues in Texas. You could do a general search for gambling on Texas Web sites. Such a search would look like this:

```
+gambling +site:tx.us
```

TIP

There's no law that says you can't use these URL formats to try to guess the URL for a city or county you're interested in. If you're wondering if the city of Fairbanks in Alaska has a Web site, by all means try http://www.ci.fairbanks.ak.us/. This trick doesn't always work, but it works enough that it's a handy tool.

(Notice that I'm using the site: special syntax instead of the inurl: special syntax. The site: special syntax allows you to easily search all of the tx.us site. Using `inurl:tx.us` will work just as well, but has an outside chance of generating "false positive" results.)

You'll find 1,980 results. You can narrow that search down by narrowing it to city-level information:

```
+inurl:www.ci.*.tx.us +gambling
```

You'll get 152 results, including crime stats, city council meeting notes, and zoning information. Now, back that up to the state level:

```
+inurl:www.*.state.tx.us +gambling
```

You'll get over 2,580 results, including survey results and answers to questions on compulsive gambling. Do you see how the "tone" of the results is very different from the city-level information on gambling? (There's a lot more of it, too!)

Of course, you can get as specific as you like, too. For example, if I need information on permits in Cumberland County, North Carolina, I can use this query:

```
+inurl:www.co.cumberland.nc.us +permit
```

and narrow it right down.

It's rare that I want to find information from more than one state at a time, but I can see where you might need to do it. You may, for example, want to compare gambling laws across several states, and want to get a general sense of what's available. (You *can't* use this technique to get a full list of all gambling laws in all 50 states without a lot of work; you'll have too many results to narrow down.) In that case you can use two wildcards in the URL search. Let's go back to the gambling example. To expand your search to all 50 states, try this search:

```
+inurl:www.*.state.*.us +gambling +ordinance
```

Because I suspected that the results would be greatly expanded by removing the "tx" from the search, I tried to narrow them down again by adding the keyword "ordinance." And for the most part I succeeded; this search gives me 4,110 results, and the first page includes results from Minnesota, Rhode Island, Missouri, Vermont, and Illinois.

It's very difficult to keep in your head all the services that might be offered by a particular state, and besides, states may have different names for departments that offer the same services. So it's important that you know a technique for doing general searches across a wide group of state Web pages.

Federal

The U.S. is one country, so there's just one Web site you have to know about for searching country information, right? Yes and no; on one hand, the U.S. government has established a great clearing house for government Web sites with their site FirstGov. On the other hand, plenty of other folks have tried to map essential U.S. government Web sites too, and some of those resources are very good as well.

If state Web sites have a lot of resources, then the idea of finding anything on a government Web site might seem overwhelming—especially if you don't know from which department you should seek your information! Here's the strategy I use: I find the general kind of information I'm looking for at FirstGov, and if I need additional information I go to either a government-oriented search engine or a government-oriented searchable subject index. But I start with FirstGov.

FirstGov--http://www.firstgov.gov

Whether you need to browse or search, FirstGov is a good jumping-off point. The best way to use the site depends on what you need. If you know the department your research is related to, browse the department list. Say you're looking for statistics on labor. Go to the A–Z department listing and look up the Department of Labor. When you do that, you'll see that there's also a Labor Statistics department, so you can go to that site.

If you're not clear on what you want, you can do a full search. You'll notice that in addition to a federal search option, you'll also have the option to search for state information, or federal and state information. A federal search for `"labor statistics"` found more than 1,000 results, which is why you want to use the department listing if at all possible. You also have the option to use the advanced search.

When you look at the advanced search, it may occur to you that the advanced search looks much like a search engine's advanced search—there are options to limit search words to Web page titles, page size, language, and so on. With that in mind, when you're trying to narrow down your search, treat this as a regular search engine. Getting too many results for "labor statistics"? Limit your search to page title. Want to find resources that are oriented toward Hispanic Americans? Limit your search to documents in Spanish. Like a general search engine, these techniques will not work perfectly, but they will bring your search results down to a more manageable level.

I find that FirstGov provides very good results for the government information searches I do. But if you want to go beyond it, you can try Google's government search engine.

TIP

I've already mentioned .gov, which is a top-level domain for the government. But there's another government-oriented top-level domain: .mil. Can you guess what that's for? Right—military pages.

TIP

You may find some April 14th that you need some tax forms, and you need them right away! In that case you'll get a lot of use out of the IRS site at http://www.irs.gov. But what happens if a few million other people need forms, just like you do, and the site is crowded and slow to respond? Visit Yahoo's directory of tax form sites at http://dir.yahoo.com/Government/U_S__Government/Taxes/Online_Tax_Forms/ and try to get the form from somewhere else.

Google's Uncle Sam--http://www.google.com/unclesam

Google's Uncle Sam is just like the regular Google search, with the difference that the materials searched are government-related Web pages. The search syntaxes are just like Google. Here a search for "labor statistics" gets over 350,000 results (wow!) and includes results from both federal and state sites. Use Google's special syntaxes to narrow down the search, especially intitle:.

Hey, if Google has Uncle Sam, why did I suggest you do your state searching from the main Google site? A couple of reasons. The first is that I have more faith in the longevity of the general Google Web search than in a Google specialty search. The second is that I'm concerned that the Uncle Sam specialty database won't be as complete as Google's full-text engine.

If you're feeling a little overwhelmed by the vast amount of information available at the FirstGov site, you might want to try one of the U.S. government searchable subject indexes or directories.

Other Places to Look

GovSpot, at http://www.govspot.com/, provides links to sites, searches, and statistics. The main sites include the largest government sites used on a regular basis, while the searches connect to various government services (getting Social Security benefits, locating government resources, etc.). There are articles, questions answered (How much are my savings bonds worth?), and even trivia.

I've already mentioned another Yahoo Directory, but also check out the Yahoo U.S. Government directory at http://dir.yahoo.com/Government/U_S__Government/. This directory has several subcategories including categories for all three branches of the government, a Web directory, taxes (of course), and employment. And remember, you can confine your search to just one category, so it's easy to search just the sites listed underneath the U_S__Government directory.

In the last few years the U.S. government has developed some dynamic, useful Web sites. If you haven't visited them lately to see what they have to offer, start with FirstGov. If that proves too intimidating, try GovSpot or the Yahoo Directory. I'm sure you'll find something useful.

International

As a researcher, and especially a researcher who respects the fragility of the Internet, I try to maintain several favorite spots in a research category. If I want to research cars over a long period of time, for example, I try to be aware of several different spots for researching cars.

But when it comes to international research—that is, research on individual countries—there's only one place I want to go, and that's the awesome CIA World Factbook. Once you've visited the Factbook, you can take just one bit of information from it and do some detailed Google searches. And if you're looking for information on groups of countries, there's another Google trick I can show you. But it's all going to start with the CIA World Factbook.

The CIA World Factbook--http://www.cia.gov/cia/publications/factbook/

Why do I like the CIA World Factbook so much? Three reasons: 1) It's very credible. 2) It's updated often. 3) It's put together in such a way that the information is very easy to scan and extract from.

Let's take a look. The Factbook's front page has a drop-down menu that allows you to select a country from Afghanistan to Taiwan. From the front page you can also access groups of information (Flags of the World), download rank-order pages (highest population, debt, military expenditures, etc.), and get a guide to the country profiles.

Pick a country. You'll see that the page starts with a map of that country, and then moves through information in a series of categories, including geography, people, government, economy, and military. Each chunk of data (and there are several chunks per category) has two icons above it; a book icon (which takes you to a page explaining that particular chunk); and a page icon, which takes you to a list of all countries with each country's data chunk.

If you're using this page for research, note that there's a print-friendly page, and note the appendixes if you want to do extensive research across several countries. If I want to research a country, I always start here. It gives me an extensive overview of the country in capsule format, and I'm always sure the information is relatively recent. And then there's that one bit of information that unlocks very relevant Google results.

What am I talking about? Look at the Government section. Now, look for the country name. (If there are several versions, look for the conventional long form.) You'll see that the official country name is often longer and more formal than the regular country name. Let's take Belgium as an example. The conventional long form of the country of Belgium's name is Kingdom of Belgium.

Now, let's do a Google experiment. Do a Google search for "Belgium." Now do a Google search for "Kingdom of Belgium."

You should notice two things. The first thing you'll notice is that your search results are cut down drastically! The second thing is that your search results will be for the most part focused on Belgium and in some cases from the country of Belgium itself.

Using the official name of a country is your first step towards narrowing down/focusing results when you're doing country research on Google. The second step is to use a country code.

TIP

For the most part, a Web site's country code indicates some kind of country affiliation; either the creators of the content are located in that country, or the content has something to do with that country. But there are a couple of exceptions to this. A few countries—most notably Tonga (.to), and the Cocos (Keeling) Islands (.cc)—have licensed their domains specifically for public registration. In other words, just because something is registered with a .cc or a .to address doesn't mean it's located in Tongo or the Cocos Islands or has anything to do with Tongo or the Cocos Islands: in fact, odds are that it isn't and it doesn't. Keep that in mind if you run a search on a country code and get results all out of proportion to what you would expect.

What's a Country Code?

You already know about the regular top-level domains—.com, .net, .org, .edu, .gov, and others. But what you might not know is that all countries have their own top-level domains.

The United States, for example, has .us (which you've seen earlier in this chapter). The United Kingdom has .uk. Japan has .jp, and so on. You can get a full list of country codes at http://www.iana.org/cctld/cctld-whois.htm.

Maybe you see where I'm going with this. You can use the country code in conjunction with the official country name to narrow down your search results to more official sites. This works with Google's site: syntax, like so:

```
"Kingdom of Belgium" site:be
```

When you do this you'll see that the Web site for the government of Belgium is http://www.belgium.be. So if you want to you can narrow down your results even further by tweaking the site syntax:

```
"Kingdom of Belgium" site:belgium.be
```

Of course, you don't have to narrow down your site syntax; instead you could start adding keywords. What are you interested in? Demographics? Trade? Taxes? Try various keywords and see if you can expand the statistics that are found in the CIA World Factbook.

TIP

Just because a country has a country code doesn't mean it has an Internet presence. You'll find that the information available from various countries varies a lot. There's more variation still as to what's available in English (or whatever language you prefer).

Finding Information for Groups of Countries

Sometimes you don't want to do research on a single country, but rather get comparative information on several countries at once. To do that you should employ the Principle of Mass Similar. You can apply it to international searches, too. In this case let's say you want to get search results about exports, focused on Asia. Apply the Principle of Mass Similar and include several Asian countries in your query along with the simple keyword "exports."


```
Japan Korea China Mongolia Malaysia exports
```

Even though you're using a lot of keywords, you're getting a lot of results. In fact, you might be getting too many. If that's the case, then narrow down your search a bit:

```
Japan Korea China Mongolia Malaysia exports
              "circuit boards"
```

That worked beautifully! But always start with a general keyword in this case. You're already narrowing down your searches with the several country names. Don't over-narrow your search results right off the bat.

This search works well for a region in the world. How about the world itself? Sure. The only thing you need to do is to include countries from every point of the globe; don't concentrate them in one region. Let's go back to the exports question, only let's try a different set of countries:

```
Japan Denmark Canada Brazil "South Africa"
          "Saudi Arabia" exports
```

You'll notice that these results aren't as neat as the results for the first country search you did; that's because this set of countries isn't easy to categorize. But as you add additional keywords, the search results will start getting more focused.

Because of its intimidating size and constant expansion, it's not easy to think of the Internet as a source for local information. But as you can see, it's easy to get information on an area as small as a zip code or as extensive as a country. The trick is to know unique identifying numbers (in the case of a zip code) or potential ways to group large items (in the case of countries).

PART IV
SEARCHING FOR MULTIMEDIA

17 Finding Images

Long gone are the days when the Internet was mostly just words. Now the Internet is all kinds of multimedia—audio, images, and even video. Though many of the principles you're learning in this book will work with multimedia in addition to text searches, you also have to know about the search engines that specialize in picture content. So that's what this chapter's all about: pointing you toward those search engines that search images, with a special look at large image collections and some pointers for finding image databases via text search engines.

But before I do that I have to discuss a sensitive topic briefly. I am, of course, referring to Naughty Bits.

Avoiding the Naughty Bits

Most image search engines have a filter option on them. If you do any searching for images at all you'll soon find out why there's a filter option. Even the most innocuous search terms you can think of have the potential to return search results with Naughty Bits.

For the purpose of this chapter all searches are assumed to be run with the filters on. If your tolerance is high, by all means leave it turned off. If your tolerance is very low or you're searching with someone who absolutely must not be exposed to those images (like a small child or your extremely conservative grandmother), consider searching only kid-friendly or specialized engines that are indexed by humans (not Web spiders) and are guaranteed not to have any inappropriate content. Yes, it does greatly restrict your image searching options, but it sure beats paying for ten years of therapy for grandma. We'll cover kid-safe searching a little later in the book.

Let's get back to searching, shall we?

Image Search Engines Associated with Major Search Engines

As you might expect, many search engines have image searches associated with them. Searching for images isn't too different from searching for text content, except that you might find your very specific searches less rewarding. Sometimes you'll find your search for a pink teddy bear cross-stitch pattern working perfectly, but sometimes you'll have to start at `teddy bear cross-stitch` and see what you can find.

Image search engines generally don't have the extensive special syntaxes that text search engines have, but they have other limiting options, such as image size. If you have an image search that fits within one image size (for example, you're looking for icons for your home page), be sure to use the special image search restrictions.

Google Images--http://images.google.com

Google Images searches an index of over 800 million images at this writing. Its search interface looks much like Google's—a plain query box. If you go to the advanced search you'll see the additional options to limit your search results to images of a certain size, a certain file format (Google Images only searches for images that are PNG, GIF, or JPG format), or certain color (color, grayscale, or black and white). You'll also see the option to limit your search to a certain domain or top-level domain.

What you don't see is that you can also use some of Google's other special syntaxes. For example, you can search for a word in the URL of the graphic (`inurl:cat`). You can search for multiple instances of a word, which will change your result count and order (`cat cat cat`). For the most part I find the site: search tends to do the most limiting—searching only in .edu sites tends to provide more academic results, etc. (though that's only a guideline—remember, students publish their home pages on university sites!).

NOTE

It should go without saying but I'll say it anyway: Images on the Web, unless otherwise specified, are protected by copyright law. Please don't take stuff from one site for your site without getting permission first.

Google Images provides search results in "thumbnail" format, 20 per page. Click on a result and you'll get a framed page, with the image on top and the original page on the bottom.

AltaVista--http://www.altavista.com/image

AltaVista gives you a few extra options when it comes to figuring out what you're going to search for. Instead of searching for certain sizes, you can search (from the front page) for photos, graphics, or buttons and banners. There are additional search options in pulldown menus for searching for color, sources (there are a couple of specialty collections here, including *Rolling Stone*), and sizes. You'll notice that the size option for AltaVista image search giving four basic sizes (small, medium, large, and wallpaper), and then "wide wallpaper," allows you to search over a dozen different sizes.

> **TIP**
>
> Note that AltaVista has a video search too. Try that at http://www.altavista.com/video/default.

You'll also notice that the results are somewhat different than Google's image search. You'll see a thumbnail of the image, the filename, its dimensions, and the file size. If you click on the image itself, you'll go to the page where it appears. If you click on More Information, you'll get a few additional bits of information about the image, including the format and an abstract of the page (I don't find the abstracts very useful; I suggest you go straight to the page).

When you run image searches, you'll get a lot of results that not only aren't useful but are really far off. Sometimes this doesn't distract from your search efforts but sometimes you can't do the extensive searches you want to with a huge collection of nonrelated images collected by a spider. In that case you can take one of two more steps: you can either use a specialized image search engine or you can use a specialized image collection.

Specialized Image Search Engines

PicSearch--http://www.picsearch.com/

When you first see PicSearch you might think to yourself, "Hey! Where's all the search options and pulldown menus?" They're not on the front page; all you can do here is a simple keyword search.

If you go to the advance search page you'll see a familiar search option for size, only the size option provides the size (in pixels) of the images that you'll be looking for. You'll also see an option to search for images, animations, or both. The found images are animated GIFs that will display in all current browsers without additional software (unlike, say, Flash animations).

I find PicSearch's image search to provide fewer results than Google's image search, but at the same time it's nice to be able to search for animations separately, and to be able to see what large, small, and medium actually mean. Note also that PicSearch's adult content filters are integrated into their service and cannot be bypassed; if you're looking for content that might be accidentally considered adult content (images related to breast cancer, for example), you might want to use a different search index.

Ditto--http://www.ditto.com/

Ditto, like PicSearch, has always-on filtering, so this is not a place to deliberately find adult content.

In addition to doing keyword searching, Ditto also allows you to browse through images by category; categories here include Homelife, Entertainment, Health, etc. Unfortunately their search results leave a bit to be desired for the serious researcher; all you get for your results is a thumbnail, file size, and a link to the source. I recommend you review the source URL before you go to any Web pages holding pictures. I also recommend you skip this site if you have advanced searching to do; this site doesn't offer an advanced image search form.

Specialized image collections have, in my experience, the advantage of giving somewhat more relevant results for a search, and the ones I've shown you here have built-in filters to help minimize the chance of getting inappropriate content. But you may find that even these searches are not helping your particular research needs. In this case, you'll want to search specialized image collections.

Giving you a semi-complete list of specialized image search collections would take up an entire book. I'm going to give you some collection highlights and then provide you with some guidance on finding image search collections related to your own search interests.

NOTE

There are several places that have interfaces to use several different image search engines—handy if you want to do a lot of searching without a lot of surfing. Try http://images.langenberg.com/ for a pretty good list of interfaces and FaganFinder's image search page (http://www.faganfinder.com/img/) for a really good list.

Specialized Image Collections

Specialized image collections generally have all their images maintained on one site. This is important for a few reasons: 1) pages will not expire as they might for pages with images gathered from all over the Web, 2) images can be indexed in more elaborate ways, as they and their information are maintained on one site, and 3) image collections can be confirmed as family-friendly since all the images are in one place and can be reviewed, instead of coming from all over the Web. (Of course, there is no guarantee that such a collection *will* be family-friendly, since there might be tens of thousands of images and nobody to review them.)

Another consideration for specialized image collections is that they are generally under some restrictive copyright laws. Though you should always be mindful of copyright when researching images, you should be doubly considerate when searching a specialized image collection.

Remember what I told you about machine filtering being susceptible to error? It's still true. These "always filtered" search engines may strive to avoid showing you adult content, but there's no guarantee they'll always be successful.

Corbis--http://pro.corbis.com/

You'll get the idea about the copyright stuff the first time you go to Corbis. Instead of checkboxes for searching by size, color, or file type, you can limit your searches to royalty-free images or model-released images. There's also an option to limit your search to very broad categories including commercial, editorial, and historical. Search results appear as a series of thumbnails, and clicking on a thumbnail shows you a larger version of the picture in a pop-up window.

Getty Images--http://www.gettyimages.com/

Getty Images is actually an aggregate of several different image collections, including the Time Life Picture Collection, National Geographic, and several stock photography collections. You can search an entire category of images (like Creative or News) or search individual collections. You can do a keyword search or use a really complicated search that includes item orientation, color, release status, and whether or not the image is on CD. Since that kind of information doesn't have much relevance to an Internet researcher, and since specialized Internet collections have a limited number of results, I recommend you stick with the simple keyword search.

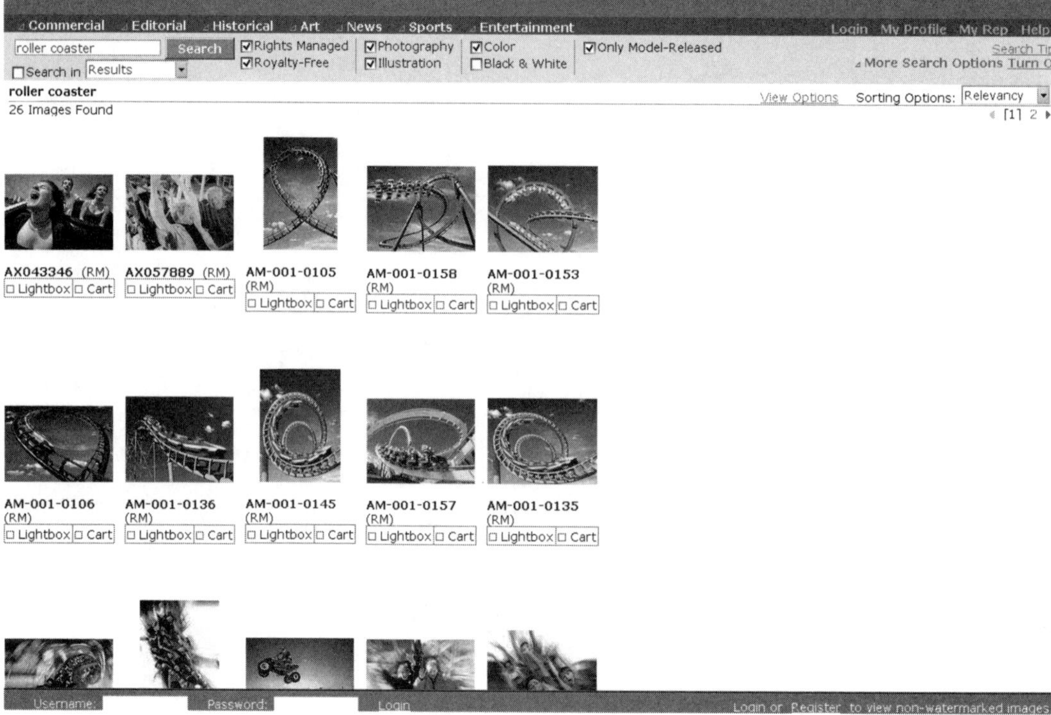

17–01

You can get all kinds of pictures from Corbis—even roller coasters! (Image from http://pro.corbis.com/search/searchFrame.asp.)

Getty and Corbis are best for when you're looking for pictures of people and simple pictures of common things (for example, if you wanted a picture of a giraffe or a steam-powered locomotive). General image search engines might find you these things, but they'll have a lot of irrelevant and just plain wrong stuff mixed in at the same time.

LOC Collection--http://memory.loc.gov/ammem/mdbquery.html

LOC stands for Library of Congress, and if you have any research to do related to the history of the United States, I urge you to look here first.

This collection actually spans all of the Library of Congress's collections. To limit it to images, choose the "Photos & Prints" option on the upper right side of the page. The resulting search form will give you a query box, a couple of pull-down menus to help you narrow down your query, and then a list of all the available collections with photos and print in them; at this writing that's "Adams, Ansel ~ Japanese-American Internment ~ Photographs ~ 1943" to "Wright Brothers ~ Multiformat ~ 1881-1952." As you can tell by these titles, they're usually enough to give you an idea of what a collection contains, but if they're not helpful enough you can click "Show Descriptions" on the right side of the page and get a more thorough overview of a collection.

Your search results will show a table with the name of the exhibition and the title of the matching item. Click on the title of the item and you'll get a lot of additional information including a summary and any relevant notes. Click on the picture and you'll get a much larger picture; sometimes archival pictures are available, but they're a long download!

I find that the LOC collections work particularly well when searching for famous Americans of the 19th and 20th centuries. You're likely to find surprise results. For example, do a search for the phrase "Babe Ruth"—you'll find over 40 results and dozens of pictures of the famous ball player.

> **TIP**
>
> I know I said that with picture collections you'll have to be careful of copyright issues, but the LOC collection is a little different, since it's your tax dollars at work! See the LOC's copyright information at http://memory.loc.gov/ammem/copyrit2.html to get an idea of how the copyright works for their collections.

Yahoo News Search: News Photos--http://search.news.yahoo.com/usns/ynsearch/categories/advanced/index.html

What am I doing mentioning Yahoo News in an image search chapter? Check out the advanced search and you'll see: one of the search options is for news photos.

As you might expect, this search is best for contemporary news searches; Yahoo does not keep its news photos indefinitely. So do searches for currently famous people (rock stars, media personalities), perpetually famous people (heads of state), and current events (Olympics, elections, holidays). Note that the search will sometimes return strange results, as the search looks for the keyword in the entire caption. At this writing, for example, a search for "George Bush" returns a picture of U.N. Secretary General Kofi Annan (because the name George Bush is in the caption).

I've given you pointers to some extensive image collections, but they're not going to do you any good if you have very specific image needs. In that case fire up Google and do some serious specialty searching.

Finding Image Collections Via Web Searches

You'll need a little time and several searches to zero in on exactly what you want, but you can find specialty image collections with a few Google searches. Pick a general word to describe what you're looking for and then add a few different phrases. I tried "microbiology" here:

```
microbiology "image search"
microbiology "image finder"
microbiology images pictures search
```

If that doesn't work, try putting the general word in the title and then searching for images and phrases that define image collections.

```
intitle:microbiology images
```


As you've seen from this chapter, the Internet's far more than just text. And as you'll discover in the next chapter, it's far more than just images, too—there's lots of audio as well!

18 FINDING AUDIO ON THE WEB

I may lose all my street cred for this, but I'm going to go ahead and tell you anyway: I've never used Napster or any of those other music-swapping services. I know, big geek like me, you'd think I'd do all that peer-to-peer stuff. But I never did. However, that doesn't mean I've never had a use for music and sound online.

Ever since I used an early version of RealAudio *cough* years ago, I've loved sounds on the Internet. More and more these days that means music, but it can mean other sounds too—sound effects, quotes from television shows, and historical speeches, among other things.

Let's start at the beginning: sound formats.

Sound Formats

In the beginning there was *beep*. And it was good. But man, it was boring! The Internet's come a long way since the first sound formats back in the early 90s. Now there are lots of different sound formats. Some of them are very popular and you'll see them every day, and some of them are less popular than they used to be.

Popular Sound Formats

MP3

Unless you've been living under a rock, you've heard about MP3. It's a very popular sound format for music. Why? Because the MP3 format allows for lots of compression with very little sound loss, leading to great-sounding music in fairly small sizes. In my experience downloading music (from Emusic.com), it seems to come out to about 1MB per minute of music. Howstuffworks.com has a great article on how MP3 music works: http://www.howstuffworks.com/mp3.htm/printable.

WAV

The WAV audio format creates much larger sound files than MP3, but it's a much older format. It's also much friendlier to regular CD players—if you "burn" a CD with WAV sound files, you can play it on most CD players (in my experience). On the other hand, if you burn a CD with MP3 files, you'll need a special CD player that can play CDs containing MP3 files. The WAV file format is the standard Windows audio format; if you record something with your sound recorder, it's going to be recorded in WAV format.

WMA

WMA stands for "Windows Media Audio," and as you might expect it was developed by Microsoft. I understand that it compresses files even smaller than MP3, but I've never tested that. There are several different WMA players available, but in my experience it is not as popular as the MP3 format. You can download the Windows Media Player from http://www.microsoft.com/windows/windowsmedia/players.aspx; despite its name it is available for both Windows and Mac.

RealAudio (RA or RM)

RealAudio, also known as Real, is an extremely popular streaming media format. What is streaming media? Streaming media means you can play it almost immediately after clicking on it; you don't have to wait for the entire thing to download like you often have to with WAV or MP3 files or other downloadable file formats. The quality for RealAudio is sometimes not as good as WAV or MP3, but it's good for listening to news broadcasts and other spoken-word audio.

Less-Popular Formats

There are other formats floating around, but they're not as popular as the big four I've outlined above.

AU—This is the Sun audio format. It was more popular several years ago. If you're using a halfway-recent version of IE, Opera, or Netscape, you should be able to play AU sound files no problem.

AIFF—This format was developed by Apple computer and is the standard audio format for Mac computers, I understand. You'll see this format occasionally online; not often.

MIDI—"MIDI" stands for "Musical Instrument Digital Interface" and it's rather different from the other sound formats I'm describing here. You don't record a sound and then save it in MIDI format. Instead, a MIDI file is a set of musical commands that are played back by your soundcard. Since it's just a set of instructions, you can create songs that fit into very small files. There's a great page about how MIDI works at http://www.hybridproductions.org/dave/writing/midi.html.

On the Horizon

There is one sound format on the horizon that I haven't covered here, but which you may see more of in the future. It's called Ogg Vorbis, which has an extension of .ogg. Ogg Vorbis is an unpatented audio format that claims to have better sound quality than MP3; you can read more about it at http://www.vorbis.com/. I have a seen very few music files available in Ogg format, but it does seem to be gaining some momentum.

Now that you know something about the available formats, let's talking about using general search engines to find sound files.

Playing Sounds

Let's look at some software you can use to play these formats, in case your browser can't handle what you're trying to throw at it.

But first a small explanation. I could easily just list a million software packages here and let you explore. While I do want to give you some leads on doing your own exploring—I'm including a list of software sites at the end of this section—I'm only going to cover in-depth those programs that I've used myself. There won't be as much variety in operating systems because of that, but on the other hand I want to give you more firsthand information than a simple software roundup would provide. Okay? Let's talk about the big three: playing WAVs, playing MP3s, and playing RealAudio. And let's talk about the big mystery: recording RealAudio.

Playing WAVs

If your browser/OS doesn't play WAV files, color me stunned. I figured pretty much everybody had built-in WAV support. But goodness knows I've been wrong before. And besides, you may find your WAV player a bit puny. You may want to do some editing or suchlike that a player won't allow you to do.

I've used GoldWave (http://www.goldwave.com/, Windows 95 & up) for ages. There's a shareware version you can download and try, or you can register and buy the program for $40. I've done all kinds of things with this program—cleaned up the static from audio recorded from vinyl, added some basic effects to WAVs, and cut up a WAV into individual words.

Playing MP3s

I have a lot of MP3s, but I don't use the same program to play them all the time. In fact, I use three different programs. What makes me determine which one I'll use? The programs are each good for slightly different things.

Winamp—http://www.winamp.com/ (Windows; Linux "in the works")

This MP3 player is free and supports Shoutcast and Windows Media formats in addition to MP3.

Why do I like it? A few reasons. You can customize Winamp's appearance with a huge number of different "skins." You can specify a file to play or a directory to play—so if I want to launch my "bemused at the universe" mix in a particular directory, it's the matter of a moment. There's also a very nice shuffle function.

Musicmatch—http://www.musicmatch.com/ (Windows)
Musicmatch has come with the last two computers I've purchased, so I've always used a bundled version, and I'm probably using a somewhat old one.

I sometimes use Musicmatch for playing MP3 files, and I don't have any complaints with it in that regard (though I will say I like Winamp better), but what I use it for most—and what I like a lot—is its ability to "rip" songs from CDs.

It works very simply. You put a CD in your CD drive, launch Musicmatch, and view the recorder window. Pick the tracks you want to pull from the CD, and Musicmatch records them. If you're using the free version like I am, it takes a little longer to rip tracks than it does with the paid version, but it's not a terribly long process.

My favorite thing about Musicmatch as an MP3 player is the fact that it saves the playlist. So if you play a couple of songs and shut down the application, the same songs are on the playlist when you open the application later.

Windows Media Player—http://www.microsoft.com/windows/windows media/players.aspx (Windows, Mac, Palm, Pocket PC, Solaris)
The Windows Media Player also came with my computer. I use it occasionally, not as often as the two MP3 players mentioned above.

As you might expect, the Windows Media Player has a sturdy connection back to a Web site that allows you to browse new song offerings as well as radio stations. The program's way of organizing available media is pretty good, too.

Playing RealAudio

If you want to play RealAudio files, you don't have much in the line of options besides the Real player itself. If you go to the main site for the player, it tries to get you to buy the player, but you can download the free version there, too. Look for the RealPlayer download link—RealPlayer Plus is the one that costs money.

Real works. I try to avoid using it. Why? Because I hate that chirpy little pop-up box that sends you marketing stuff. I remember using Real circa 1997 or so and I loved it. I am not as enamored now. But RealAudio is a pretty standard format online, and you're going to have to use this player if you want to access a variety of audio services—especially news.

RealAudio is what's called a "streaming" format. That means that instead of waiting for the whole sound file to download, the file starts playing as soon as a certain amount has filled the playing buffer. Now, this is great if you've got a slow connection, or the sound file is very large, or if it doesn't have a clear ending (a live feed, for example). However, if you want to record the audio to listen to later, it's a pill.

Recording RealAudio

I have tried a couple of different ways to record streaming RealAudio, and I've settled on Total Recorder. It's not perfect, but it's a fairly easy and inexpensive way to get streaming audio into a burnable format.

Total Recorder—http://www.highcriteria.com/ (Windows)

Total Recorder isn't free, but it's very inexpensive—all of $11.95 U.S. for the standard version (there's a professional version with a few more features for $35.95 U.S.).

Total Recorder works by setting itself up as a "virtual sound driver." Sound is played through the virtual driver and passed on to the sound card, so the sound that's going to the sound card can be recorded—by RealAudio, Winamp, QuickTime, whatever. Once you're using the virtual driver there's a small control panel that lets you turn recording on and off, etc. The program also has a scheduler that you can use to set up recording events.

For the most part, I've found that Total Recorder works very well. There are two slight problems with it, though. The first one is that the RealAudio streams I recorded weren't that great in quality. A recorded 28.8 RealAudio stream doesn't sound better just because it's saved as a WAV file. The second thing is that the virtual driver had problems with one program. With most programs it worked fine, but with one game it made the sound act choppy and occasionally cut out. But since deactivating the driver is the matter of a moment in a control panel, this slight problem doesn't make me any less likely to use the software.

Other Sources for Software

Maybe after reading this chapter you're feeling a bit adventurous and you want to find some other music software to experiment with. No problem. Here are some other sites to check out.

DailyMP3.com—http://www.dailymp3.com/main.html

As you might expect from the URL, this site focuses on MP3 software. Categories include players, CD rippers, skins, and a bevy of other utilities that aren't necessarily related to MP3. There's also a brief section for MIDI software and MP3 news as well as featured listing. Plenty of stuff!

Partners in Rhyme—http://www.partnersinrhyme.com/

If you just glance at the front page you'll think that this site is just about music loops and royalty-free samples. Check out the link on the left of the page for links to sound utilities for both Mac and Windows. Not tons of listings here, but they're pretty well explained.

Shareware Music Machine—http://www.hitsquad.com/smm/

Heavy duty; tons of stuff on this site. The front page is low on graphics but heavy on the sound software categories, including audio editors, audio restoration, music calculators, and tuners. Software is divided out by operating system. There's a lot of advertising and pop-ups on this site, but there's enough good material here that I'm willing to wade through it.

Searching for Sound

Searching for text is soooo 1996. (Well, yes, it's vital and useful, too, but stay with me. I'm trying to do a humorously elitist and ironic intro here.) There's more to search online than just—words, for crying out loud! There's audio, too.

Search engines do not index complete audio files. That is to say, you can't expect Google to have indexed an MP3 that contains all the words to a Tina Turner song. When you search for a sound, you have to use a little savvy.

How you search depends on what you're looking for, and what you're looking for might be a sound effect or a quote from a TV show. Except for songs, I find that most of the sounds that are online are in WAV format.

If you're looking for sound effects or certain types of sound, your search can be fairly straightforward—try searching for the keyword and the keyword "wav." The other day I was looking for windchime sounds. I got plenty of results just searching for `windchimes wav`. Then I thought about potential spelling issues and changed my search to `(windchimes | "wind chimes") wav`, which gave me over 1,200 results, the front page of which looked very relevant. A search for `chimes.wav` led to disaster; chimes.wav is a Windows sound file, so references to that were everywhere.

Sometimes you won't find what you want with such a specific search. In that case you need to back up and get more general. For example, say you're looking for the cry of a red-tailed hawk. Now, if you actually search for `"red-tailed hawk" wav` you'll get plenty of sound files, but let's pretend that didn't work, or that you weren't able to find a file you like. In that case you could back up your search using the Principle of Onions.

There are several ways to back it up. You could get a little less specific with the query `hawk wav`. You could get very general with `bird wav`. You could try plurals, with the query `bird wavs`.

With some sound searches, like quotes, it's a little more difficult. I recommend that when you search for a quote, you pick a little tiny part of a specific quote and try searching for that. For example, say you're looking for a wav of the Mystery Science Theater 3000 quote, "We've got movie sign!" Don't try to search for the whole thing. Instead, pick a little part of the quote—as small as you can get it so it's still unique—and search for that and the string wav. So for this search we could try `"got movie sign" wav` and find several dozen relevant results.

Of course, you can go beyond general Web searching to find sounds. In fact, some general search engines have audio search options, and there are a huge number of specific search engines and directories that deal with just sound. Let's start with the sound search offerings from AltaVista, AlltheWeb, and Lycos.

Regular Search Engines Offering Sound Search

I know, nobody goes to AltaVista anymore. But go anyway because they've got a decent audio search at http://www.altavista.com/audio/default. This interface searches for MP3 files, WAV files, RealAudio, Windows Media, AIFF, and "other."

I did a quick search for "Mississippi Mass Choir" and got 11 results. Results include the title of the clip (sometimes these are helpful, like the title of the song, and sometimes they're something nonhelpful, like "Track 10"), the clip's "author" (sometimes this is available and sometimes not), length of the clip, page URL, and the option to get more media information from that page. Be sure to check out the search options below the query box, which let you narrow your search by kinds of media (MP3, WAV, Windows Media, Real, Other) and checkboxes to toggle whether the sound should be more or less than a minute.

AlltheWeb allows you to do MP3 searching at http://www.alltheweb.com/?cat=mp3 . Information in the search results includes the size of the download and the date of the file.

I must say I don't visit Lycos much any more, but their multimedia site (http://multimedia.lycos.com/) has a lot to offer. There are search options for both audio and MP3. A search for "rock" found tens of thousands of results, with the results listings including a snippet from the page (not very useful in the ones I found), file name, file size, URL, and a direct link to play the file.

Sound search engines run by general search engines are good to use when you're searching for general titles and popular stuff, or when you want the ease of using an interface with which you're already familiar. But don't stop here. There are some great sound search engines that stand alone.

Sound Search Engines and Directories

Before I get into the listings, let me say that I could literally write a book on finding sound/audio on the Web. I'm just scraping the surface here.

FindSounds—http://www.findsounds.com/
I love easy-to-understand domain names. FindSounds features a checkbox-heavy interface for finding audio online. File formats include AIFF, AU, and WAV. You can specify that sounds found be mono or stereo, their minimum resolution (8-bit or 16-bit), their minimum sample rate, and their maximum file size (which only goes up to 2MB, so this is not the place to find songs or extensive recordings).

A search for "click" found over 100 results. Results include the full URL of the sound, the name of the sound (some of them were just named "click," but some of them were named "mouse click," etc.), information about the sound, and links to view the entire page or to e-mail the sound. This site isn't fancy but it's fast-loading; nicely done.

Wav Central—http://www.wavcentral.com/
As you might expect from the name of the site, Wav Central indexes only WAVs. It's set up as a tabbed site—look across the top of the page for navigation.

Here you'll find WAVs divided up into several categories, including TV, FX, and commercials. Some of the sounds are mixed together—I found an MST3K WAV listed under FX. Listings include title, a brief description, date added, number of times the item has been downloaded, size, and user rating (you can use a pulldown menu to rate the WAVs you download). The Search tab allows you to search by keyword, with result listings that look like what you see when you browse. Note that the search engine automatically stems—if you search for "crow" you'll get results that include "crowd."

SoundAmerica—http://www.soundamerica.com/

Instead of being tabbed like Wav Central, SoundAmerica is set up like a file directory. From the front page you can explore a variety of categories including cartoons, spoofs, movies, and sound effects. (All the categories I looked at had extensive subcategories.) Listings look just like directory listings—that is, you'll see the name of the file, the date it was last modified, and its size. Unfortunately there are no descriptions, which makes it hard to follow what some of these files are.

Naturesongs—http://www.naturesongs.com/

Getting away a moment from the eight hundred billion *South Park* WAV depositories out there, we have Naturesongs. This site offers categories like bird sounds, animal sounds, insect sounds, and even a few human sounds. Some of the categories have subcategories, and some of them don't.

Unlike the fairly plain listings on the directories we've looked at so far, these sound listings actually feature commentary. The site's writer explains what you're hearing, where the sound was recorded, and provides the size of the recording. Not only will you get to hear some cool nature sounds, you'll learn something too!

Ljudo—http://ljudo.com/

Not a helpful domain name, is it? Ljudo is a directory of over 1,200 sound effects in MP3 and RealAudio formats. Ljudo is different from many of the resources I've covered here in that it's available in several different languages.

Once you've picked the correct language and entered the front of the site, you'll get a search box. Enter a keyword—I tried "bell"—and you'll get a list of results. Results include filename, file size, and the option to hear it in either MP3 or RealAudio format. There's no annotation to the file names but they're usually self-explanatory. I like this site because the results load quickly and it's focused on one thing: sound effects.

Speechbot—http://speechbot.research.compaq.com/

From this site you can search over 17,000 hours of content from a variety of Web sites. There are a couple ways you can access the content on this site. You can do a simple keyword search, which can (but doesn't have to) include topic restrictions (advice, sport, paranormal, etc.). You can also do a power search, which allows you to restrict by media type and by date, and to do a little Boolean tweaking.

A search for "Tom Peters" found 22 results. Results include a link to play the extract, the Web site, date, and an extract from the transcript. The extracts are rather short and range from very helpful to not helpful at all. Fortunately there's a "Show Me More" link for more extensive transcripts. If you're doing current event research, or looking for topical audio, look here first.

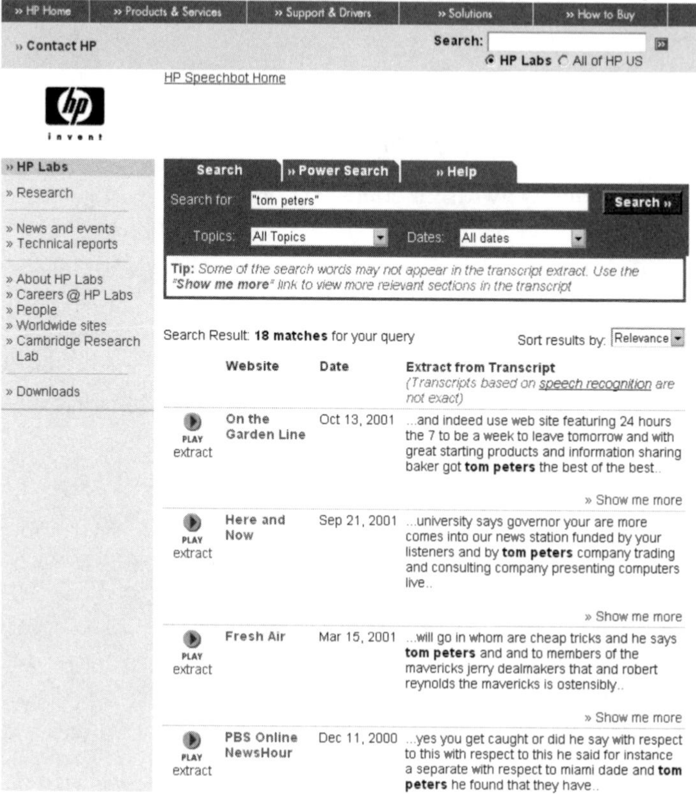

18–01

Speechbot has a huge number of audio transcripts. (Image from http://speechbot.research.compaq.com/?q=%22tom+peters%22&topic=%2A&dr=%2A.)

The Earchives—http://www.the-earchives.com/

The Earchives is a WAV depository that allows some extensive searching options. You can search by actor, character, title, or WAV description. You can also browse, getting the top 150 downloads, random WAVs, and a list of wanted WAVs. You can also, heaven help you, browse the sound files in alphabetical order.

A search for "Daffy" by character found 15 results. Results show the title of where it comes from (in this case Warner Brothers Cartoons), the date added, the character and actor, and a description of the file that shows a transcript, the length of the file, a link to download it, and the number of times it's been downloaded.

Other Fun Audio Sites

The Daily WAV—http://www.dailywav.com/

Heh! If you're looking for clever, quippy WAVs to use to signal incoming mail or whatever, this is where to look. This site features a new WAV every day (well, the weekends are doubled up) with a variety of sayings from a variety of pop culture celebrities. Selections include Mr. T., *Star Trek*, Darkwing Duck, and Mr. Rogers.

You can view archives chronologically (back to January 1999) or alphabetically (the clips are listed by show/movie/whatever name). The archives aren't quite complete (looks like the Webmaster got hit by a C&D from *The Simpsons* people—there are no *Simpsons* WAVs on this site), but you'll find yourself browsing for hours.

Historical Sounds Archive—http://www.webcorp.com/sounds/

I don't know who these folks are, but they've got a nice mix of audio and video at their site. You'll find a lot of sound bites from Nixon, but there are several other historical figures here, too, including Winston Churchill, Malcolm X, and Bill Clinton. Materials here are in RealAudio and WAV format. There's also some video in AVI format as well.

Interactive TTS Demo—http://www.research.att.com/projects/tts/demo.html

Sometimes you can't find a WAV that says quite what you want it to say. That's when you can use this experimental text-to-speech (TTS) generator. Why search endlessly for a clip of a Monty Python Gumby saying "My brain hurts!" when you can create your own?

What you do is enter the text you want spoken into the query box, then you choose the type of voice you want the words spoken in from a pulldown menu (choose from U.S. English, U.K. English, French, German, or Spanish). The site generates a WAV that you save to your local machine. I found pronunciation to be fairly straightforward; if you want a silly-sounding WAV, you'll have to do some phonetic experimentation ("my brayyn hurtz!").

PART V
SEARCHING FOR PEOPLE

19 PEOPLE SEARCHING

There are over six billion people on the planet Earth! But they don't all have Web addresses; it just feels like it. There have been phone books for decades; now many of them are available online in large searchable collections. If you're trying to get a phone number, the Internet makes it easier than ever. In some ways that's a good thing, and in some ways that's a really bad thing, so we're going to start this chapter with an admonition on privacy.

A Few Words on Privacy

In this chapter I'm going to point you toward phone books, address finders, and some mapping resources. They're very powerful tools. And because of that you need to treat them carefully. Don't violate people's privacy with these tools. If they want to be left alone, leave them alone. Don't use these tools to find phone numbers for the purpose of telemarketing—that could lead to a big ol' fine from the FCC. In other words, be sensible and treat people courteously. All right?

Now that we're all on the same privacy page, let's talk for a minute about what you'll find in this chapter. Mostly you'll find offline contact information, which is gathered from credible sources. There's some discussion of finding people via search engines in the Principle of Nicknames, which discusses the different types of information you'll find when searching for different variants of names.

The thing is, there are many people who just don't have personal Web sites. If you've got your own LiveJournal, Webcam, and you know your e-mail address better than your phone number, you might find this hard to believe, but it's true.

If someone's famous, you've got a better shot at finding information about them online. Sometimes you can just try to plug in their name as a domain name. Take for example the musician Elvis Costello. If you try to go to the domain name ElvisCostello.com, you'll be redirected to an Island Records information page about Elvis Costello. Trying to go to StephenKing.com will take you to the official Stephen King Web site. Sometimes you'll end up at an unusual or unexpected Web site. In that case try searching for the famous person's name and the word "official":

```
"Terry Pratchett" official
```

which will often bring them to the top of a search.

You also have the option of searching for someone within the context of what they're famous for, if you don't want to start your search in a general searchable subject index like Yahoo. If I wanted to search for Clark Gable, for example, I could start with the Internet Movie Database at http://www.imdb.com/. From there, search for Clark Gable and see what you can find. You might find enough relevant keywords to start a general Web search using the Principle of Onions.

> **TIP**
>
> How to find databases relevant to the famous person you want to research? Decide what they're famous as (in Clark Gable's case, as an actor), make a plural of that keyword, and search for that keyword with the word database. For Gable your Web search will look like this:
>
> ```
> actors database
> ```
>
> If this doesn't work for you, you could try different keywords related to Gable's career choice—movies, films, etc.—in conjunction with the word "database."

Finding in-depth, credible information about non-famous people would take its own book, so let's limit our searching in this chapter to basic, credible information that everyone can use as contact information. That starts with phone numbers and addresses.

General People Searching

You might think it odd that I point you to a search engine for phone number lookup, but what can I say? Google's got all kinds of specialty syntaxes that come in all kinds of handy. The one we're going to discuss here is phonebook.

Google has two syntaxes for finding phone numbers. One is rphonebook: for finding residential phone numbers, and the other is bphonebook: for finding business phone numbers. We discuss the business syntax elsewhere in the book; for this chapter we're going to stick with rphonebook. Using it is simple.

Enter "rphonebook:" and a name, a city if you wish, and a state, like so:

```
rphonebook:john doe san francisco ca
```

You don't have to include a first name or a city in your search. It can be this simple:

```
rphonebook:doe ca
```

> At this writing, unfortunately, Google's phone book search only finds American phone numbers.

TIP

Feeling a little freaked out about your phone number being available via a Google search? You can request to have it removed at http://www.google.com/help/pbremoval.html.

TIP

Non-U.S. readers, don't worry—I'll be getting to phone book resources for you in just a moment.

You can even search by area code instead of city or state name:

```
rphonebook:doe 510
```

Or, if you're feeling *really* obscure, by zip code:

```
rphonebook:doe 90210
```

That last one would be good when you have an address for someone but don't have a phone number and want to narrow down your possibilities.

Google's phone book listings come with full addresses as well as links to two different map sites for driving directions.

I find that most of the time when I need to look up a quick phone number, the Google search does just fine. But there are other phone books available. I tend to use WhitePages most often.

General Phone Books

WhitePages.com--http://www.whitepages.com

WhitePages.com opens with a simple people search—first name, last name, city/state, and zip code. The advanced search allows you to specify that the first and last names begin with a particular sequence of letters. While it's possible to get a "too many search results" error (try searching for Smith in California), generally only last name and state are required for this search.

Search results include phone number, address, and zip code—all the standard results you'll get from a Google phone book search if your search is there to be found.

Where WhitePages differs from Google is its specialty search offerings.

Reverse Phone Lookup

WhitePages.com offers two kinds of reverse phone lookup—phone number and state and phone number. With the phone number lookup, you're required to use the state and phone number. With the state phone number lookup, you're required to provide the state and phone number; area code is not required. Presumably this would lead to multiple listings, but I never saw that in the experiments I did.

TIP

Some WhitePages.com features require that you register with the site. Registration is free.

Reverse Address Lookup

Reverse address lookup is just what it sounds like: enter an address, and get the name and the phone number of the person living there. What this feature doesn't make very clear to you is that you can also enter a range of addresses on the same street, or just leave the street number blank. If you leave the street number blank and it's a small street, you can get the addresses of everyone on that street. If the street is a large one (like Pennsylvania Avenue in Washington, DC), you will get a "too many results" error. In that case you can enter a range of street numbers. If you search for 1500-1520 Pennsylvania Avenue, Washington DC, you'll get 27 listings. (You'll see that these results show mostly business addresses; reverse address lookup works for business and residential addresses.)

Area and Zip Codes

Finally, WhitePages offers several searches you can do with area and zip code. There's reverse zip and area code (enter a zip code and get its corresponding city, or enter an area code and get two lists: one of major cities in that area code and one of all cities in that area code). There's an area code and zip code finder (enter a city and state, get its area or zip codes). And there's an international calling code lookup—select a country and get its calling code.

Google provides a very simple phone number lookup, while WhitePages adds a whole 'nother set of ways to find phone numbers and addresses. But

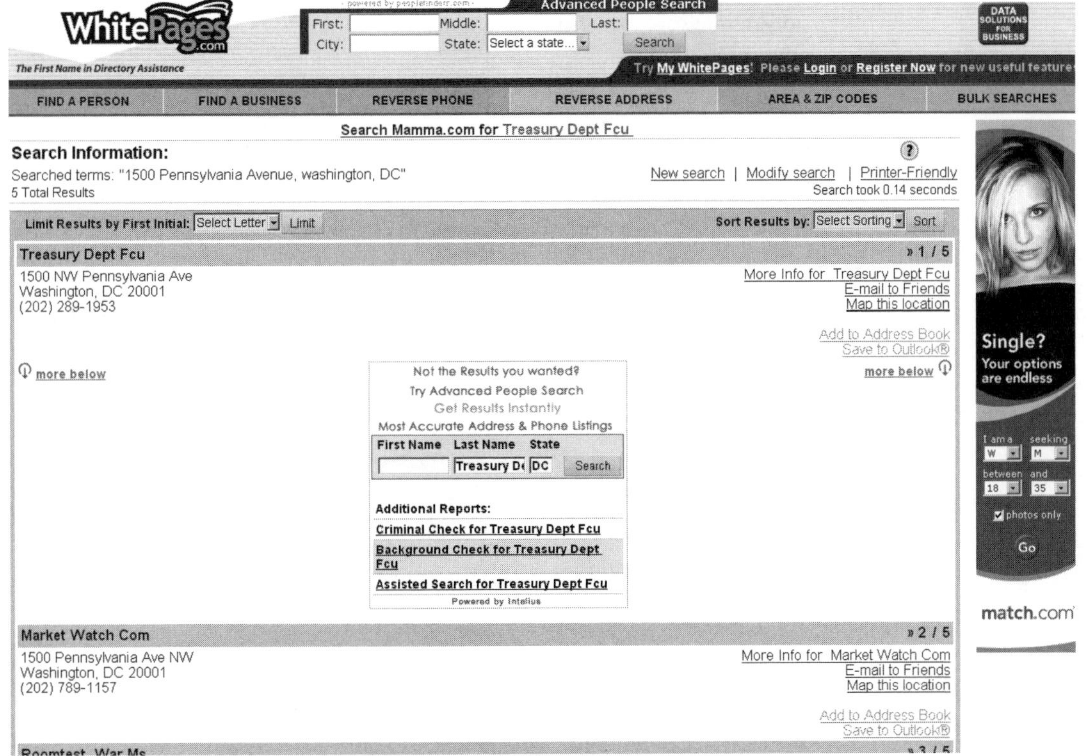

19–01

Business reverse lookup in Washington DC. (Image from http://www.whitepages.com/search/Reverse_Address?housenumber=1500&street=Pennsylvania+Avenue&city_zip=washington&state_id=DC.)

you'll notice that these tools are limited in a couple of very important ways: they often don't search institutional phone numbers, like you'd find at universities, and they're depressingly American-centric. Well, we'll fix that with a look at specialized phone books.

Specialized Phone Books

Phone lookup doesn't stop at U.S./Canada listings. There are plenty of international phone book lookups as well as other institutional and business phone book lookups. And let's not forget all the government phone numbers . . . but let's start with international listings.

International

International white and yellow page lookups often—not always, but often—have English interfaces. Even when they don't you can usually muddle through the lookup based on form clues—phone book lookups are pretty standard no matter what the country. Try these sources.

International White and Yellow Pages—http://www.wayp.com/
This site contains listings for people and businesses, but instead of hosting a phone number index on its own site it links to other listings. From the front page pick the continent in which you're interested and you'll get a listing of the countries on that continent and the available online directories for them, and notes as to whether they're white or yellow page listings. Some countries have several listings (like the United States), while some countries have only one or two listings or even none.

White Pages Global—http://www.whitepagesglobal.com/
White Pages Global doesn't have its own database either, but instead of linking directly to other sites it frames other sites' search pages within its site. In a way this is good—it means you can stay at one site and search several different phone listings. The bad thing about it is that it lists only one phone book lookup per country.

InfoBel World Listings—http://www.infobel.com/World/
InfoBel contains a variety of lookup information beyond just white and yellow pages, but what it offers depends on what country you're searching. For example, France offers yellow and white page listings, street maps, and other business information. The U.S. offers even more information, including employment and shopping lookups. Be sure to check the International category on the front page for a complete country list.

TIP

They're almost an endangered species, but public pay phones still exist! There's a directory of them available at http://www.payphone-directory.org/. Most of them are in the U.S. and Canada, but there are other countries listed, too. This site also has a gallery of pay phone pictures and several recordings related to pay phones.

Universities

Universities are not as populous as countries, but there are more of them, and man do they have phone systems. Unfortunately their listings often aren't in the phone book, or, due to the seasons of a school year, the regular white page listings don't keep up with the actual phone numbers. In that case you can use a university phone book lookup.

You can find links for university phone books on the majority of larger universities out there. Look for pointers to "phone books" or "faculty lookup" or "people search." Sometimes universities have their faculty and student lookups separated, sometimes they're together. The pointers are usually on the front page or on a "search" page. There's a nice lookup for Canadian university phone books at http://www.physics.mcmaster.ca/resources/CanUniv.html. If you just can't find the phone book from the university's Web page, try doing a Google search. For example, if you were looking for a phone book at Duke, you could search for `"phonebook" site:duke.edu`.

You thought universities were bad. Consider government and large businesses. Sometimes their phone books are even more extensive—and daunting!—than college phone books.

Large Business and Government Phone Books

When it comes to getting the phone numbers for large businesses, I've found my efforts are hit and miss. Very very very large companies—like IBM, for example—might not publish their phone numbers in order to protect their employees against junk phone calls. Very very very small companies might rely on the yellow pages to distribute their phone numbers instead of the Web.

Here's how I deal with it. If I need Joe Smith's phone number, and he works at IBM, I generally try to e-mail him first and ask him for his phone number. If I have absolutely have no other alternative I will call the main business phone number. For businesses over a certain size there's always a phone number somewhere. It may be for sales, it may be for a switchboard, or it may be a press contact. (I tend to use those last because press people tend to get grumpy when non-media folk call them, but if you are desperate, and you have no other contact options, it may be all you can do.)

Looking for 800 numbers? Try the Internet 800 number directory at http://inter800.com/.

Sometimes I'll try to search Google. For example, if I need Joe Smith's phone number, and he works at IBM, I might try:

```
joe smith phone site:ibm.com
```

(Why didn't I put Joe Smith in quotes? Because I don't know if he's listed as "Joe Smith" or "Smith, Joe.") If this search didn't work I'd follow up with "Joseph Smith."

As bad as businesses are for phone numbers, governments can be a lot worse. On the other hand, I've found I have a better chance of finding the phone number for any given government function over any given business function. There are a couple of Web sites you can refer to for phone numbers, but if you're looking for local (city or county) phone numbers, it's better to start with your local government's Web site (which we've covered earlier in the book). If you're looking for federal phone numbers . . .

> **TIP**
>
> Ever wondered what your phone number spells? Find out at PhoneSpell (http://www.phonespell.org/). You can also enter some letters and see what the corresponding phone number would be. It's interesting to note that 867-5309 spells absolutely nothing of interest.

FCIC National Contact Center—http://www.pueblo.gsa.gov/call/phone.htm

This Web site from the General Services Administration points to several different federal phone books, including Federal Government Blue Pages, phone books for members of Congress, Cabinet Agencies, and frequently requested 800 numbers. Some agencies have phone numbers on this page, but if you click on the agency name, in most cases you'll go to a page with additional phone numbers. Most of your basic government phone lookup needs will be met on this page. If you can't find it here, try FirstGov.

FirstGov—http://www.firstgov.com

FirstGov's got a "Phone" option on its main menu (left side of the screen). There you can find pointers to some of the same resources as were available at the FCIC Contact Center, with an additional link to U.S. contacts organized by agency and topic.

After this section you're probably feeling up to your eyeballs in phone numbers, so let's move on to something different: address and zip code helpers.

Address and Zip Code Helpers

In Chapter 16, "Finding Local Information on the Web," we looked at several things you could do with a zip code. But we didn't look at how zip codes could help you with making sure you have the correct address.

Zip Code Helpers

Since the zip code is administered by the post office, the first thing you want to do is visit its site at http://www.usps.gov. Here you'll find several zip-code–related tools, including zip code lookups, all zip codes for a particular city/town, all cities and towns covered by a zip code, and a zip code for a given company. There's also a list of zip code FAQs. Refer back to Chapter 16 for several other cool things you can do with an address.

Driving Directions

Do you know where you're going? Know how to get there? Say you don't. There are several options on the Web to give you driving directions; I really like MapQuest (http://www.mapquest.com).

The front page asks you to provide an address to see a map. (You don't have to provide the zip code if you don't know it.) Once you've done that, you'll have the option of getting a more detailed version of the map or getting driving directions to that address. (If you don't know exactly where you'll be coming from, you can provide just a city and state.)

20 Genealogy Research Online

When I first got on the Internet back in nineteen-coughity-cough, the idea that the Internet could be used for genealogy was a new one on me. I knew there were interest groups for genealogy, and I knew there was a small body of information out there. But the largest holders of genealogy data—birth and death certificates, census, and so on—are usually government institutions, and they hadn't quite gotten that far in their discovery of the Internet.

Fast-forward to 2004. If you're a genealogy researcher, now is a wonderful time to be alive. Not only is more and more source information becoming available, but even secondary sources of genealogy data—like obituary collections—are being archived.

An overview of all genealogy data online would—literally—require a book. (A big book.) So instead we're going to take a bird's eye view, looking at source material: birth and death records, and census records; and secondary materials: service records, obituary collections, and old newspapers. This is not material you can usually find using Google, but searching Google can be an important part of genealogy research, so we'll cover that as well. Finally, we'll take a look at a pay service that has large aggregates of genealogy-related data, if you have some money. Throughout this chapter I'll be scattering some tips of other places you might want to look for genealogy information. And may all your searches be fruitful, and all your ancestors brilliant and wise.

Source Material

When I say source material, I mean material that can be authenticated by a record-keeping entity—usually the government, but sometimes a church in the case of some marriage certificates. Source material includes birth certificates, marriage certificates, death certificates, census data, and military service records.

You can usually find birth and death certificate information, or at least pointers to information. The marriage certificates, census data, and military service records are more iffy and vary by state. Some data is not available online simply because it isn't yet available publicly; census records as well as birth and death records are not released to the public until several decades after they're established. So unless you're reading this in the 2020s, don't think you're going to go online and find the 1950 census.

We'll start with what you'll find in a minute, but let's start with one meta-site that's administered by the Church of Jesus Christ of Latter-Day Saints: FamilySearch.org.

Meta-Site for Source Material

FamilySearch—http://www.familysearch.org

You do not have to be a member of the LDS either to search this site or to have ancestors listed in it. Their search page is an "all resources" search that includes birth and death records, census data, contributed data, etc.

The only information you *must* enter in this search is the first and last names of the person you're looking for. If you can, however, enter at least the name of the spouse or any information about the parents that you know. If you don't know any of that information, at least enter the country and state of the person for whom you're searching—that will narrow down your results a lot. (If you think there are a lot of John Smiths around now, just consider how many there have been across history!) I recommend against checking the "use exact spelling" box—errors get made in transcription. Even John Smith can be spelled different ways.

Search results will be divided into several categories: census results (only the 1880 census), the International Genealogical Index, and the Social Security Death Index. Different data will give you different levels of information. You won't be able to see original copies of the records, though some are available if you go to Ancestry.com (more about Ancestry a little later in the chapter).

One thing you're going to find as you do your genealogy research is that you'll get a lot of information and sometimes it can be hard to keep track of. FamilySearch offers a bunch of data templates for you at http://www.familysearch.org/Eng/Search/RG/frameset_rhelps.asp. These templates include blank census data sheets that you can use to fill out information on your ancestors, genealogy terms in different languages, pointers to a variety of data types, etc.

Once you've done your overview on FamilySearch, you can move on to more specific data, starting with birth records.

Since the data search does include contributed data, there's every possibility that some of the data has errors in it. I found one of my great-great-great-grandfathers listed in two different family trees with death dates over a year apart. So be a little cautious with the data in the International Genealogical Index part of the search results.

Birth Records

Birth records are kept both by state Web sites and local historical societies. There are two ways to start looking for them: via a Google search or via a couple of clearinghouse guides. A Google search is simple enough: search for the state name in which you're interested and the phrase "birth records":

```
california "birth records"
```

You'll see that there are about ten billion pages offering to give you clearinghouse data on births in California. Unfortunately a lot of them are sites that just point you toward the variety of databases available at Ancestry.com, which won't do you a lot of good if you don't have a membership. Look for official state sites (which often have URLs ending in .us or .gov), which (sometimes) have the information available in an online index or (always) have information on what you need to do to order a copy of a birth/death certificate.

Often states have their historic vital records and their current vital records separated; try searching for the word "genealogy," the phrase "state library," and then the name of the state in which you're interested:

TIP

If you just want information on where to go offline for records, check the National Center for Health Statistics. They have a list of states and how to get vital records for each: http://www.cdc.gov/nchs/howto/w2w/w2welcom.htm. Cyndi's List, one of the oldest and best genealogy sites on the Web, also offers a vital record clearinghouse listing and links to relevant state sites at http://www.cyndislist.com/usvital.htm.


```
genealogy "state library" oklahoma
```

While this won't always give you pointers to data, it can give you information on how to find very local sites that do contain data, such as genealogy groups dedicated to particular counties. If the search is giving you a lot of noise, try narrowing it down by searching for the state's domain code as the site instead of the state name:

```
genealogy "state library" site:ok.us
```

This'll get you really narrow results for all state vital records.

Birth records are chockablock with great information—parent names, parent birthplaces, and parent occupations—but death certificates can be very useful, too. And often there's more to be found.

Death Records

What do I *mean*, death records can be very useful? Often death records contain cause of death (useful if you're trying to get a handle on your family medical history), name of parents, last place of residence, and other basic person data. And in addition to death records, you can also find death information in obituary data as well as cemetery records.

Using the tricks above for birth records, you can often find death records as well. What you may not find are cemetery and obituary records. So I will help you out.

Obituary Records

Obituaries are by no means error-proof, but the services I'm going to show you here come directly from newspapers. That means there's less chance for errors in transcription and a better chance for completeness. What actually appears in an obituary is up to the one who places it—you'll see everything from just brief information on birth and death to complete histories and genealogical information.

ObitsArchive—http://www.obitsarchive.com/

ObitsArchive is brought to you by Newslibrary, a newspaper archive service. They've stripped out the obituaries and put them into this online database. You have a few different ways to search here. You can narrow down your search by region, by keyword, by name, or by year span. Since most of the time you're looking for one person in particular, I don't see why you'd want to search for anything but name and possibly year span (year span comes in handy when you're trying to narrow down the results for a common name). Searching is free but to review the full obituaries you'll need to subscribe to the service; it costs $3.50 to retrieve a single article but you can buy a "pass" for 30 days' worth of access to the archives for $14.95, or 90 days' worth of access for $29.95.

ObitMessenger—https://www.legacy.com/ObitMessenger/Default.asp

Like ObitsArchive, ObitMessenger pulls its obituary information from participating newspapers. Unlike ObitsArchive, ObitMessenger allows you to specify keywords and then receive e-mail when an obituary mentions your keyword. If you have a genealogical interest that might be counted as obscure—a very unusual last name, a small town, etc.—this e-mail service might be useful. Just be careful not to use broad keywords or you could get overwhelmed with e-mail!

Also like ObitsArchive, ObitMessenger is a pay service. In this case the cost depends on whether you're searching a single newspaper for keywords, all newspapers for keywords, or all newspapers for a last name. (Searching all newspapers for keywords is the most expensive option, costing $199 a year with a free 30-day trial.) Be sure to check the participating newspaper list before you sign up for this service! There's no point in signing up if there are no newspapers that would have obituaries in which you're interested.

Cemetery Records

Unlike death records, which are required, and obituaries, which are easily archived when published, cemetery records are iffy. If you're looking for an ancestor from very long ago, you may find that their cemetery is lost, or their gravestone irrevocably broken. Cemetery records can be useful when they have more information than a birth or death date, and sometimes they can give additional family clues, but don't worry if you can't find an ancestor's grave site. On the other hand, these Web sites may help you.

Find A Grave—http://www.findagrave.com/

When I first became aware of Find A Grave, it was for famous people's graves. And it still is—you can search for thousands of people here. What's available at each listing varies, but most famous people have a brief biography, a picture of their gravesite (if they have one), and sometimes other pictures from their lives. Site visitors also have the option to leave virtual flowers and notes, and those are available to be read as well.

Find A Grave also allows you to search for less-famous people, by name, birth or death year, and the state in which their cemetery is located. These listings are much less detailed than the listings of famous folks. However, they do include basic information such as grave location and transcription, with the option to add pictures or virtual memorials.

Interment.net—http://www.interment.net/

Interment.net is a worldwide directory of cemetery transcriptions. It contains over 3 million records from over 7800 cemeteries. You have the option on this site to either browse the records by region or search by keyword (name). When you search by keyword, you won't get single entries but rather transcriptions of the cemeteries where the name is found.

Cemetery Junction—http://www.CemeteryJunction.com

As you might be realizing, cemetery transcription is a very common thing for genealogists. This site links to over 42,000 U.S. cemetery transcriptions, over 2,000 Canadian cemetery transcriptions, and Australian and Family cemetery transcriptions as well.

Veteran's Affairs Cemetery Listings—http://www.cem.va.gov

If you have an ancestor who was a solider and who is buried in a veteran's cemetery, this is the site for you. Established and published by the U.S. government, the Veteran's Affairs Cemetery Listings allow you to search by first and last name, either exact spelling or "begins with." Search results include the veteran's service dates (if known), date of death, date of interment, location in cemetery, and location of the cemetery.

Ellis Island & Immigration Records—Ellis Island (http://www.ellisisland.org) has a great collection of source material—immigration records of people coming to the United States through Ellis Island. I've found that I had to do a lot of guessing about how names might be spelled when using this site, but if you can get through that, you can find out when your ancestor came over, who was with them—even what ship they came on!

Census Data

The depth of census data varies depending on what year the census was taken. Some very early census have little information, while the most recently released census have a lot. And of course sometimes there are town- and state-level census as well as federal census. Census are scattered all over the Web, so I'm going to give you three pointers to roundup sites.

Census Finder—http://www.censusfinder.com/

Census Finder contains over 25,000 links to census online, both from the U.S. and from all over the world. Some of the sites here are free databases, while other ones are paid.

Census Links—http://censuslinks.com/

Census Links contains news and links to census all over the world. It's set up like a searchable subject index with both links to census and general census sites.

Census Online Links—http://www.census-online.com/links/

This site concentrates on U.S. and Canadian census links, with a small selection of links to other countries. Overall there are over 41,000 census links on this site.

Great "Roundup Sites" for Genealogy Information

As the Internet has become more and more mainstream, more and more people are using it to exchange information about genealogy and establish genealogy information sites. If I tried to cover every type of genealogy information available, this book would be about 2,000 pages long. But thanks to the Principle of the Reinvented Wheel, I don't have to do that. Instead I can point you to some great roundup sites.

Ancestry.com--http://www.ancestry.com

I have tried not to cite too many pay sites in this book, but Ancestry has such a wealth of information that I feel like I must include it here.

Ancestry.com has fifteen sets of census, many city directories, passenger rolls, historical newspapers, and lots, lots more. Some of its information is free (just searching is free), while some of it requires a subscription fee. Subscriptions vary on the amount of access, from $9.95 for a single search of the people finder database to $199.95 for the "U.S. Premier Collection."

Cyndi's List--http://www.cyndislist.com/

I've mentioned Cyndi's List earlier, but I like it so much I'm going to mention it again. This site has almost a quarter-million links devoted to genealogy in over 150 categories, from Acadian and Cajun & Creole to Writing Your Family's History. The categories are divided into subcategories, and the site is frequently updated.

RootsWeb--http://www.rootsweb.com/

While Cyndi's List is more of a single-person effort, RootsWeb is run by a huge community of people. It contains information on millions of names contributed by literally tens of thousands of online genealogists. Among the databases here are the RootsWeb Surname List, U. S. Town/County Database, and World-Connect Project (family trees.) RootsWeb is funded by Ancestry.com, but information access here is free (of course, there are not as many things available here as there are at Ancestry.com).

Genealogy at About.com--http://genealogy.about.com/

If you want to keep up with what new resources are available and get pointers to articles on how to actually use all this great genealogy information, check out

Genealogy at About.com. You'll find links to resources, articles, and how-to's at this site.

If you like the process of Internet research—the deliberate searches, the organization of information, the satisfaction of assembling various bits of data into a usable whole—you'll enjoy genealogy. And thanks to the Internet's ever-expanding variety of genealogy resources, the two hobbies overlap a lot. See if you can spot one of your great-great-great-grandparents in cyberspace!

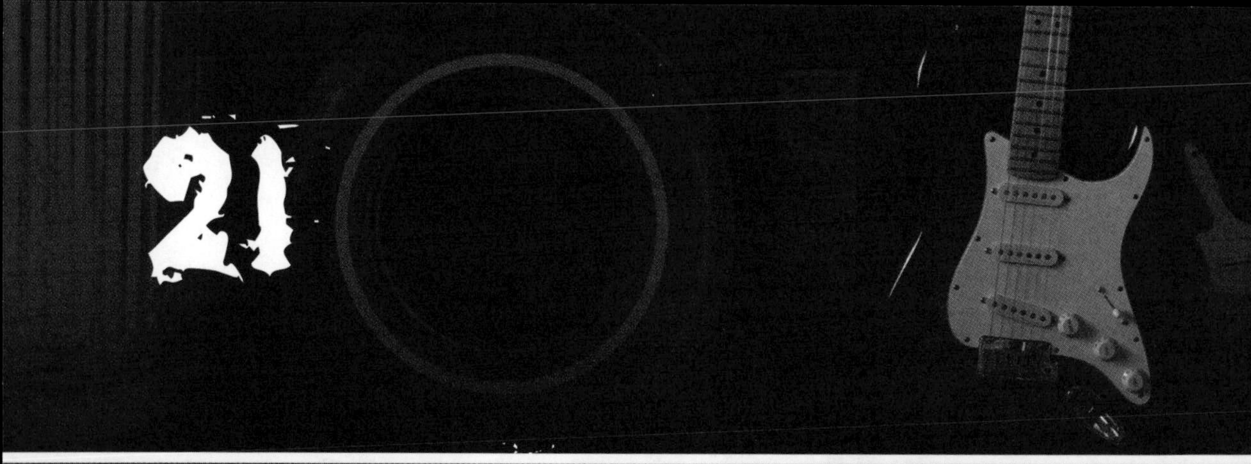

21 Ready Reference

Much of this book deals with extensive research projects—tasks that might take several search sessions and a lot of work. But equally valid, and even more useful for day-to-day searching tasks, are those Internet searches that are for quick tasks—dictionary definitions, encyclopedia entries, almanac listings, and other ready-reference–type services.

As you might imagine, the Internet is as good for that as it is for the more complicated searching—there are several Web sites devoted to ready reference information. What you may not know, however, is that search engines themselves have some ready-reference tools. We'll start with those.

Search Engine Tools for Ready Reference

> **TIP**
>
> If you have a hard time remembering all of Google's various search offerings, try Soople (http://www.soople.com). It offers dozens of different interfaces to Google's search tools; there's a whole page just for the calculator!

Google's got a couple of ready-reference tools. The first is a calculator. It works very simply: enter your calculation and Google will spit out the results. For example, you might enter, without quotes, `one billion divided by fifty-nine`. (Don't use caps when you're using this feature, either; Google doesn't like that.) Google will include the result at the top of the regular search results (in this case, 16,94,152.5). In addition to calculator functions, the Google calculator also does conversions (miles to inches, ounces to quarts, etc.).

Google's got a couple of different dictionaries. The first one you can use as you search. Enter a search term. At the top of the results you'll see a blue bar containing "Searched the web for" and then your search words. If the dictionary Google uses contains the words, they'll be clickable, and you can click on them and get a dictionary definition. If you're using a phrase that is recognizable by the dictionary ("per se," for example), then the whole phrase will be clickable as a definition. Otherwise individual words will be clickable.

Google also has a "define" syntax. Enter `define:keyword`. When you do this you won't get regular search results or a blue bar at the top of the results page; instead you'll get definitions pulled from all over the Internet. Because definition results are pulled from all over the Web, results are sometimes kind of strange, but there's usually something that provides you with a definition.

Unfortunately, sometimes the results are confusing enough that you realize it's best to restrict your searches to predefined sets of data and not to use search engines.

Don't forget Yahoo! Remember that in Chapter 1, "Search Engines," I mentioned Yahoo's shortcuts. Some of them, including a currency converter, dictionary and encyclopedia lookups, and a zip code lookup, make excellent ready-reference tools. Get a list of search shortcuts and instructions for using them at http://help.yahoo.com/help/us/ysearch/tips/tips-01.html.

Roundup Tools

There are literally thousands of reference-type Web sites online—dictionaries, almanacs, encyclopedias, and more. Because of this you'll get a lot of use out of a site that aggregates a bunch of the best ones together into a reference desk. Here are three I recommend.

RefDesk--http://www.refdesk.com/

RefDesk has been around for ages, and it's still great. It contains over 20,000 links. When you visit the front page you may find yourself a bit overwhelmed. Have no fear; it's simple. On the left you'll see some search boxes for popular search tools (like Google) and links to site information and "Quick Find" for specific information types like jobs, economic facts, and obituaries. In the middle you'll see daily features (x-of-the-day) as well as links to current event resources and, at the bottom of the page, RefDesk subject categories. Finally, on the right you'll see lots of news links, "help and advice" links, and pointers to reference resources in popular categories like almanacs, biographies, etc.

ReferenceDesk--http://www.referencedesk.org/

ReferenceDesk is a lot less cluttered than RefDesk, but it doesn't have all that cool stuff on the front page either! The front page is laid out more like a searchable subject index, with categories like Almanacs, Law and Legal, Quick Searches, and Biographies. On the left and right side of the category list, you'll see a variety of link lists, including Quick Useful Links, Today in History, and even television listings.

LibrarySpot--http://www.libraryspot.com/

LibrarySpot is one of the 'Spot family of sites, and there's plenty of good stuff here. This site is not so much about ready reference as it is about library-type information. Because of that you'll find some unusual features here, including asked questions, trivia, library listings, and a huge number of lists (top 100 movies, 2004 college rankings, etc.). Be sure to check out the pulldown menus at the top of the page, which will direct you to a number of reference tools as well as to library news, reference information, and more.

When you need a variety of information at one time, or you're not quite sure what you need, these all-in-one sites are great. They point you to a ton of information at once, and for the most part they're fast-loading and don't clutter your surfing with pop-ups or a lot of unnecessary graphics. On the other hand, the volume of information can be a little *too* much if you know what you want—a definition, a biography, an encyclopedia entry—and you don't want to wade through thousands of nonuseful links.

Dictionaries

OneLook--http://www.onelook.com/

OneLook dictionary encompasses over six million words in over 950 dictionaries, which you can search either by definition or by "reverse lookup," which allows you to put in a definition and get possible words that fit that definition. There's also a "Word of the Day" if you're looking to expand your vocabulary.

Your Dictionary--http://www.yourdictionary.com/

Your Dictionary links to over 280 language dictionaries, from Abenaki to Zulu. There's also a quick dictionary lookup on the front page (if you're just interested in English), a "Word of the Day," courses in grammar for a number of languages, a huge number of glossaries, what's referred to as "'Nyms and Such" (rhyming dictionaries, thesauri, etc.), and even more. If you're just a plain word nut like I am, you'll find this site a pleasure to wander around.

VoyCabulary--http://www.voycabulary.com

VoyCabulary is a site to use when you're trying to read a page and most of the words are completely beyond you. Instead of entering a word to look up, you give the URL of a Web page. VoyCabulary then processes that entire page and presents it to you with all of the words clickable. (Obviously, words that are part of graphics are not clickable, as VoyCabulary can't recognize those as words.) Click on a word, and a new page will open up with the definition of that word. If the word is not in the dictionary, then alternate possible words will be recommended.

Of course, reference is about more than just dictionaries. Once you know what the word is, you may want more in-depth pointers to its meanings. That's where encyclopedias can come in handy.

Encyclopedias

Encyclopedias were, early in the days of the Web, all the rage. There are not as many of the general encyclopedias online now, and many of those available cost money. But there are still some fairly good free versions available.

Britannica--http://www.britannica.com/

The Encyclopedia Britannica site is not your grandfather's 35-volume, drop-it-on-your-toe-and-deeply-regret-it encyclopedia. You can search many different kinds of information here (encyclopedia information, Web sites, multimedia, and so on). The snag is that there's not a whole lot of encyclopedia content that's free. If you search for something, you'll get an excerpt of the first part of the encyclopedia article, but not more than that. If you don't mind shelling out some money, subscriptions to give you complete encyclopedia access are $9.95 a month or $60 a year. Free trials are available.

Encyclopedia.com--http://www.encyclopedia.com/

Encyclopedia.com is a service of eLibrary, which in turn is a pay service. Unlike Encyclopedia Britannica, however, you can get the full text of encyclopedia articles from this site; they're just fairly short articles. From the front page you can view some "Today in History" information, browse the encyclopedia alphabetically, or search by keyword. Articles as I mentioned are fairly short, with no multimedia or additional information. Each article also has recommended resources from the eLibrary online database, which does cost money to access.

TIP

Want to try an encyclopedia that's completely free and has extensive articles? There's one snag, though: it's pretty old. Almost a hundred years old, in fact. The LovetoKnow Free Online Encyclopedia, at http://www.1911encyclopedia.org/ is based on the 11th edition of the *Encyclopedia Britannica*, which was first published in 1911. You can browse this site alphabetically or search it by keyword (the searching is a little awkward since it's administered by Google). For fun, search this encyclopedia for contemporaries of the time. Thomas Edison, for example, is noted here as having been made a chevalier of the Legion of Honor by the French government in 1878, and for his development of "quadruplex and sextuplex transmission" in telegraphy. Generally not stuff you're going to see in a twentieth-century encyclopedia. On the other hand, you can't research anybody from within the last hundred years or so in this encyclopedia. Keep it to (very) historical people and (very) historical events only.

TIP

Perhaps the encyclopedias listed above are too general for you. Perhaps you would like an encyclopedia of cheese or an encyclopedia of bowling. Sometimes you can find specialty encyclopedias simply by searching a full-text search engine for a keyword and the word "encyclopedia":

```
cheese encyclopedia
```

or, if that doesn't work, try searching for the keyword in the title and the word "encyclopedia":

```
intitle:cheese encyclopedia
```

Be sure to use a fairly common word when you're trying this technique. You're probably not going to find an encyclopedia of Especially Runny Brie (though it's the Internet, so who knows?).

Almanacs

Don't give almanacs a bad rap. You may remember riffling through them when you were a kid, seeing the weather predictions for the upcoming year and all the old-timey "folk wisdom" about what you should take for a stomachache and when you should plant pumpkins under the full moon. But almanacs are much more than that; they contain lots of snippets of useful information about people, places, and things. And there are plenty of them available online.

The Old Farmer's Almanac--http://www.almanac.com/index.php

This is one of my favorites. The Old Farmer's Almanac starts off with information about the day in history and other topical information on the front page, while the tab at the top divides other site information into several categories, including Gardening, Astronomy, and Weather. Be sure to check the site map for an overview of all the things that are available here.

InfoPlease Almanacs--http://www.infoplease.com/almanacs.html

InfoPlease is a "roundup reference" site, like RefDesk, and it's got a nice almanac page. Almanac information is divided into categories, like Sports, Biography, and Government. There's several years' worth of information here—lists of celebrities who passed away over the last several years, the final NFL standings back to the late 90s, and so on (sometimes information like that is considered very transient online, so it's good to find it here in such a useful format).

More Ready Reference

The previous resources, while useful, are just scratching the surface of what's considered reference. And you and I might have entirely different needs. I might want a bunch of atlases for my ready reference shelf, while you might need a rhyming dictionary. Because of this, some of the most diverse parts of the Yahoo Directory and Open Directory project are at http://dir.yahoo.com/Reference/ and http://www.dmoz.org/Reference/, respectively. Here you'll find a huge variety of reference information, including maps, flags, books, an archive, a bibliography, and lots, lots more.

The Internet is just as good for quick-hit snippet searching as it is for the more complicated, in-depth searching. You just have to know where the good reference sites are.

PART VI
CONSUMER SEARCHING

22 Consumer Help

I know you know that one can do all kinds of shopping online. But what about when you're trying to decide what to buy, or trying to decide what to do when you've bought a clinker, or when you've been ripped off by a business? The Internet has a lot of product information you may not have considered—recalls, opinions, complaints, and even product manuals. Let's start with something basic: Where do you go when you decide you want to buy something?

Finding Product Information

Sometimes I'll decide I want to make a purchase but I don't have any strong opinions on what exactly to purchase. For example, I might be in the market for a digital camera. I have no strong opinions about *which* digital camera I want to use. So I first wander over to Amazon.com.

Yup, Amazon.com. If Amazon carries the thing I'm interested in buying, even if I have no intention of buying it at Amazon, I will go there first. Why? Because everybody goes there. Which means everybody posts opinions there. Which means I can get plenty of reviews for a product before I decide to get serious about buying something.

I wander over to the Electronics section and look at cameras. I list cameras by their bestselling status. You'll note that Amazon product listings also include the average ratings for each product.

When I see something I'm interested in, I view the product page, paying close attention to the following things:

- The full name of the product ("Hurrah WidgetZoom 12MP Digital Camera"). This'll come in handy in a moment.
- The Amazon Review, which is a product review done by an Amazon-approved reviewer. They're not always available, but when they're available they're usually very good.
- The user reviews. These vary a lot in quality. The best ones list definitive pros and cons for products, give thorough explanations for why the reviewer did and didn't like something, and avoid sweeping generalizations ("best product ever") or irrelevant statements ("All WoWidget products are terrible"). I generally give less credibility to anonymous reviews, and to the reviews that are written in all caps or with terrible spelling and grammar.
- The product manual. If I am really serious about buying something and I intend to do a lot of research before spending my hard-earned moolah, I'll download product manuals from Amazon (when they're available) and skim through them.

After a fair amount of rummaging around at Amazon, I usually have some products I want to get more information on. I'll take the full product names and go into a Web search.

Web Searching for Products

Start by plugging the entire product name into a Google search. For example, `"Sony DSC-F828 8MP Digital Camera with 7x Optical Zoom"`. When you run this search, check and see if all the results you get back are from online stores. If they are, your product name is too specific. Try shortening it to incorporate a specific model name, then add the keyword "review":

```
"Sony DSC-F828" review
```

Unless the product is brand new, a search like this will bring you lots of results from all over the Web. I'll go through these and add them to my consideration. Finally I'll run just a search on the model in Google Groups:

```
"Sony DSC-F828"
```

The reason I search in Google and in Google Groups is because of Google Groups' threads. People have discussions on Google Groups. If someone doesn't like the "Sony DSC-F828," there's going to be a discussion about it. Also, there's discussion over time. You might find that Widget A got terrible reviews when it was first released, but then Widget Co did an upgrade to it and Widget A2 is getting raves.

Getting Other People's Opinions

Another thing I do in the course of my shopping, as I've noted, is read other people's opinions. A well-written, thoughtful opinion can really sway me toward one

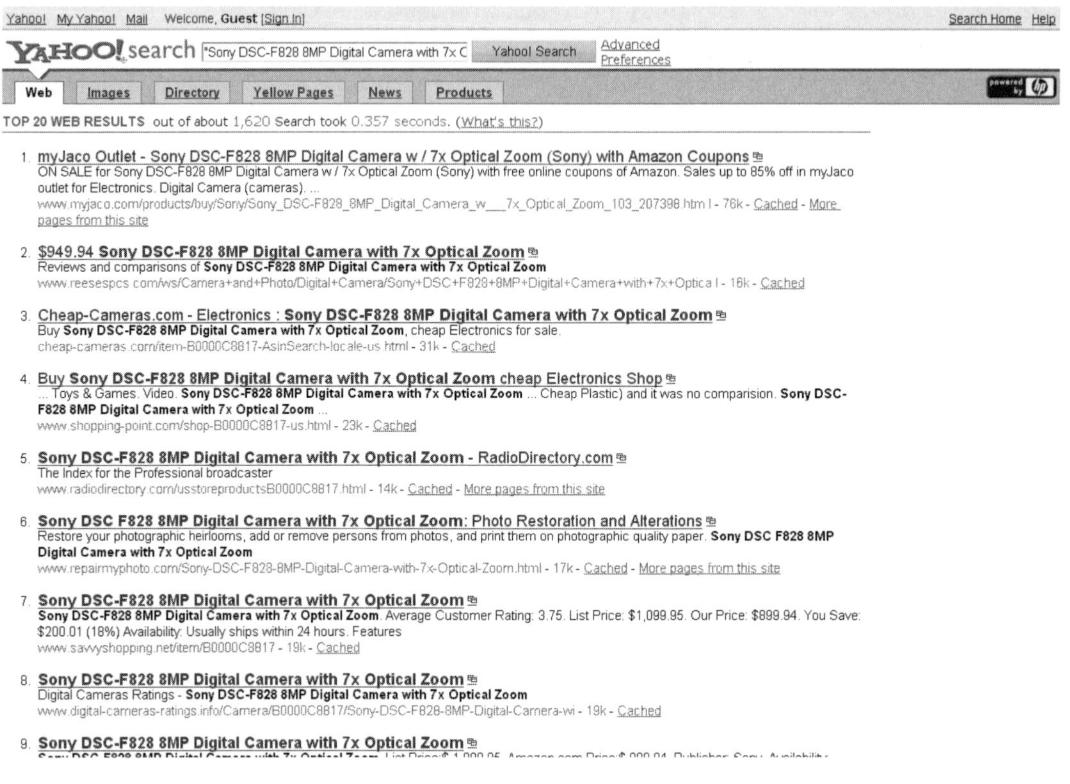

22–01

Searching for entire product name gives very precise results, usually product catalogs. (Image from http://search.yahoo.com/search?fr=fp-pull-web-t&p=%22Sony+DSC-F828+8MP+Digital+Camera+with+7x+Optical+Zoom%22.)

brand or another. Amazon is a great place to look, but there are other places on the Web that are entirely devoted to opinions. If a Google search for opinions doesn't move you one way or the other, try these sites.

Epinions--http://www.epinions.com

There are several nice things about Epinions: they've been around a long time so have built up a considerable database; they cover a wide variety of items; their reviews tend overall to be thoughtful, articulate, and detailed; and, if you want to buy something that's mentioned, it takes only a moment to hop over to one of the stores they link to and buy it.

From the front page of the site, you can choose to browse by category or search. When searching you can do a full-site keyword search or search by keyword within categories. Results include the name and picture of the product, the average rating (from 1 to 5 stars), the number of reviews (not all items have reviews), and the lowest price found for the item.

If you're not interested in searching and want more browsing, Epinions has a small selection of "top ten lists" and listings of new products added to the site. I love to browse around Epinions when I'm in the market for a new product but I don't know the brand or model I'm interested in.

Ratings.Net—http://www.ratings.net/

Epinions is more about products you can just go out and buy. And that's cool. That's their niche. Ratings.net seems different in that it will rate a much broader range of items. For example, you can rate Prozac. Yes, the drug. Ratings.net doesn't seem to have the sheer breadth that Epinions has, but their pool of potentially reviewable items seems larger. You can, like Epinions, browse by category or search by keyword.

Eventually you decide what you want and how you want to purchase it, be it through eBay, Yahoo Shopping, Amazon, or something else. Once you've done that I hope you have no problems with your purchase and that you and it live happily ever after. Unfortunately that rarely happens, so let's talk about consumer protection, whether it's local, statewide, or around the Internet.

What About Retailers? If products have their own review sites, then you'd expect online retailers to be reviewed, too, wouldn't you? And you'd be right. Check out Resellerratings.com for user-submitted reviews of over 5,000 merchants. Yahoo Shopping (http://shopping.yahoo.com) also offers user-submitted reviews of its merchants.

Consumer Protection

Compared to five years ago, there are good things and bad things about shopping on the Internet today. One good thing is that there is a wide variety of stores available. Another good thing is that PayPal and other online payment services make it easier to buy things online. A bad thing is that there's more fraud—at least in volume if not percentage of transactions—at online auction sites. Another bad thing is that "phishing" e-mail scams, where spam e-mail tries to persuade you to give up your credit card, PayPal, or other financially related information, are rampant. If you're going to do any kind of shopping online, it'll behoove you to keep your eyes open and remain aware of scams and other things that might affect you.

TIP

Where you decide to buy a product is up to you, whether you want to use eBay, Amazon, or one of the thousands of smaller shops on the Internet. If you want to get the most bang for your buck, consider using one of the many shopping comparison engines available. These sites provide you with information on prices for the items you're shopping for, helping you track down the lowest prices available online. There's BizRate at http://shop.bizrate.com/, Shopping.com at http://www.shopping.com/, MySimon at http://www.mysimon.com/, and lots more. While price is important when you're shopping, bear in mind there are other factors as well. If you find a place that ships promptly, always gets your order right, and has great customer service, who cares if it's a few dollars more?

Local

There's not much local information on scams that might be taking place in your area, but you can make your own with a good Google News search. Try this in Google News:

```
"attorney general" [state name] (scam | fraud)
```

So if you live in Georgia try `"attorney general" Georgia (scam | fraud)`. If you live in a city large enough, you could substitute a city name for a state name (Atlanta for Georgia). If you're not getting enough results, try swapping `(warning | warns | warned)` for `"attorney general"`. Thus:

```
(warning | warns | warned) [state name] (scam | fraud)
```

You can also add in a topical word if you have an idea of what you're looking for. For example, every time North Carolina has a significant hurricane there are local stories and warnings about home repair scams or tree removal scams. If you were looking for stories like that, add the word "hurricane" or "tree."

State resources are also important. In all the states I know about, fraud and similar information is handled by the attorney general.

State Resources

To find information on fraud and scam protection, first go to your state's home page. (Remember that you can get to pretty much any state home page by opening http://www.state.xx.us, where xx is the postal code of the state you want.) We'll do South Dakota as an example. So go to http://www.state.sd.us. There's no immediate information on the front page of the site, so use the search function to search for "scam." (You can also search for "fraud," but I find that search brings too many results for things like welfare fraud and fraud legal issues.) You'll find within the first few results a link to the AG, which takes you to consumer protection information.

Exactly how much information is available on a state site at any given time varies. There may be tip sheets to avoid more "routine" fraud and ripoff issues. There may be a seasonal press release about charity scams. It'll vary a lot over time. If you hear about a scam on your local news, this is a good place to follow up and see if it's statewide. (Sometimes your local news source will also link to state government information, so check there, too.)

Webwide Resources

Sometimes the frauds and scams that you encounter aren't confined to your local area. The Internet, unfortunately, is full of scams and ripoffs. You've probably heard of phishing (when you get a fake e-mail that's supposed to be from a legitimate company, but it's just a setup to try to get your financial information) and auction scams. While there are many, many legitimate merchants on the

Internet, there are tons of scammers as well. Here are a few things you can do to protect yourself.

1. Never ever ever ever ever ever ever ever ever give your PIN number, credit card number, or other personal finance-related information via e-mail.
2. If you get an e-mail claiming that your account has been suspended, or you need to install a software update (that comes in an attachment), *throw it away*. If you're very concerned that the alert you've gotten is real, either forward it to the company it claims to be from and ask or (better yet) call them and ask.
3. Realize that nobody legitimate from Nigeria is ever going to contact you asking for your help in laundering several million dollars.
4. Realize that nobody legitimate from Switzerland is ever going to randomly e-mail you with the news that you've won a sweepstakes.
5. When it comes to online auctions, especially online auctions for expensive items (personal electronics, collectables, etc.), approach them with suspicion. If items are unusually inexpensive, be suspicious. It may be that everything's fine, but if it is you won't be hurt by checking out the seller thoroughly—check their seller feedback, use an escrow service, etc. If everything checks out but you still feel funny, search for the seller's alias on Google. That's not foolproof (aliases can be common, and they can be changed), but you might find something you wouldn't have seen otherwise.

Of course there are plenty of online resources that'll help you in your quest to avoid getting ripped off.

BBB Database—http://www.bbb.org/

If there's a business you want to check out or just something that doesn't feel right, use the "check out a company" link at the Better Business Bureau. This database is not complete—that is, it doesn't list every business in the United States—but it lists plenty.

You can search in three ways: phone number, Web site address, or by name, city, and state. An advanced search allows you to also limit your search to members only as well as to search by business category keywords. You won't get full reports of what people complained about, but you'll get indications of whether there have been any complaints lodged against that business and whether they responded or not. BBB sites are regional; some of them report how many complaints have been lodged against a site, while some of them just report whether a business has a satisfactory or unsatisfactory record.

FTC—Bureau of Consumer Protection—http://www.ftc.gov/ftc/consumer.htm

This site is a directory of consumer protection publications covering both online and offline issues. Topics listed on the front page include Credit, Travel, and Telemarketing. Click on a topic and you'll get a list of publications available in text or PDF. Some are even available in audio. When I clicked on Telemarketing I got links to publications like "Ditch the Pitch: Hanging Up on Telephone Hucksters," and "When Yellow Pages Invoices Are Bogus." Not all material is available in all formats, but it looked to me like all of it was available in at least text. You can also file a complaint from this site.

Consumer.gov—http://www.consumer.gov/

Consumer.gov is the United States portal on consumer issues—that's consumer issues in general, and not necessarily computer protection issues. You can find out about signing up for the national do-not-call list here. You can check out the topics at the top of the page, which include Food, Health, and Children. And in the middle of the front page you can see the latest news that affects consumers—a lot of it appears to be fraud-related. If you just want to keep an eye on the government's comments about consumer affairs, this is a good, single page to monitor.

Scam Warnings from the RCMP—
http://www.rcmp-grc.gc.ca/scams/cfraud_e.htm

If you don't want the U.S., there's always Canada. Slightly to the north we can take in the scam and fraud warnings from the Royal Canadian Mounted Police. Here you'll find information about some scams that sound familiar (phony job scams, house repair scams) and some that probably don't (Canadian Gemstone Scams?).

Sometimes you'll have a perfectly fine transaction, only to find out later that the product you purchased had some kind of problem.

Recall Information

Before I show you a few places where you can look up recall information, bear one thing in mind: Just because a product is recalled doesn't mean it's necessarily bad. I'm not allergic to peanuts or to eggs. Therefore, a product that has been recalled because it contains undeclared peanuts or eggs is not hazardous to me. When you read that a product has been recalled, do not assume, especially in the case of food, that the recall means that product is bad.

Consumer Product Safety Commission Product Recalls--http://www.cpsc.gov/cpscpub/prerel/prerel.html

This is the central place for recall information online. There are several ways to go through this information. Product recalls are listed by month, company, and type. Categories include Appliances, Clothing, and Sports Products. Click on a category and you'll get a list of items in that category, backwards by date. Unfortunately there's no date on the items, but if you want to get an ongoing list of the recalls this site does offer an RSS feed. Click on the item and you'll get a full press release including a description of the item, the reason for the recall, and a summary of any problems that consumers have had with the item thus far.

The CPSC does not oversee all products, and as such has a list of links to government agencies that do regulate those products (like the FDA). If you want a more extensive list of product recalls, you can get it at http://www.pueblo.gsa.gov/recallsdesc.htm, but the recall list only goes back a couple of months.

Safety Alerts--http://www.safetyalerts.com/

Safety Alerts doesn't appear to be an official recall site. Instead it pulls information from government agencies to create this site. From the front page you can get a clickable list of the most recent recalls (at this writing: pound cakes, cookies, crab meat). You can also view recalls by category, which include Food and Food Allergy, Drugs, Clothing, and Car Seats.

FDA Food Recall Alerts--http://www.fda.gov/opacom/7alerts.html

The food recalls here are much like the ones you'll see at Safety Alerts, but you'll get them straight from the source—the FDA. The front page contains the last 60 days' worth of recalls, and the items on the front page are dated.

The archives go back to 1999. (If you want reports earlier than that, check out the enforcement report index, which goes back to 1990.) Other features on the Web site include medical product safety information as well as links to other agency recalls.

Food Recalls in Canada--http://www.inspection.gc.ca/english/corpaffr/recarapp/recaltoce.shtml

This site is from the Canadian Food Inspection Agency and provides information on recalled foods in Canada. From the front page you can see the last six months or so of food recalls. Recalls on the front page are dated and fairly succinct ("HEALTH HAZARD ALERT - PRICE CHOPPER brand store packaged frozen MEATBALLS may contain harmful bacteria"). Click on an item and you'll get a press release with more details about the recall. The nice thing about this site is that it separates allergy recalls from health hazard recalls.

National Highway Traffic Safety Administration: Recall Search--http://www-odi.nhtsa.dot.gov/cars/problems/recalls/recallsearch.cfm

The name's almost as long as the URL, and the site's about as extensive. Here you can search for vehicle recalls going all the way back to 1949 (car model year, that is). The search for vehicle defect report goes through five steps if you don't care to do the quick search, which provides all new recall information since a certain date or all the information associated with a certain campaign ID number.

With the first steps you pick the type of search you're doing (vehicle, equipment, child safety seat, or tires). With the next search you pick the year. Next you'll pick the make, model, and component with the problem. On the last tab you'll be able to specify whether you want to see a summary of the problem or not. I recommend you do; it puts everything neatly on one screen.

Where to Complain

TIP

Before you start filing complaints everywhere, contact the merchant and see if they can resolve your problem. Don't assume that the merchant is evil and is out to rip you off. E-mail is not reliable. Sometimes you just didn't get the delivery notification or the mail requesting additional information. Try to work it out with the merchant first.

Did you have a terrible purchase experience? Unfortunately it happens in the online as well as the offline world. And you do have some options to deal with it. Here are some resource options.

The first place you should go is the online site for the Better Business Bureau, at http://www.bbb.org. Search the database first to see whether the online merchant you want to complain about already has a listing (use the Web site address for the search). Then lodge your complaint. This method of complaining may or may not get you results, but the information will be recorded for a long time, and the BBB itself has a lot of online credibility.

There are other places that also offer complaint outlets that don't have the long track record of the BBB but do give satisfying outlets to vent, including those discussed.

PlanetFeedback--http://www.planetfeedback.com

PlanetFeedback actually has two sides: a side for businesses (so they can hear what people are saying about them) and a side for consumers (so they can complain). When you visit their site you can choose to either search through public messages or create your own. You'll be amazed at how many letters have been left for certain companies—over 5,500 letters have been left for Wal-Mart alone! (Note that PlanetFeedback includes letters indicating *positive*, as well as negative, experiences.) Complaints range from price issues to delivery problems to customer service. Visitors get to comment on letters that are left, so be sure to use your best spelling and grammar!

TIP

Apply the same kind of credibility filters to complaints that you do to online reviews. Sometimes folks have axes to grind that they don't make clear in their reviews or their complaints. Look for rational, thoughtful, well-documented complaints (and try to write them, too!). When in doubt, imagine that someone walks up to you on the street and starts relating the complaint that you see on the site. Are you compelled to listen carefully or back away slowly?

Complaints.com--http://www.complaints.com

Complaints.com isn't as fancy as PlanetFeedback. You can do a simple keyword search or you can browse the archives (which go back to the year 2000). Sometimes the complaints feature extensive correspondence between complainer and company. Further, some of these folks went to great length to document their complaints!

Watch Your Step

I really, really wish I could tell you that every single transaction in which you engage will be perfect, and that you will love all the merchandise you order and all the merchants you deal with. I wish I could say that, but I can't. I *can* say, though, that if you use your common sense and the resources included in this chapter, you can reduce your chances of getting burned.

Sometimes, if the merchant is large enough, you'll find entire Web sites devoted to someone's dislike of them. (To use the vernacular, these are called "sucks sites.") You can get a list of these kinds of sites at http://dir.yahoo.com/Society_and_Culture/Issues_and_Causes/Consumer_Advocacy_and_Information/Consumer_Opinion/Individual_Companies/. Are these kinds of sites worthwhile? While I'm sure that they help relieve some emotional stress, and while they might get attention for the person who took the time to put the site together, they probably won't be very useful to you.

23

Drugs and Medical Information

The Internet is not a boon for a hypochondriac. A quick Google search might convince you that you've got everything from athlete's nose to toe termites. But if you're struggling with a real condition, the Internet has a tremendous amount to offer. Not just medical reference information but also news and a huge supportive community of people who may be in (or who are supporting loved ones who are in) the same situation as you.

I've discovered that when I have medical issues to research, the research usually evolves into two broad paths, either searching for information on general medical conditions or searching for information on specific drugs. The drug search is usually a little easier, as there are some very good general resources available for that. But before I get into either one, a quick warning.

Tara's Quick Medical Warning

A computer is not a substitute for a doctor. The Internet is not a substitute for a doctor. In the right frame of mind, reading lists of symptoms procured from Google might convince you that you have a piranha bite—even if you live in Arkansas and don't swim in anything wilder than a bathtub. If you're sick, please, go to the doctor.

General Medical Searching

But that's not to say the Internet isn't useful. Recently I scratched my eye. After a trip to the doctor and a couple of days of wearing a very chic eyepatch, I got online and researched eye scratches. I discovered what causes them, how they are treated, and how to avoid them in the future. In other words, I used the Internet to support a trip to the doctor by getting additional information that the doctor didn't have time to give me and in some cases that I didn't know enough to ask.

Start your search by either searching for the condition you had or as close a description as you can. Let's use the example of tinnitus, the very annoying problem of ringing in the ears. To start your search you could use either the name of the condition or the symptom. Thus, either one of these searches:

```
"ringing in the ears"
tinnitus
```

would be sufficient. If you run these searches you'll discover that the first search is more oriented toward stories and pages of introduction to tinnitus, while the top results for tinnitus are for either support pages or communities of people who suffer from this unfortunately very common disorder. You can change your search results a bit by adding the word "FAQ" or the phrase "support group." Try searching for

```
tinnitus "support group"
```

You'll see when you search for this that there are a lot of support group listings. So many, in fact, that you could probably search for a state and get a result.

Another couple of useful phrases you can add to your medical query are "caused by" and "symptoms of." Add them as separate phrases, like this:

```
tinnitus "symptoms of"
```

Why don't you just search for the phrase "symptoms of tinnitus"? Because you'll miss a lot. There are a lot of words that could appear between "of" and "tinnitus": "symptoms of chronic tinnitus," "symptoms of acute tinnitus," and so on.

I use a full-text search engine when I'm trying to get a sense of what a medical condition is, and sometimes when I want to understand the symptoms of a particular disorder. (Something that may not be" an illness so much as a condition—hypothyroid, for example. But the Internet is still no substitute for a doctor!) But sometimes I want to skip the searching and go straight to a medical site. In that case I generally have three choices: consumer-oriented Web sites, government sites, and news sites. If I want to do ongoing research, or ask questions, I'll look for a community or support site.

NOTE

In this chapter I'm discussing general searches for condition information. But you can also try searchable subject indexes, as long as you use just the name of the disorder. For example, search Yahoo's directory for "tinnitus." It won't give you as wide a scope of information as Google, but it'll give you some basic information to get started.

NOTE

Tinnitus has support groups because it's a chronic condition. If you're searching for something that isn't chronic and ongoing, you're far less likely to find a support group for it. There might be a Head Colds Anonymous out there, but it's not as likely as a tinnitus support group.

Consumer-Oriented Health Sites

> **TIP**
>
> HealthWeb, and many other online sites, do not have spell suggestions built into their searching. So if you're searching for something and you get no results, try the search in Google. Google might inform you that you're actually misspelling your search query.

HealthWeb—http://www.healthweb.org/
It's not fancy, but it's extensive. HealthWeb opens with a query box and a huge list of categories for you to choose from—from AIDS & HIV to Women's Health. You can either browse through the listings here or search by keyword. Don't miss the user guides, which are listed from the top of the page! They'll teach you how to use other Internet medical resources well.

WebMD—http://www.webmd.com/
WebMD is a very consumer-oriented resource that is built more for searching than browsing—at least that's how I've found it the most useful. You have to be careful when you're searching, however. A search for tinnitus found a recommend search (which was fine), Ad Links (which as you might guess are ads), and regular search results. On the search results page you might also want to spend some time exploring the left side of the page, which can point you to disease and symptom lists, an interactive application to help you determine symptoms, and a set of calculators and quizzes.

There are huge numbers of consumer sites online; the two above are a couple I happen to like. But in addition to consumer sites from commercial entities, the government also, as you might expect, has a large number of medical information sites online.

Government Sites

Healthfinder—http://www.healthfinder.gov/default.htm
Healthfinder is also consumer-oriented. On the right side of the page you'll find pointers to health news and online checkups (at this writing there are 50 of them). On the left side of the page you'll find a health library; health topics (divided up by gender, age, and ethnicity); information about health care professionals, institutions, and outlets; and selected organizations. There are also additional versions available in Spanish and for kids. Search results are ranked and there are no ad results anywhere.

Healthfinder is for consumers. Medical professionals will probably find it too pedestrian, though with plenty of stuff they can recommend to their patients. For more advanced medical searchers, or for laymen who want to do deeper research, I can't recommend too much the National Library of Medicine.

The National Library of Medicine—http://www.nlm.nih.gov/
There are several sets of information here: health information, library services, research programs, general information, and what's new announcements. For the sake of online research I recommend you focus on PubMed. PubMed provides references and abstracts from 4,600 biomedical journals. A search for tinnitus here will get you an overwhelming number of results (at this writing, over

four thousand!), so apply the Principle of Onions to your PubMed search. In my searches I try to apply one topic to my initial search. For example, I might wonder if tinnitus is caused by nutrition deficiencies, so I'll search for tinnitus nutrition and get a more reasonable number of results (seven). Search results include the title of the article as well as its date and source. Sometimes there are abstracts available. A link on the right points to related articles and links. For more information on using PubMed, try the tutorial on the left side of the results page.

There are other databases at the National Library of Medicine you'll want to explore. There's a database of clinical trials (which you can search just by disorder; tinnitus here found two trials in progress), a directory of health organizations, health information for older adults, and databases of toxins and information on toxic substances. There are also several databases available for specific diseases and disorders. All the resources I'm aware of offer tutorials and/or extensive help systems.

TIP

Some people can't stand PubMed's search interface, or find the search results hard to navigate. Metasearch engine Vivisimo is offering ClusterMed, which groups PubMed results into searchable groups. A `tinnitus nutrition` search here, for example, provides the results in three groups: disease, blood/hormones, and deafness. If you're unregistered you can get up to 100 clustered results. Registered users can get a 30-day trial with up to 500 results. If your search query is specific enough, that 100-result limit won't present too much of a problem.

Doing a News Search

PubMed and similar medically oriented databases aren't the only places you can get news about diseases and disorders, especially common complaints. Try regular news search engines like Google News and Yahoo News. A Google News search for tinnitus, for example, will get you all kinds of results from news on treatments to advice to research updates.

Medical literature searches are good, and even general news searches are good when you're trying to find medical information online. But there's a place for general Web searching, too. When you search consumer health sites like WebMD and literature sites like PubMed, you are generally getting only two sides to a medical disorder. You are getting research information and you're getting professional health advice. You are not getting the experiences, advice, and problems of people who have to live with a disorder, or care for someone who's living with a disorder, day after day. To get that kind of information, you're going to have to find the communities and mailing lists where medical disorders are discussed. But that kind of research leads to its own problems.

Community and Support Sites

I think that finding and joining support groups and mailing lists is an essential part of medical research, especially when you're living with a disorder or you're supporting someone who's living with a disorder. But at the same time there are pitfalls to beware of. Be careful of the information you review; don't take it as credible just

> **TIP**
>
> You may wish to join a support group for the purposes of research. Perhaps you're writing a paper about a particular disorder or doing research for a class. In that case please disclose to the group—or at least to the list owner—what your purpose is. Please do not join a group and pretend to either have the disorder or be supporting someone with the disorder. It's unethical and it damages all support communities by breaking down trust.

because it's part of a support group, and bear in mind that some information might be shared incorrectly, misunderstood, or just plain wrong. A community of patients discussing medical issues can be very useful, but it's possible—even likely—that accidental misinformation can become part of that information exchange. Be aware of that and be wary of that.

That having been said, let's look at medical support groups.

Finding medical support mailing lists is as simple is looking in the major mailing list sites, like Yahoo Groups. Searching at Yahoo Groups for tinnitus will find support groups, but also fan groups (there are apparently bands named Tinnitus) and other irrelevant information. Pay attention to the number of members in the group; support groups aren't that supportive when they only have four or five members. If you don't want to join a group but only want to get information, look for public archives. In my experience there are fewer support groups with public archives.

While you might be interested in doing specific medical searches occasionally, you might find yourself doing searches for drug-related topics more often. Let's take a look at some quick ways you can get good drug search results.

Drugs and Web Searches

You might find yourself doing drug searches a lot more often than you do regular medical searches. You might want to know what your headache remedy's possible side effects are, or you might be considering changing your blood pressure medication, and you want to get more information about different medications available. Or you might simply see a drug commercial on television and be curious. In that case you'll have a lot of search options.

General Web Searches

When you do a regular Web search for a drug name, what you'll get will vary a lot. If you're searching for a common though not widely known drug, like Synthroid, you'll get mostly useful results from several different kinds of sites. (If you find an overwhelming number of sites to be commercial in nature, add site:edu to your search.) If you search for a drug that's more well known, like Prozac, you will get everything from anti-Prozac sites to commercial sites to informational sites. If you find your search getting gunked up with a lot of irrelevant material, I've got a few suggestions for you:

1. Misspell the drug name. Sometimes if you misspell the drug name you'll get support and informal information pages. With the more popular drugs, though, you can get garbage results.

2. Add symptoms of the disorder that's supposed to be treated. If you were searching for Prozac you could add the words "depression" or "depressed," or the phrase "social anxiety." The more medically oriented the term you add, the better your search is going to be; if you're searching for Prilosec, adding the query "acid reflux disease" will get you better results than "heartburn."
3. If you know the full, "official" name of the drug, use that. Zoloft is the "brand name" for sertraline. Searching for sertraline will get you far different results than Zoloft.

There are also some words you can add to your search to change the results some:

"Controversy"—Finds articles about drug controversies, and is more slanted to finding news stories and roundup pages than more general drug pages.

"FDA"—This term removes results rather than narrows the results to a new category. It removes a lot of "online shopping" links, especially for very popular drugs. If you're still having trouble with too many shopping links, try removing these phrases from your search: "shopping cart" or "no doctor." ("No doctor" is short for "no doctor prescription required," a phrase used on many overseas drug sites.)

"Risk study"—These words will provide both stories about controversial aspects of a particular drug and stories about diseases related to that drug. For example, the Google search `Xanax risk study` provides information about Xanax effects and more general pages and news on mental illness. If you want even more medically oriented pages, try adding the words "percent," "dosage," or "placebo" to your search.

"Tried x"—If you're looking for discussion from consumers of drugs, this is the phrase to try, where "x" is the name of the drug in which you're interested. This will lead you to mailing list archives and online discussions from different disease support sites. Try misspelling the name of the drug when you use this phrase and see what turns up.

TIP

At this point you may be wondering about all those advertisements for drugs that you can get "without prescription" from any number of places, often overseas. You may be wondering if this is something you want to try. I can't tell you what to do, but I can tell you I'd be very wary of a drug I ordered from overseas with no assurance that it came from a doctor or pharmacy or anybody remotely connected to a medical profession. There is a problem with counterfeit drugs all over the world; are you sure you're ingesting what you think you're ingesting?

Some Good Web Sites

There are many places that contain overview information about drugs.

RxList—http://www.rxlist.com/

RxList is kind of funny. On the one hand, I'm thrilled to be able to search for a keyword, side effects, interactions, and so on. On the other hand, the idea of almost weekly "comix" on a pharmaceutical site is strange. But there's enough information here to overlook that.

You might not even have to do a search; the top 150 searched drugs are already on the front page. If you do search, you'll see that you can search by several different things, including keyword, generic or brand name, imprint code, and so on. (There's also a simple name search on the front page.) You'll be surprised; you'll get a lot of results for a single drug search, but that's because there will be different results based on dosage. One link on the results page will give you a page of basic information about the drug, including how it's taken, possible side effects, warnings and precautions, what to do if you missed a dose, what to do if you've overdosed, etc. Another link takes you to a search results list for possible side effects and interaction problems. As you might imagine, there's a lot of information here.

Drugs.com—http://www.drugs.com/

Drugs.com allows you to either browse drugs by first name or search by keyword. They also have news about recent additions to the database and news about recent drug FDA approvals. Drug information includes extensive information about the drug, what it's supposed to do, and how to take it. In addition to the drug information, this site also offers news and articles, an interactions checker, an image search, and several bulletin boards.

Yahoo Health—http://health.yahoo.com/health/pdr_drugs/a.html

Yahoo Health's information is not as detailed as the other sources I've mentioned here, but the results are very quick and easy to read. There is a huge amount of information here on proper dosage and storage, as well as pointers to information from other parts of Yahoo.

Both doctors and pharmacists are very busy; if all you get with your prescription is a brief information sheet, you'll learn a lot more by checking out one of these resources online. But remember, there's no way that the Internet can substitute for the advice of a flesh-and-blood doctor. If you're confused about information you find online, or need more details, consult your health care provider.

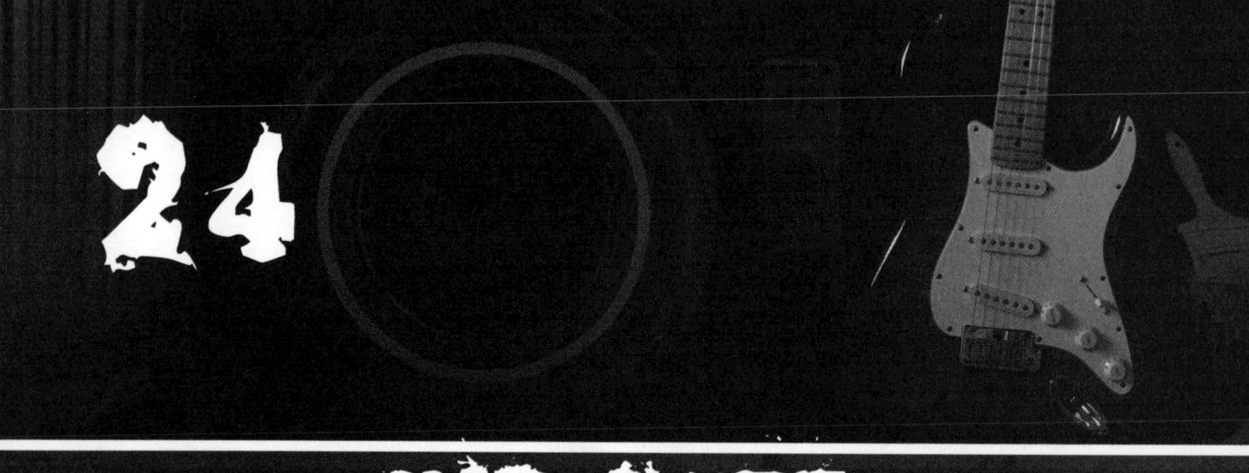

24 KID-SAFE SEARCHING

If you've got kids, you know that searching the Internet with them can sometimes lead to some awful discoveries. Though most search engines have filters of one kind or another, I'm not that fond of them. To do really kid-safe searching, the best bet is to either use very specific Web searches or limit yourself to kid-safe, human-edited subject indexes.

Tara's Rant About Kids and the Internet

Don't worry, it's a short rant. Please. Please. Please. If you've got kids, surf with them. Don't just stick them on the Internet and let them wander around. There are all kinds of things on the Internet and it's just too easy to accidentally come across some strange stuff. Would you let your kids wander around a huge city all by themselves, talking to just anybody and peeking in all the shops? No, you wouldn't, so don't do it online.

Using Full-Text Searching

Every full-text search engine I know that offers filtering offers machine filtering. That means instead of having humans filter the search results, the results are filtered by computers. These filters are pretty good, but they are not perfect. While I appreciate filters to help eliminate results I find distasteful, I do not trust them to remove all prurient results from my searching. And you shouldn't either: machine-filtered search results aren't perfect.

If you want a strong assurance that you're not going to run into any search results that'll make your head hurt, I recommend against using full-text search engines and instead focusing on human-built search indexes, which we'll get into later in this chapter. If you are willing to take some risks, I can make a few suggestions about limiting your searches such that you can get mostly good search results, with a minor risk of some bad ones.

> **TIP**
>
> Bear in mind that machine filters are used for filtering things that may generally be considered offensive—adult materials, alcohol information—anything that's inappropriate for people under age 18. If you find something offensive outside that range—say, you're deeply offended by Pez or you don't like cumulous clouds—filters aren't going to help you. You'll need to stick to searchable subject indexes and avoid keywords that might trigger the things you find offensive.

A Guide to Doing Kid-Safe Full-Text Searching Without All Your Hair Turning White

1. Turn the machine filtering all the way up. No, the machine filtering doesn't always work, but it doesn't hurt. So be sure to make sure it's activated. Google has different levels of filtering available; be sure to use the highest level. Filtering options are usually on a site's advanced search page.
2. Use potential trigger words carefully. You don't always know what a "trigger word" is—a trigger word in this case means a word that you mean to use innocuously but that ends up getting you pornographic results. Let's do an easy example: breast cancer. Sometimes this'll trigger results that you didn't intend. In this case be sure to search for the entire phrase: "breast cancer." Furthermore, try to add query words that won't narrow your results, but will keep them from being prurient. Like "medicine" or "treatment," or breast cancer–related words like "biopsy." Use your query words to steer the result in the right direction.
3. Stick to special searches when you can. If a site is offering special searches, and they're relevant to your topic, try those. If your kid is researching Washington, DC, and you want to do a full-text search, then try searching the Uncle Sam special search that Google offers instead of Google's main search.
4. Slant your search with syntaxes. There are some search syntaxes you can do that'll make your results less likely to get adult-oriented results. Limiting your search to certain top-level domains—including .edu, .gov, and .mil—will help. Using non-trigger words and restricting them to page titles will help. Using your syntax to tighten up your searches as much as possible can really lessen the chance of inappropriate search results.
5. Be sure to use the feedback feature. If you stumble into some content that not only is inappropriate but really doesn't belong (it's been indexed with the wrong keywords, or uses fraudulent methods to get a high search results, or something else), be sure to take advantage of any feedback mechanism offered by the search engines to report adult-oriented results that come up for nonadult searches.

> **TIP**
>
> Though the .us domain isn't as safe as it used to be, searching for `inurl:k12.*.us` on Google can be very useful. That assures that your search results will be limited to k12 school sites. Those aren't completely safe, but they're safer than the Internet as a whole.

Kid-Safe Subject Indexes: A Better Way to Go

While there are ways that you can do kid-safer searching on full-text search engines, I recommend that you use kid-safe searchable subject indexes and subject guides—those that have been established by humans and that have pages added to them by humans. Though these kinds of sites aren't foolproof either (an expiring domain might be bought by an adult-oriented site, a page might get hijacked, etc.), they tend to be much-reviewed and a pretty safe place for kids to go. My personal favorite is Yahooligans.

Yahooligans--http://www.yahooligans.com

Yahooligans, as you might imagine, is a Yahoo Web site. It isn't as far-reaching as Yahoo, but it offers sites, games, news, and an "Ask Earl" section to which kids can submit questions. There's also a parent's guide and a teacher's guide for making the most of Yahooligans and avoiding kid-unsafe information

Ask Jeeves for Kids--http://www.ajkids.com/

Yup, Ask Jeeves has a kids' site. Like the regular Ask Jeeves site, this site allows you to ask natural language questions and get answers. So here you can ask things like, "How does a car work?", "Who was George Washington Carver?", and "Why is the sky blue?". This site also offers a nice set of links to ready-reference materials as well as pointers to kid-appropriate news sources and a bunch of fun and games.

4Kids--http://www.4kids.org/

Though it doesn't have the brand recognition of Yahoo or Ask Jeeves, this actually isn't a bad site. Here you'll find weekly issues of a kids' newsletter spotlighting interesting sites, a site search helper column called "Ask Amy," and pointers to safe surfing resources. This is a good resource to check regularly to help your kid build up a library of useful, safe sites.

ALA Great Web Sites--http://www.ala.org/greatsites

ALA stands for the American Library Association. This is another great collection of kid-oriented sites. This one is arranged more like a searchable subject index, with categories like Animals, Science, and History & Biography. All sites are nicely annotated and marked with an icon to specify for what age group they're appropriate. If you like Yahooligans but don't like the pop culture references, try Great Web Sites.

The Internet is not all commerce, news, and unmentionable Web sites. It just seems that way sometimes. Fortunately, with millions of kids already using the Internet for everything from keeping up with their family to getting help with their homework, there are already plenty of sites out there that are friendly, safe, and kid-oriented. You just have to know where (and how) to find them!

PART VII
TECHNICAL SUPPORT

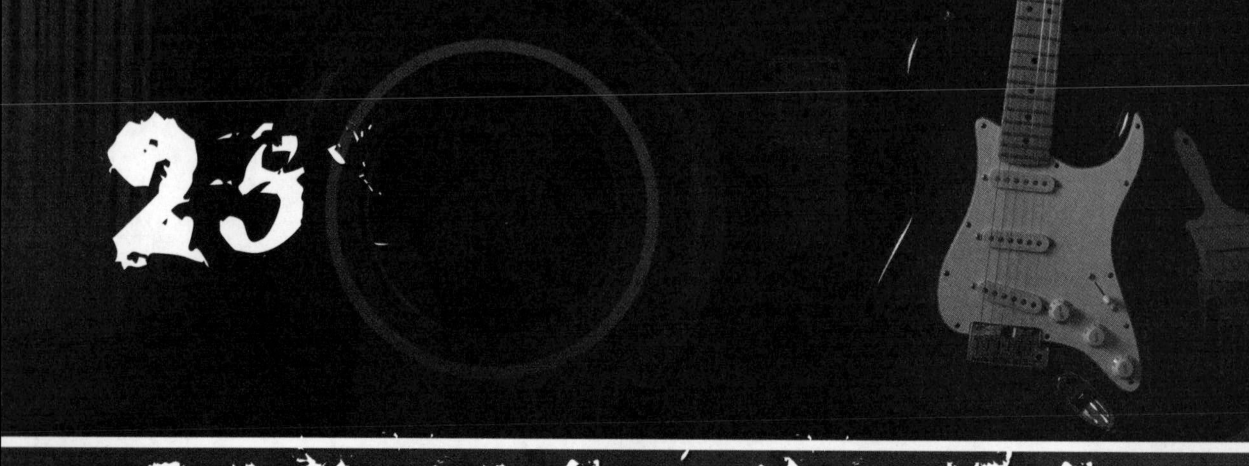

23 DRIVERS, CHEATS, HELP, AND MORE

Since you're reading this book, I'm going to assume that you either have a computer or have access to one. And if you own a computer or have access to one, you also own or have access to computer problems, because that's the way computers work. There are several strategies for finding technical support online.

There may not be anything wrong with your computer specifically. You may be stuck on a game, or a peripheral may not be working the way you want, or you want to get more power out of a program. As you might imagine, the Internet has a huge community—well, several huge communities—of computer whizzes, and much of the time they're eager to help newbies. Sometimes, if you have a specific question, you need to access this community.

If you're looking for more routine information, like about device drivers, you can refer directly to the Web.

Finding the Community Help

To find community help you first must find the community. Google Groups is the largest site for getting computer help, specifically in the comp* newsgroups.

Google Groups

You can limit your Google Groups search to the comp hierarchy of newsgroups by adding "group:comp*" to your query. Start with that and then add any keywords that might be relevant. If you want to find information on passwords in Windows XP, try:

```
password "windows xp" group:comp*
```

When you get your search results be sure to list them by date so you're not reading very old or outdated information. Notice that the search results include the newsgroup where the post appears. You may find that a particular newsgroup or set of newsgroups contains relevant information, and you'd like to limit your searches to those groups. In that case you can tweak your search to include just those newsgroups. Want to limit your search to operating system newsgroups? Search for `comp.os* password "windows xp"`.

To try to get the fewest results possible, search for model numbers first. If you're having trouble with the scanning function of widget 5000, try your search first with the words "scanning," "widget," and "5000." That doesn't always work, either because people don't include model numbers in their posts or because several model numbers may share the same problem. On the second pass remove the number but keep the brand name and try again. Use descriptive words for the problem but try to keep your search to the brand name and model number of the item you're having problems with and only a few descriptive words.

SPECIAL DOUBLE TIP

The asterisk (*) at the end of the group syntax merely means that you're looking for all groups that start with the string you specify. You advanced searchers are going to be wondering to yourselves, "Is this stemming?" Yes it is, but unfortunately it's limited to Google Groups. If you're not sure what groups are available, review the extensive group hierarchy at http://groups.google.com/groups?group=*&hl=en.

If you must use descriptive words, try to describe the problem as plainly as possible. I know this is difficult sometimes; how do you describe the fact that every time you play Freecell your hard drive makes a weird noise? Start with what you think are the two culprits: "Freecell" and "hard drive." Those two are unusual enough that you might start finding pointers to solve your problem. If that doesn't work, add "sound" or "noise." Don't add an adjective, like "weird," because there are even more adjectives than nouns that could end up in a discussion of your problem.

Once you've found an answer that fits your problem, take the relevant, distinct parts of the answer (the name of the troublesome file, the name of the patch you should apply, whatever) and *run another search*. Just because one person makes a recommendation doesn't mean that it's right, or that it will work in your situation. Run the search again with the "solution words" that you've found and see what other people say. If you can't find information in Google Groups, try extending your search to mailing lists (we'll discuss those in a minute) and the Web as a whole (if your solution words are specific enough you won't get a whole lot of junk results). Once you've found a potential solution for your problem, it's a lot easier to search for information related to the problem and the solution.

TIP

Why use model numbers and brand names in a search? Because when it comes to slang and technical terms, computers and software beat all. Fortunately, though, there's a severe limit on slang for brand names and item numbers.

I find that Google Groups helps me with a lot of general tech support questions related to Windows and other OSes, some peripheral help, and some game help. If you have a problem related to a very specialized program, or an esoteric system, Google Groups may not offer you much. But there are other resources to turn to, like mailing list archives and online communities.

Technical Mailing List Archives

You can find technical mailing lists at the community sites we've discussed throughout this book—Yahoo Groups, Topica, and so on. Generally you'll find mailing lists on general topics, with occasional secondary topics. You might see several mailing lists about Excel, and a couple of mailing lists about generating business information with Excel. Unless you find a very, very, very targeted mailing list (you have an advanced-level macro problem and you find an Excel mailing list that deals with nothing but macro issues), I would recommend you stick to the general mailing lists. Why? Two reasons. First of all, a lot of computer problems are general in nature—you need a patch, or you've got a virus, or a hardware component is going awry. Even when they're unusual, it's hard to pin down why they're unusual (if you're having a problem getting a macro to execute in Excel, do you *know* that it's an advanced macro issue or have you missed something really simple?). Second, general mailing lists tend to have more people on them. More people can mean a better chance of getting your question answered.

In addition to mailing lists, there are also online communities that are Web-based. They're a little tougher to find, but they're also useful.

Online Communities

I start my search for online communities with a simple "name of software" online reply forum search. If the software is an actual English word (Excel), this makes the search a lot more complicated; add the name of the company and turn it into a phrase ("Microsoft Excel") or just add the company to the search (Adobe Photoshop). If that doesn't work, try removing "forum" from your query. Now, the results you get will be a little strange so let's look at them. We'll do a search for Photoshop:

```
Photoshop online reply
```

You'll see in these results that you'll get two kinds of results out of those relevant ones: those that are pointed to individual messages and threads, and those that are more pointed to the top of forums, either at topic categories or messages within a category. From here you have two choices: 1) continue your Google search, or 2) start investigating individual forums you find.

Which you do depends on what you're looking for. If you have a specific question that you need solved (every time I try to change the contrast in an image it turns completely green), then add some keywords to your initial search and do another Google search. If you have a more general question or issue—you're not good at manipulating images, you want guidance on using plugins, etc.—then look at the forums this Google search has turned up more closely and see if there are topics or categories of information you should explore.

Finding Help for Routine Things

When you have specific questions or advanced questions, online forums are great. But unless you're involved in very basic forums, there are certain kinds of questions it's sometimes hard to ask: basic questions. Often forums and communities assume a critical mass of knowledge, or the dynamics of the group make it difficult to ask a basic question without getting razzed or causing controversy. But, of course, there are lots of beginners online. In addition to basic beginner questions, you may find you have lots of "routine" needs—looking for software drivers, say, or trying to get a handle on current virus alerts. And, of course, there's the gamer's need for cheats and walkthroughs.

Don't worry, I can hook you up with pointers to all these. Let's start with basic help. If you are a beginner, or you are assisting a beginner, consider the following sites to help you understand some basic computing problems.

TIP

If you need to help someone with really basic computer skills—like, how to move a mouse around—try this site: http://northville.lib.mi.us/tech/tutor/welcome.htm. Library and university Web sites offer some amazingly good basic computer help. Try searching for the name of your hardware or software, and then modifying the search with site:edu or site:us. You can come up with some good stuff that way.

Computer Hope--http://www.computerhope.com/

Those of you who are trying to troubleshoot older computers will appreciate this site. There are hardware and software listings pointing to both basic troubleshooting ("When attempting to read from a Zip diskette I hear continuous clicking from the Zip drive") and hints for more details on older manufacturers ("What happened to the Conner hard drive company?"). The site also offers forums and a chat room, as well as a dictionary and some basic Web help.

Tech Tutorials--http://www.techtutorials.com/

Sometimes you don't need help with a problem so much as you need to know how to step through a particular process. Tech Tutorials provides several categories of tutorial pointers, including programming, networking, and all kinds of different operating systems. Tech Tutorials is just one of the tutorial sites out there; there's also FindTutorials at http://www.findtutorials.com/, which offers free and paid tutorials and is quite good.

TIP

Why don't I just search for a product name/number while I'm searching for a driver page? Because all the driver sites I've seen have very useful internal search engines (more useful than Google's because you know they're complete) or easy-to-navigate driver lists.

Finding Drivers

When most of the Internet was on dial-up, getting drivers was tough. Either sites wouldn't offer them via download (I remember Hewlett Packard drove me crazy a few times by making some drivers available only by postal mail) or they were huge and took hours and hours to download. But things are much easier now. I can't think of any hardware companies that don't have Web presences, and I can't think of any of those that don't offer driver downloads.

> **TIP**
>
> Many software programs offer the ability to update themselves from within the program. You can choose Update, and they'll connect to the Internet, download the appropriate files, and install them. While this can save you a lot of time and hassle, make sure you trust the program that you're allowing to access the Internet and download software.

Make your driver search from Google super-simple: search for the name of the company and the word "drivers." Sandisk drivers, Seagate drivers, whatever; this search has never let me down. The only time you need to modify it is if you are looking for Linux drivers; sometimes there are "unofficial" Linux drivers that cannot be found on a company Web site. In that case I would simply add the word "Linux" to my Google search:

```
Linux Soundblaster Drivers
```

Software Updates

Finding software updates isn't much different than finding drivers. If you're using Windows, of course, you can use the built-in Windows update; or if you're on a network, your network administrator might take care of updates. When I'm looking for a software update, I usually know the site for the software, and I go straight there. If you don't, try searching for the name of the software and either the word "patch" or the word "update":


```
photoshop (patch | update)
```

Security Issues: Viruses and Such

> And *use* the virus scanner! Scan your system for viruses at least weekly.

If you're on the Internet you need to have good anti-virus software and a firewall, period. And you need to keep them updated. If you use Windows you need to use the Windows Update feature at least monthly to make sure that any discovered holes are patched. This goes triple if you use Internet software that integrates closely with Windows, like Microsoft Outlook or Internet Explorer.

This will cover you for the vast majority of security problems out there. I also review CNET news and Yahoo's most popular news items to see if there are any other security issues or rampant viruses I should be aware of. There are millions of teensy other security issues that will pop up, but unless you're a system administrator, a Linux user (since Linux security issues don't get the mainstream media play that Windows issues do), or a very very advanced user, I wouldn't worry about tracking security issues further. If you must, don't bother with Web searching—this stuff changes too quickly. For Macs try SecureMac (http://www. securemac.com/), for Windows try the Microsoft Windows Update site (http://windowsupdate. microsoft.com/), and for Linux and other open source OSes try the Open Source Vulnerability Database at http://www.osvdb.org.

Cheats and Walkthroughs

I love playing computer games, but I'm not very good at them. So I rely a lot on the Internet to help me when I get stuck. Luckily I end up playing the popular games years after they're actually popular, so I don't have trouble finding cheats and walkthroughs. If you're playing a game that was released within a month, you might have trouble. It depends on how popular it is and how many other people are playing it.

Finding help when you're stuck on a game is very similar to finding help when you're stuck with anything else. You name the item you're having trouble with and describe the problem. You may be playing Squiggletronica but can't find the DoomSquiggle. Your search in that case is simple:

TIP

Sometimes you're looking for information about a game, but you're not really looking for help. You might want maps. You might want to find a community. You might want to get more details about a particular aspect of a game. In that case use Yahoo. Just search for the name of the game. If you go to Yahoo and search its directory for Everquest, you will get (and I'm not kidding) 51 results. Some of them are official sites, some of them are community sites, and some of them are even for fan fiction! But they'll all give you more detailed information than you might get at a cheats site.

```
Squiggletronica DoomSquiggle
```

This is really the Principle of Unique Language in action; "Squiggletronica" is a proper noun, and the DoomSquiggle is an item within Squiggletronica related only to it. So it'll narrow down your search results to exactly what you need.

When you're not stuck, but instead want a walkthrough of the game, try searching for walkthrough and the name of the game:

```
Squiggletroncia walkthrough
```

Or sometimes you don't want a walkthrough but need a couple of cheat codes to give you a boost over the tough parts. Just add "cheats" or "cheat codes" to your search:

```
Squiggletronica "cheat codes"
```

Don't forget, these kinds of searches work just as well for console games (PlayStation2, GameCube, etc.) as they do for computer games!

I find that these searches are more than enough when I'm stuck with a game, but in case they're not enough for you, try the Yahoo Directory's Cheats, Hints, and Codes category at http://dir.yahoo.com/Recreation/Games/Video_Games/Cheats__Hints__and_Codes/ for pointers to several cheat and walkthrough sites.

As you've figured out from this chapter, the Internet is a great place to get technical support. And if you think about it, that makes sense; the Internet is built out of people and computers, and therefore the Internet is full of people who are really good at computers. So before you rip your hair out over the weird whine in your mouse, try your research skills.

PART VIII
SEARCHING THE WORLD

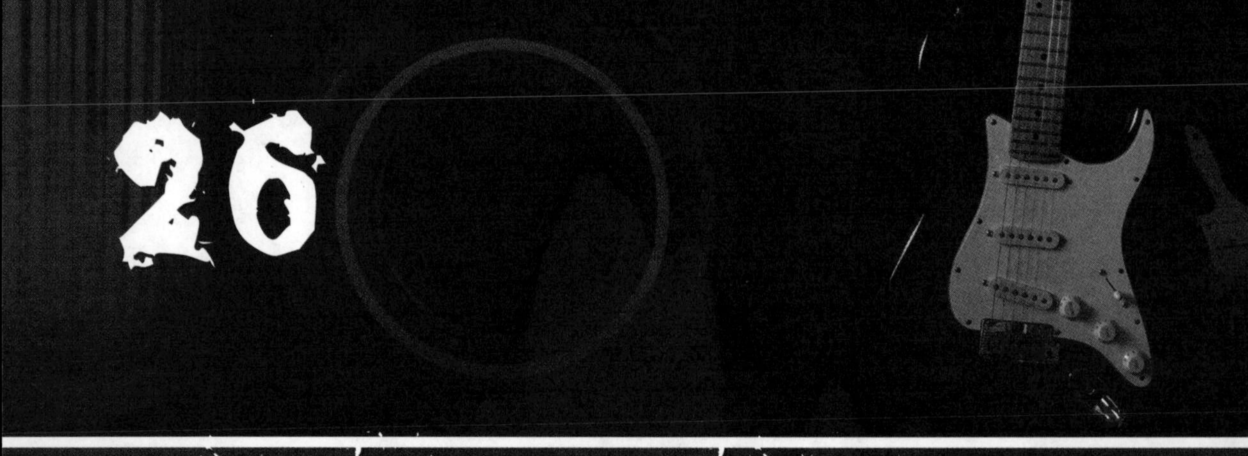

26 International Information

TIP

If you really want to limit your search results, try searching for documents in one country and limiting your results to a language that's not in that country. (search Japanese Web sites for documents in Spanish, for example). In the cases where that kind of search has relevance—you're looking for information on Spain's exports to Japan—doing a cross-language/country search can work wonders for narrowing results. Of course, if you don't speak Spanish you have an additional problem, but we'll discuss that later in this chapter.

Back in Chapter 16, "Finding Local Information on the Web," we covered some ways to get international information. In this chapter we're going to look at other ways to get international information, including search engines' offerings, specialty directories and where to find them, and translation tools when your interests and the available languages just don't intersect.

What Search Engines Offer

When you go to Google, where your browser actually ends up depends on what country you're located in. Google can redirect your search to country-specific sites. But if you're in one country and you want to get information on another country, you'll have to go to Google's language tools page at http://www.google.com/language_tools?hl=en. Here you can limit your search both by country and by language.

Yahoo also has a huge selection of international country sites. See their list of Yahoos worldwide at http://world.yahoo.com/. Yahoo's world sites provide content in the local language. In the cases where there's more than one language—like Hong Kong—Yahoo will sometimes offer more than one language site and mark it appropriately.

Many search engines have country sites available. Try searching a full-text search engine for the name of the search engine and the name or abbreviation of the country in which you're interested. For instance, if you search Google for "Ask Jeeves" UK you'll get a pointer to Ask Jeeves' U.K. site. Not all search engines offer sites for all countries, but there are a lot of country-specific search engine resources out there.

Strangely enough, though, when I'm looking for country-specific sites focused on a single topic, I don't use Google or Yahoo. I find the Open Directory Project very useful.

Specialty Sites and Directories for Country Information

Though Yahoo and other subject indexes are good, I prefer the Open Directory Project at http://www.dmoz.com for my country searching. Start your search there by searching for the name of the country and then narrowing your search down by category. For example, I might want information on health issues in South Korea. Searching for `"South Korea" health` would bring me some results, but there's no guarantee that a thematic keyword and the name of the country would find useful results. On the other hand, searching for `South Korea` immediately brings a pointer to South Korean–oriented categories, and from there you may "drill down" to a set of health-related categories.

Of course you can do this same kind of search on Yahoo or any other searchable subject index. I've found that the Open Directory Project works for me in the searches I do for international information; you might find that Yahoo suits you better. To each his own.

For searching about a wide variety of international information, I find using the Open Directory helps, or using the CIA World Factbook and some specialty Google searches as I mentioned in Chapter 16. But there are also a couple of other places that I can go to find country overview information and pointers to other sources, though their usefulness varies a lot by country. Those are embassies and national libraries.

Embassies

An embassy, as defined by the *American Heritage® Dictionary of the English Language*, Fourth Edition, is "A building containing the offices of an ambassador and staff." It's a point of contact between a country and the rest of the world. As you might imagine, a Web site for an institution that acts as a point of contact between a country and the rest of the world is going to have a lot of great information available. Finding the embassies to find the information is simple; I've got two suggestions for you.

Embassy World—http://www.embassyworld.com/ embassy/directory.htm

Embassy World offers not only links to embassies but a variety of other information about embassy-related sites and information related to those embassy countries. Each country has its own embassy page, with links to lists of embassies related to that country, information on relocating to that country, and maps and references for that country. Embassy information includes both online contacts (Web pages, e-mail) and offline contacts (phone numbers, address). Other information available on this site includes international search tools and United Nations Permanent Missions.

Embassy.org—http://www.embassy.org

Embassy.org was developed for the Washington, DC, area embassy community. Here you'll find a list of embassies in Washington, from Afghanistan to Uzbekistan. Offline contact information is included as well as Internet information (most of the time) and a link to that country's information at CountryWatch.com.

While embassies are very useful and contain a huge amount of country information, I find there's an even better country-level institution for finding research materials and historic information. Take a wild guess. You got it—national libraries!

National Libraries

Not all countries have libraries with Web sites, but a great many do. Try searching for "Library of Countryname" to find a country's library site. This doesn't always work; `"Library of Peru"` takes you to Peru's national library, but `"Library of Benin"` takes you first to a page of offline contact information for the National Library of Benin.

Many Library sites will offer at least some services and information in English, but many won't, so keep that in mind when you're doing your search.

What You Can Expect

What you can expect from a national library site varies depending on the library. I have found census data, digitized periodicals, card catalogs, digitized photos, and more on national library sites. The United States' Library of Congress, at http://www.loc.gov, has a wealth of information. Outside the United States, the Library of Scotland (http://www.nls.uk/) has a huge amount of information and is always adding more. I find that most library sites I visit, no matter how limited, offer something of interest. And they're not going to get anything but more extensive as time goes by.

> **TIP**
>
> If you just can't find the national library you're looking for, try the list at http://www.library.uq.edu.au/ssah/jeast/.

Of course, one problem with getting library information or embassy information or information from a certain country or whatever is that you can't always be assured that you can read what you can find. That's where translation tools come in.

Translation Tools

Before we get into translation tools I have to tell you one thing: translation tools usually aren't very good. A translation tool is for a gist, not for a deep meaning.

And if there's a sense of humor or an overload of idioms in what you're trying to translate, forget it—it'll be a mess. That having been said, when you just want to get an idea of what someone is saying, translation tools are great. There are two I really like, one from Google and one from AltaVista.

Google Language Tools--http://www.google.com/language_tools?hl=en

Google's language tools allow for quick translation of either pages or chunks of text. While the translations are fast and I've found them useful, the number of languages available for translation is limited. If you want a wider variety of languages to translate, including Chinese and Korean, use Babelfish.

Babelfish--http://babelfish.altavista.com/

Babelfish is a service of AltaVista and one of the oldest and best translation services out there. A wide variety of languages are available for translation here, including Greek, Korean, Japanese, and Russian. A special "world keyboard" is available to enter nonstandard characters that you might not be able to find on your physical keyboard. Note that the block of text option will translate only up to 150 words—after that you'll have to choose the option to translate the entire page.

D

E

N

O

P

T

U